Cooperatives in the Global Economy

Cooperatives in the Global Economy

Edited by
Tapas R. Dash

LEXINGTON BOOKS
Lanham • Boulder • New York • London

Published by Lexington Books
An imprint of The Rowman & Littlefield Publishing Group, Inc.
4501 Forbes Boulevard, Suite 200, Lanham, Maryland 20706
www.rowman.com

6 Tinworth Street, London SE11 5AL, United Kingdom

British Library Cataloguing in Publication Information Available

Library of Congress Cataloging-in-Publication Data

Library of Congress Control Number: 2021934265

ISBN 978-1-4985-5522-7 (cloth)
ISBN 978-1-4985-5523-4 (electronic)

Dedicated to cooperatives across the globe
for their relentless service to mankind

Contents

Acknowledgments

It is my great pleasure to present the book *Cooperatives in the Global Economy* in its final form. Many individuals supported the book during its conception and production, without whom the book would not have been possible. First of all, I would like to acknowledge the support of Mr. Joseph C. Parry, Senior Acquisitions Editor, Lexington Books, USA, for believing in the book proposal, putting it through the review process, and finally accepting it to publish. I am also grateful to the authors for contributing to the book by writing excellent chapters on timely topics in engaging styles; the reviewers for taking the time to painstakingly review the chapters in a timely manner through their meaningful comments and observations, specifically Ms. Alison Keefner, Assistant Editor, Lexington Books, USA; and, the production staff for turning the manuscript into a beautiful book.

My special thanks are also due to Professor Casey Barnett, president of CamEd Business School, Phnom Penh, Cambodia for extending constant support for research development, and Professor Satyendra Singh, University of Winnipeg, Canada for providing valuable input throughout the publication process.

I would like to express my deepest sense of gratitude to my family members for their continuous encouragement, and particularly my wife, Malabika, for tolerating my incessant disappearances into my research work. She makes both the journey and destination worthwhile.

My heartedly thanks to all of you!

Tapas R. Dash
Professor & Research Advisor
CamEd Business School
Phnom Penh, Cambodia

List of Figures, Tables, and Text Boxes

FIGURES

TABLES

TEXT BOXES

Introduction

Tapas R. Dash

Cooperation is a worldwide movement. Globally, millions of people have chosen the cooperative model of business to achieve their personal and community development goals. Today, the movement brings together over one billion people around the world (ICA 2017). According to the International Organization of Industrial, Artisanal and Service Producer Cooperatives (CICOPA 2017), on the basis of data from 156 countries, employment in or within the scope of cooperatives concerns at least 280 million people across the globe, which means that cooperative employment contributes toward 10 percent of the total world employment. Thus, the livelihoods of millions have been secured by cooperatives as they play crucial economic and social roles in their respective communities.

Cooperatives across the globe have been able to elevate their position as a powerful economic model. In a number of countries, a significant position has been assigned to cooperatives through the tasks of alleviating poverty, creating employment opportunities, and improving the socioeconomic standards of people in general and the disadvantaged section of the society in particular. The nonexploitative character of cooperatives, voluntary nature of their membership, democratically controlled organization, decentralized decision-making process, equitable contribution to capital, and a fair share of risks and benefits dignify them as agents for socioeconomic development. Although cooperatives cover a large gamut of activities to serve the interests of producers, consumers, and other stakeholders of the society, the so-called liberalization, marketization, and globalization of the world economy have thrown numerous challenges to the development and management of cooperatives. Therefore, in the present context, the cooperative sector needs thorough consideration and understanding.

Cooperatives in the Global Economy is a timely text which voices the emerging issues of cooperatives throughout the world. It presents a unique collection of written pieces contributed by leading social and economic thinkers and researchers who provide critical insights into how the cooperative business model meets complex global problems in today's competitive economy. Apart from theoretical arguments in favor of the value-based cooperative business model, the book presents the performances of various forms of cooperatives, their potentialities, and the challenges they face across borders. In the globally competitive economy, the challenges for cooperatives are enormous due to their particular value commitments, forms of incorporation, and organizational structures. Thus, the constraints and challenges in managing cooperatives whose perspectives have received little attention, need a clear understanding in an international context. Again, in spite of the presence of several challenges, cooperatives promote economic growth and social justice worldwide.

The chapters in this book focus on how cooperatives, through their performance, meet complex global problems. Part I of the book comprises chapters focusing on why do we need the cooperative business model, commencing from the thought-provoking introductory ideas to an elaborative discussion on the management of cooperatives in emerging markets. Part II of the book includes chapters with the different types of cooperatives as viable business models along with their performances, potentialities, and challenges in countries such as Tanzania, India, Post-Yugoslav space (Bosnia and Herzegovina, Croatia, Kosovo, Montenegro, Macedonia, Serbia, and Slovenia), the Philippines, Argentina, and Latin America, South Africa, and the Republic of Armenia. Together, the chapters give a rich overview of the performance and critical roles of various forms of cooperatives in balancing economic, social, and environmental concerns, along with the obstacles they face, challenges they undertake, and opportunities that nourish them in the process of building a better world.

Part I

THE COOPERATIVE ENTERPRISE: WHY DO WE NEED IT?

Chapter 1

Why Do We Need Cooperatives to Make the Business World Plural?

Vera Zamagni

BEYOND CHANDLER

Until the 1980s, the winning paradigm of business history internationally was Chandler's corporation-public company model, which separates ownership from control and has a managerial hierarchy and a multidivisional structure (Chandler 1980; 1990). This type of enterprise became very competitive as a result of containment of costs due to the economies of scale and scope and claimed such an imposing part of the market that it created concern about growing so large as to become a monopoly, convincing governments to issue rigorous antitrust laws. These laws, however, did not thwart entirely its potential to expand, because corporations can grow in sectors other than the one they started in, turning into conglomerates and internalizing goods and services previously acquired in the market; more importantly, corporations can expand abroad and become multinational/transnational enterprises. The Chandlerian enterprise's aim is that of maximizing quantities of goods produced with a high level of standardization at prices unbeatable by other forms of business. It originated in the United States, where there was a rapidly growing internal market without customs barriers, receptive to extensive mechanization of production and parceling of labor in assembly lines (Zamagni 2015). Chandler claimed that the corporation was the most modern and efficient form of business destined to replace all other forms, which would live on only in backward countries with inadequate laws and inferior returns.[1]

In American literature, very few dared for a long time to challenge the Chandlerian paradigm, except to note that this business model was not effective in all sectors (Sabel and Zeitlin 1997) or to point out the fact that not even in America had other forms disappeared entirely (Scranton 1997). The first dent in the Chandlerian paradigm on an international level was made by the literature on business groups, which developed between the 1980s and 1990s and mostly applied to Japan. Japanese scholars of economic history had to account for the particular development of Japanese enterprises, which, first with the *zaibatsu*, and after World War II with the *keiretsu*, were consistently inclined to form closely knit groups with a house bank and a common trading company (Morikawa 2001). It was not until 1995, however, that an important article by Mark Granovetter laid down a general framework to establish the business group paradigm.[2] Granovetter claimed in his article that the business group was not necessarily a second-best enterprise model to Chandler's integrated enterprise (as Chandler had always argued), rather, it had come into being to minimize the cost of transactions among businesses—just as the enterprise emerged to reduce the costs of transactions among individuals participating in a production process—and can reach levels of network efficiency competitive with the economies of scale and scope enjoyed by the integrated corporation.

At this point, the literature that has analyzed European state-owned enterprises (SOEs) must be briefly mentioned because they are another form of enterprise different from the classic private corporation. The literature on SOEs has not developed a true alternative to the Chandlerian paradigm, limiting itself to demonstrating the inferiority of SOEs to private companies (Toninelli 2000; Aharoni 1986). However, there is no shortage of paradoxes with reference to the SOEs, because quite a number of them have performed well, especially in the auto industry (for example, Renault and Volkswagen), in the oil industry (Eni and many others), and in the aerospace and defense industries, with the very admirable achievement of the formation of EADS (now Airbus) in 2000 in Europe to compete with the American Boeing company. In reality, the tight relationship with politics sometimes made management of SOEs inefficient because managers were forced to pursue "inappropriate" objectives and worked in monopolistic markets. However, the fact that managerial practices within SOEs did not differ much from those of a classic private corporation and could enjoy a higher propensity to invest over the long run explains the cases of success. Another shortcoming was that managers of SOEs had narrower maneuvering room which substantially limited enterprise configuration because they could not consider the option of expanding or consolidating abroad. Therefore, in the era of globalization, the dismantling of state-owned businesses was considered inevitable and led to extensive privatization starting in the 1980s, with different approaches and outcomes in various countries. No one can deny, however, that many of the largest European corporations now in existence were former SOEs,[3] and that SOEs still perform positive roles in developing countries.

Another more radical alternative to the Chandlerian model evolved with the development of research on "industrial districts," explaining how small- and medium-sized enterprises (SMEs) bunching together in numerous areas have specialized in particular processes of a specific industry, often with a long history. Industrial districts have put in place complete processing chains for particular types of products in which differentiation and customization have a dominant role,[4] with a highly flexible approach in using factors of production, creativity in product models, and in the technology employed. There are numerous examples: chairs, glasses, leather, shoes, jewelry, machinery of every sort, ceramics, furniture, sofas, special fabrics, and quality clothing, to name but just a few of their current specializations. Knowledge of the industrial district model is not widespread, partially because few studies on it are available in English,[5] but especially because its dissemination is hindered by the sociohistorical entrenchment that the districts have demonstrated until now, which makes it difficult to separate them from the context in which they originated and replicate them in other places. Recently, however, the European Union has shown great interest in *clusters*,[6] that is, geographic concentrations of enterprises of different size specialized in a specific type of production,[7] which are one of the pillars of European industry. The first studies in this direction have found that one-third of the industrial labor force in many European countries is concentrated in clusters, especially in Italy, Germany, the Czech Republic, Sweden (home to the European Cluster Observatory), and Spain. The European Union has lately shown great interest in promoting policies to strengthen the technological advancement of clusters.

Only at the end of the past century and the beginning of the new millennium, however, has a more radical revision of the Chandlerian interpretative paradigm evolved, as it was clearly stated by Jonathan Zeitlin.

> The point of departure for the historical alternatives approach is the rejection of the "narrow track" models of industrialization and economic development in all their forms, from Smith's division of labor and Marx's mechanized factory system through Rostow's stages of growth to Chandler's three pronged investments in mass production, mass distribution and professional management. In contrast to both classical economists and modern historians alike, the historical alternatives approach thus denies the existence of a unilinear logic of material progress which must be adopted by all those wishing to advance to higher levels of productivity, income and wealth. (Zeitlin 2008)

This revision has developed in two main directions, which have crossed paths in various ways. The first direction noticed that the rising standards of living and market instability of the present world puts large-scale standardized production at risk. Given the new global conditions, product diversification better meets the needs of the market, and thus "flexible" production processes, aided by electronics that can reprogram machines, have become more competitive than rigid ones. Enterprises can be subdivided into smaller units and become footloose. SMEs have become competitive once again, at least in many sectors, whereas some of the "thick-skinned" businesses of the Fordist era have lost their dynamism up to the point of risking bankruptcy.

The second direction of the Chandlerian paradigm revisionism has been the recognition that there is no "teleologism" in forms of business. As a recent article finally acknowledged (Lamoreaux, Daniel and Temin 2003), between the market (small Smithian enterprises coordinated by the "invisible hand") and the hierarchy (the integrated corporation, organized by the "visible hand" of managers) there are networks of enterprises, differently organized in terms of ownership, but bound to one another through various kinds of relationships. It is precisely these networks that, in the current historical phase of the world economy, are proving to be more able to deal with the growing diversification of demand and increasing instability. The authors of the aforementioned article do not commit the error of arguing that the Chandlerian corporation is by definition the "modern" business model, which has won against all other forms. Instead, they emphasize how the world of enterprises is made up of different kinds of businesses that coexist, with the tendency of some forms to become predominant in certain periods without, however, eliminating other forms. This approach undermines the idea that there is an "optimal" enterprise under all cultural, political, and historical conditions, recognizing that the world has hosted variety, and continues to do so.

This context, which advocates a plurality of forms of enterprise, is the right one to locate my arguments in support of the cooperative form of enterprise. I will show the "comparative advantages" of the cooperative form of enterprise in specific sectors of economic activity, in which such a form is to be preferred to that of the capitalist corporation. In a final paragraph, I will also argue that cooperative enterprises additionally have a positive spillover effect upon the entire market, in which they insert values that the capitalist corporation tends to forget.

WHERE DOES THE COOPERATIVE FORM OF ENTERPRISE SHOW SUBSTANTIAL COMPARATIVE ADVANTAGES?

The cooperative form of enterprise has been the last to come into existence, after the nonprofit form and the capitalist one. Economic activities had been conducted until the birth of the nonprofit form of enterprise in the Middle Ages on a personal basis, by farmers, merchants, shopkeepers, artisans, and moneylenders who carried on their business in premises inside or near their houses. The first large enterprise not belonging to individuals was the *hospital*, created in the early Middle Ages to host people in difficulty (ill, old, handicapped, destitute). The hospital was a big business, not only because it had to care for a large number of guests but also because it had to manage capital (often made up of real estate, buildings to be administered and fields to be cultivated) out of which to pay for the expenses of treating guests and granting wages to all the service personnel. The capital for the nonprofit enterprises was donated by wealthy people and the business was run on a not-for-profit basis, but with the use of all the best accounting techniques. Many other nonprofit enterprises were born subsequently (pawn banks, conservatories, academies, universities, libraries).

In the meantime, through the *commenda*, introduced in Venice in the twelfth century, private business could be participated in by a larger number of capital providers, who were receiving remuneration on the basis of the capital supplied. This was the antecedent of the joint-stock company, of which the first large ones were the Dutch and English commercial companies of the beginning of the seventeenth century. With the creation of stock exchanges, it became easy to buy and sell stocks so that speculation expanded and the joint-stock company became the established form of enterprise——the capitalist enterprise——which could easily gather enough capital to meet the large requirements of the new industrial plants and transportation equipment. As the shareholders were generally not working in the companies they financed, their only aim was the maximization of distributed profits and managers were instructed to run the business to this end by a board elected by shareholders. The capitalist enterprise is an enterprise that minimizes all costs to hand over the largest possible profit to capital owners. In a world in which capital was scarce and badly needed to fund investment in commerce and industry, it is understandable that those who had it could impose this tough condition on one side to workers, who would otherwise remain unemployed or forced to work in the backward sectors of the economy for meager wages, and on the other side to consumers, who had no alternative but to buy from the local shops, and to borrowers, who had to accept the conditions imposed by bankers.

This was the contest that prompted a reaction by the people who did not accept being at the mercy of capitalists and wanted to provide different conditions for their economic activity. These people "invented" a new type of enterprise, the *cooperative* form. Cooperatives differ from nonprofit enterprises because capital is not donated but advanced by members and granted some remuneration, though minimal; they also differ from capitalist enterprises, because capital is not given a key role in the company and the surplus produced is distributed to members corresponding to their activity with the cooperative. Cooperative enterprises were created in all economic fields and countries but prospered more in some activities and countries than in others. We can classify cooperatives according to the different positions and roles of members.

Users' Cooperatives

This type of cooperative is created by people who use the product/service of their cooperative and can be found in retail trade, utilities, credit, insurance, and housing. Members appoint managers to organize the business on their behalf, using dependent workers. Capital is advanced by members, who need not make a large individual contribution, being generally in very large numbers, and can get the goods and services at the best price, avoiding a costly intermediation, besides receiving the surplus produced in the form of a rebate. In addition, these cooperatives can carry on specific campaigns in favor of the goals that members want to reach (fair trade, clean environment, microcredit, co-housing, etc.).

There is little doubt that this is the most successful type of cooperative enterprise: credit and insurance, retail and wholesale trade, housing and utilities are the most widespread activities practiced by this type of cooperative. The advantage lies not only in cutting intermediation costs but also in making the service concerned available to small and scattered users at the best possible conditions, responding to the needs and preferences of users, rather than to the profit-maximizing desires of capital owners. Capital can be increased by increasing the members of such cooperatives, which can easily reach the tens or hundreds of thousands. Additional capital can be made available through members' loans.

Let us consider first *credit* cooperatives, which are easily illustrated, because of all the fields in which cooperatives are present, finance is by far the best-researched one:[8] there were 3,874 cooperative banks in the European Union in 2010, with 66,000 branches, 777,000 employees, 50 million members (10 percent of the population), 181 million clients, 5,647 billion euro of assets, and an average market share of 20 percent (Boscia, Carretta, and Schwizer 2010).[9] As is well known, credit cooperatives started in Germany in the 1840s, both in the countryside (Raiffeisen) and in the cities (Schultze-Delitzsch); as time passed major groups were also formed outside Germany, in France, in the Netherlands, Finland, Austria, Italy, and Switzerland.

Outside Europe, the diffusion of credit unions in the developed world is also substantial, in the United States and particularly in Canada. In the United States, in 2009, there were 7,600 credit unions spread across all states, with $911 billion of assets and 92 million members (one-third of the total population). Their market share can be estimated at around 6–7 percent.[10] In Canada, there were 877 credit unions (including the Caisses *populaires*) in 2010, with Canadian $256 billion (US$265 billion) of assets (around 20 percent of market share) and 11 million members (35 percent of the total population; McPherson 2009).[11] It can noted that in the United States members of credit unions are numerous because such banks mostly grant mortgages and back credit cards to families, while in Europe members are less numerous, because they generally are local businessmen. But credit cooperatives are also quite widespread in developing countries, together with microcredit often supplied with nonprofit enterprises. In the *insurance* industry, the information coming from the International Cooperative and Mutual Insurance Federation website[12] reveals that one-fourth of the world insurance market was cooperative in 2008; with Germany at 44 percent, France at 39 percent, Japan at 38 percent, the United States and Canada at 30 percent.

In the field of *retailing*,[13] consumer cooperatives developed since the middle of the nineteenth century following the Rochdale Equitable Pioneers model, becoming large enterprises by today, which rank in the very top positions among the 300 world's largest cooperatives surveyed by International Cooperative Alliance (ICA), 80 of which are retail cooperatives (cooperatives of retailers included). They are present all over the world, and not only in the United States and Canada, where consumer cooperatives have important retail corporations in the nonfood sectors (e.g., Recreational Equipment, Inc. in the United States and Mountain People's in Canada, which sell outdoor gear). In Japan, there is a special kind of consumer cooperative that caters for their clients in a very personal manner with home delivery of orders and additional services, becoming a sort of community cooperative. As they grew larger and larger, consumer cooperatives needed to improve their managerial capabilities and when this has not been adequately understood, major bankruptcies have taken place; the worst were suffered in Germany and Austria, where the survival of consumer cooperatives has even been challenged (Furlough and Strickwerda 1999). But there are also remarkable cases of success in Europe, especially in the Scandinavian countries (Ekberg 2008) and in Italy (Zamagni, Battilani, and Casali 2004), so that in 2010 consumer cooperatives in Europe were still some 4,500, with 30 million members, 36,000 points of sale, 450,000 employees and €74 billion of turnover.

There are also users' cooperatives in the utilities, especially the distribution of *electricity*, 14 of which are quite large and belong to the 300 largest cooperatives. Their presence is quite important in the United States,[14] where almost 1,000 electricity cooperatives control 40 percent of the entire electricity distribution lines of the United States, covering three-fourths of American territory and serving 37 million members and their families[15] with the production plants owned by them. They came into being in the 1930s as part of the effort by the Rural Electrification Administration to promote the spread of electricity in rural areas, but have since developed into highly organized corporations. Smaller cooperatives can also be found in other utilities in different places.[16] There is now increasing awareness that the new alternative sources of energy could give rise to new forms of cooperation.

Producers' Cooperatives

This type of cooperative is formed by members who produce something in their own private company which is conferred to a cooperative in charge of buying inputs, marketing, and often processing the output. The best example is of farmers' cooperatives, which increase the market power of farmers by contrasting monopsonies, and internalize the profits produced by the processing of the produce in dairy plants, wineries, oil mills, canneries, and so on, owned by cooperatives, although often incorporated as joint-stock companies. A special version of producers' cooperatives is retailers' cooperatives. Originally, retailers maintained their direct activity as shopkeepers (as farmers do), but cooperated in wholesale purchases and many other services. When hypermarkets appeared, however, retailers' cooperatives became a rather blurred type of cooperative, because retailers shared a capital stake in hypermarkets, some of them giving up their shop-keeping activity altogether.

The reasons for the success of cooperation in this field are clear. There is a strong interest on the part of producers (generally small and scattered) to avoid being exploited by wholesale buyers, to reap the benefits of economies of scale in the purchase of inputs and machinery, and to be able to internalize the profits of the industrial processing of their produce. The capital needed to start business is not large and can be accumulated as the business grows up. The tendency of these cooperatives to become large is well established, especially if they deal with highly standardized commodities. The important role these cooperatives can play in supporting the income of farmers is so well established that governments are often inclined in committing to cooperatives the management of the bulk of their agricultural sectors, as the cases of India and Japan show. However, if cooperation remains confined to agriculture proper, mechanization, the shrinking of the labor force and the increased size of farms tend to lock farmers' cooperatives in marginal business, so the food industry is the one granting better prospects to farmers' cooperatives of having a lasting place in national economies.

Agro-industrial cooperatives are prospering in the world, both in advanced and developing countries. ICA had already created a specialized committee in 1951 (the International Cooperative Agricultural Organization) that holds an annual meeting. Among the 300 largest world co-ops (Global 300 survey of ICA for 2008), they are 110, boosted by the large number of American (23) and French (21) co-ops. This type of cooperative started to spread toward the end of the nineteenth century, following the Scandinavian example (Zamagni and Zamagni 2010): dairy in Denmark; forestry in Sweden and Finland; wine and dairy in Italy and France; and grain and cotton in the United States. These were all examples found in thousands all over the world, with application in the most diverse crop cultivation and processing as well as in animal rearing and meat processing. In Europe, there are 35,000 cooperatives today in the field with 12 million members, a turnover of 250 billion euros and an average market share of as much as 60 percent (Juliá Igual and Martí Meliá 2008; Chloupková 2002).

In the United States, agricultural cooperatives have always been very strong since the nineteenth century as a result of widespread protests against national/multinational corporations and in support of localized development based on the "cooperative commonwealth" of farmers (Schneiberg, King, and Smith 2008, p. 638; Curl 2010). The main farmer organizations, the National Grange and the Farmers Alliance, sponsored the foundation of cooperatives, mainly in the field of common purchases of inputs and collective marketing, with a modest diversification into the foodstuff industry and no propensity to develop community services.[17] In 1986, there were 5,369 agricultural cooperatives, with 4.6 million members. There has been a decline in numbers later (in 2005, they were 3,000 with 2.8 million members), but this was mostly due to mergers and acquisitions, a few failures, and the decline of the population of farmers, while the market share remains steady at around one-third.[18]

In Japan, in the pre–World War II period, agricultural cooperatives already conducted various businesses connected with credit and better living conditions in the countryside, but in the postwar years they really developed into multipurpose community-based cooperatives and became more democratically run. Besides organizing the vast majority of the agricultural business activities (JA-Zenchu has 70 percent of market share), the JA system also provides for infrastructural development, financial services (including insurance), social services (health, public care, culture, food, and agriculture education), and retail facilities in the countryside (Rajaratne 2007). With the financial liberalization of the 1990s, things have changed and JA has reacted by trying to make the system more efficient. But the results are not satisfactory yet. Today, male farmers less than sixty-five years of age who work full time are below 10 percent of the total; the legion of part-time farmers distort the mechanisms of cooperation in various ways (Yamashita 2009). In particular, part-time farmers are not interested in reforms for increasing the scale of farms and refrain from adopting a more efficient model of farming, especially in the production of rice. This inefficiency produces a level of food prices in Japan that is 56 percent higher than the world average (Harada 2012). Tariffs and subsidies help Japanese agriculture to remain in place. The international pressures toward liberalization will change Japanese policies toward agriculture and this will certainly have an impact on the power of JA.

The cooperative presence in Indian agriculture is truly impressive. Cooperation in India goes back to the British rule. The first Cooperative Society Act in 1904 enabled the formation of agricultural credit cooperatives, soon complemented by other types of cooperatives. The movement spread in the countryside and today India has 230 million members of cooperatives generally located in the countryside (80 percent), with 14 million employees. The movement is organized into 214 federations under the aegis of the umbrella organization National Cooperative Union of India. The village cooperatives provide inputs for farming, storage facilities, marketing of produce, and processing of various crops. They also provide irrigation, electricity, transport and health services, retail facilities, pretty much as in the Japanese approach of multipurpose cooperatives. When India embraced central planning, cooperatives had become quasi-state organizations, with little autonomy. They are now striving to recover efficiency and democratic stake holding. They have strong market shares in rural credit (46 percent in 2006), in the production of sugar, rubber, cotton, milk[19] and seeds oil. Consumer cooperatives (with 22 percent market share) and credit unions are the only cooperatives having some presence in the Indian urban environment (Das et al. 2006).

Social or Community Cooperatives

It has taken a long time to have this type of cooperative officially recognized by the ICA, which added a seventh principle of external mutuality to the already-existing ones only in the 1990s. They remain a special type of cooperative, which combine workers and users of social services, and can have voluntary work in addition. They are generally run by a multi-stakeholder board. The comparative advantage of cooperatives in social services is mostly based on intrinsic motivations (Becchetti, Castriota, and Tortia 2009). The fact that social services postulate a direct contact of the producer with the clients—an interpersonal relation (Gui and Sugden 2005)—makes the personal involvement of the producer essential to the good result of the process. Having "intrinsic motivations," sometimes a true passion, for what the social service worker does is the best prerequisite to have satisfactory relationships with clients. Cooperative members who choose to be in a social service firm run by them are in the best position to develop their talents and express their "benevolence" toward their colleagues and clients, ready to tailor their services to the real needs of clients. Social service cooperatives are normally not large, precisely because of the need for customization, and rely more than other types of cooperatives on networks (Menzani and Zamagni 2010). The physical capital needed is often modest, while human capital is extremely important.

Only the Italian developments of these cooperatives have been widely covered by the literature in so far. The first "social cooperative" was founded in Italy in 1963, providing training, education, assistance, recreation, and work for disadvantaged people (members, but also nonmembers), advocating an extended concept of mutual cooperation, the "external" mutualism. Workers are often members of the cooperative, but the presence in the assembly of members also who are recipients of the services makes the classical form of such a cooperative a multi-stakeholder form, in which also representatives from the local community can have a seat on the board of directors, side by side with producers and recipients of the services. Italy has passed a law to regulate social cooperatives (No. 381 of 1991). It is estimated that as much as 50 percent of the social services provided in Italy in 2010 were supplied by social cooperatives. The system is a four-tier one, with single, smallish, highly diversified cooperatives at the bottom, coordinated by a second tier of local consortia, themselves joining in a national consortium that provides the most qualified services. On top of the national consortia, there are the sectoral associations of the national umbrella organizations, mostly providing political representation.

This model[20] has been emulated in France, Spain, Portugal, Greece but it also exists elsewhere in other forms: community cooperatives in the Anglo-Saxon countries, or multipurpose cooperatives in Japan. Social services are also offered by nonprofit enterprises, as the book edited by Borzaga and Defourny (2001) illustrates, with an undefined borderline between the cooperative form and the nonprofit, or civil form, the latter being, as mentioned earlier, the original way of delivering social services before the welfare state came into being (Borzaga et al. 2009).

Workers' Cooperatives

These are the cooperatives self-managed by those who work in them, advancing the capital which is needed. These types of cooperatives have received a lot of attention in the economic literature, starting with John Stuart Mill, because they are run democratically and directly contrast the capitalist form of enterprise.

Workers cooperatives are, however, not so diffused, for a host of reasons, among which the most important are the following: standardization of products and Fordist processes of production in industry do not need cooperators; the huge physical capital needed cannot be advanced by workers; and the large economies of scale to be reaped impose a size that cannot be governed democratically. Workers at the assembly line have to perform menial jobs, in which there is very little scope for the exercise of personal talents. What predominates in these corporations is capital, and managers are seen as instruments to serve capital.

Cooperatives in industry, however, do exist, but normally for small-size businesses. France still has, for instance, an important group of artisanal cooperatives (327), but their total turnover, according to the figures published by the *Groupement National de la Cooperation* (GNC) is only 1 percent of the total turnover of the French cooperative enterprises (Bataille-Chedotel and Huntzinger 2004). There are only five industrial cooperatives listed in the global 300 cooperatives surveyed by ICA for 2008, two in the construction industry (both in Italy), one mixed (again in Italy), so that in manufacturing there are only two cooperatives listed, one Spanish (the famous Mondragon; see MacLeod and Reed 2009) and one Italian (SACMI, Imola). There are many more workers cooperatives of smaller size, but on the whole their relevance in manufacturing is quite limited.

More workers' cooperatives can be found in services: transportation (taxis, lorries, buses),[21] catering, facility management, logistics, theaters, management of cultural resorts, media, tourism, and professional firms. The literature on cooperative activities in services is, to my knowledge, very modest, with the exception of Italy, where the Bologna research group on cooperatives has done a lot to unveil this type of cooperative enterprise. Bologna hosts a large catering cooperative, Camst (Zamagni 2002), which is the largest Italian company in the field, and a large facility management cooperative group (Manutencoop), again one of the most important Italian companies in its field. It also hosts a large consortium of service cooperatives (Battilani and Bertagnoni 2010), which aims at offering clients complete sets of services produced by different cooperatives and coordinated by the consortium.

In conclusion, it might be said that cooperatives have a comparative advantage in labor-intensive lines of production, and especially in those sectors in which there is much need for differentiation of product and service (customization) and relationships with clients. Highly standardized capital-intensive lines of production are better exercised by capitalist corporations.

WHY DO WE NEED MORE COOPERATIVES IN THE PRESENT-DAY WORLD?

There is general agreement on the fact that the world has become a more hospitable place in the past two centuries, and this is mostly the result of capitalist investments by corporations, but there are today at least three disturbing trends that raise a lot of concern. The first is the presence of too many persons who still live near or below subsistence levels and cannot enjoy their lives; the second is the alarming increase of people who are too rich; and the third is the financialization of the world that diverts capital from investments in the real side of the economy. This last problem is particularly worrisome because it is only through investments that economies can grow, be innovative, and include more people in productive work. If capital is "wasted" in speculation, the rich will become richer, but the improvement of the world is jeopardized. Capitalism does not appear at present to engage in counteracting these trends, and civil society must be ready to make appropriate legislation to stop and reverse these trends. There have recently been many discussions on raising taxes on the rich, making the intervention of antitrust agencies more rigid, introducing caps on the pay of high-level managers (Atkinson 2015) and the like.

One very effective way of limiting the worst features of capitalism is to restrict the number of corporations so they do not get control of all economic activities. Many economic activities, as argued above, can be better carried out by cooperatives, which by definition do not produce the negative spillover effects mentioned above and work to increase the well-being of their members and, therefore, are not prone to entertaining speculative activities. In fact, cooperatives are open to the membership of not so well-to-do people, because they normally require only a limited amount of capital from their members, so they are inclusive businesses. Cooperatives are run democratically and tend to reward members and dependent workers in an equitable way, avoiding major differences in remuneration. Social cohesion is the result of diffusion of cooperatives, as well as a more widespread exercise of entrepreneurship. Corporations are highly hierarchical organizations, which tend to make their complete labor force passively apply commands, while cooperatives rely on self-organization and require the participation of members, enlarging responsibility and "civicness." Also, the market at large registers a positive impact from the presence of cooperatives, because there are many more firms operating and competition is enhanced.

Governments that care for their people should understand the usefulness of promoting cooperatives with appropriate legislation. The need for this legislation arises from two reasons: on one side, cooperatives must be allowed to form networks and have their umbrella organizations; and on the other side, their capitalization must be supported precisely to allow not so well-to-do people to become members. There are various ways of supporting the capitalization of cooperatives: (1) formation of a fund made up of "indivisible reserves," namely, profits that are not taxed and cannot be distributed to members (intergenerational bond); (2) loans from members, that can be collected and remunerated at the going rate of interest in addition to the capital share of members; and (3) formation of another fund with 3 percent of the profits of cooperatives to help cooperatives in difficulty and to support start-ups. But many other instruments could be used to reach this goal.

Countries with large numbers of cooperatives are the most civilized countries of the world, also because nonprofit organizations are normally growing in the same countries side by side with cooperatives, and corporations working there tend to show higher corporate social responsibility, otherwise public opinion turns against them. We can, therefore, conclude that cooperatives, besides helping their members and effectively producing many goods and services, play a humanizing and socializing role in the entire marketplace where they reach a critical mass (Restakis 2010).

NOTES

1. The "weight" of the Chandlerian paradigm in international business history is demonstrated by a recent historiographic survey. See Amatori and Jones (2003) for details.
2. See my comment on the role of Granovetter's article in V. Zamagni, "Granovetter and Enterprises Networks." *Business History Review* 80, no. 1 (2006): 159–61.
3. Italy too has a successful enterprise in the defense industry, Finmeccanica, a former state holding company of engineering enterprises. See Zamagni (2009).
4. By their very nature, districts are not interested in standardized production.
5. See Belussi and Sammarra (2009); Becattini, Bellandi and De Propis (2009, with examples also from outside Italy); Jones, Dimitratos, Fletcher and Young (2009).
6. Here is the definition of cluster: "A cluster can be broadly defined as a group of firms, related economic actors, and institutions that are located near each other and have reached a sufficient scale to develop specialized expertise, resources, suppliers and skills" (EU 2008). The main difference between them and traditional industrial districts is that clusters also include large enterprises even though they are mostly made up of SMEs.
7. For example, automotive production, which in different countries includes auto-related industries.
8. There is an extremely large body of literature on cooperative banking, both historical and economic. I draw much of the empirical material from my essay published in 2012 (Battilani and Schroter 2012).
9. Figures come from the European Association of Cooperative Banks (www.eurocoopbanks.coop).
10. Figures from www.cuna.org.
11. Figures come from Credit Union Central of Canada and include affiliated and nonaffiliated banks (www.cucentral.ca).
12. www.icmif.org.
13. In retailing, there are other forms of cooperatives: retailers' cooperatives and workers' cooperatives. In Spain Eroski, a retail cooperative founded by the Mondragon group, is a workers' cooperative.

14. Of the fourteen large cooperatives in the utilities, only one is Brazilian.

15. One of the two 2009 Nobel prize winners for economics, Elinor Ostrom, has studied precisely the theme of how to govern "commons." See E. Ostrom, *Governing the Commons. The Evolution of Institutions for Collective Action* (Cambridge: Cambridge University Press, 1990); *Understanding Institutional Diversity* (Princeton: Princeton University Press, 2005).

16. For housing and other users cooperatives, see J. Shaffer, *Historical Dictionary of the Cooperative Movement* (London: Scarecrow Press, 1999).

17. The reason being the private nature of welfare in the United States.

18. 86 percent milk, 40 percent grains, 43 percent cotton (Williams 2007). The general figures come from NCFC (National Council of Farmer Cooperatives).

19. In the case of milk, a project was launched by the state in the 1970s—"Operation Flood"—aiming at increased milk production, fair price, and improved incomes. By the end of the project, the system comprised 43,000 village cooperatives linking 4.25 million milk producers and several dairy and cattle plants (Williams, cit.).

20. The best comprehensive book on the Italian social cooperatives is Borzaga and Ianes (2006). For a comprehensive assessment in English, see ch. 5 in J. Restakis, *Humanizing the Economy. Cooperatives in the Age of Capital* (Gabriola Island, Canada: New Society Publishers, 2010).

21. I note in passing that some of these transportation cooperatives are of the producer type, because drivers own their means of transport and share services in the cooperative. There is a good company history in P. Battilani, G. Bertagnoni, and S. Vignini, *Un'impresa di cooperatori, artigiani, camionisti. La CTA e il trasporto merci in Italia* (Bologna: Il Mulino, 2008).

REFERENCES

Aharoni, Yair. *The Evolution and Management of State Owned Enterprises*. New York: HarperCollins, 1986.

Amatori, Franco, and Geoffrey Jones. *Business History around the World*. Cambridge: Cambridge University Press, 2003.

Atkinson, Anthony B. *Inequality. What Can be Done?* Cambridge, MA: Harvard University Press, 2015.

Bataille-Chedotel, Frédérique, and France Huntzinger. "Faces of Governance of Production Cooperatives: An Exploratory Study of Ten French Cooperatives." *Annals of Public and Cooperative Economics* 75, no. 1 (2004): 265–93.

Battilani, Patrizia, Giuliana Bertagnoni, and Stefania Vignini. *Un'impresa di cooperatori, artigiani, camionisti. La CTA e il trasporto merci in Italia*. Bologna: Il Mulino, 2008.

Battilani, Patrizia, and Giuliana Bertagnoni, ed. *Co-operation Network Service. Innovation in Outsourcing*. Lancaster: Carnegie Publisher, 2010.

Becattini, Giacomo, Marco Bellandi, and Lisa De Propis, ed. *A Handbook of Industrial Districts*. Cheltenham: Elgar, 2009.

Becchetti, Leonardo, Stefano Castriota, and Ermanno C. Tortia. *Productivity, Wages and Intrinsic Motivation in Social Enterprises*. Milan: Econometica Working Paper no. 16, 2009.

Belussi, Fiorenza, and Alessia Sammarra, ed. *Business Networks in Clusters and Industrial Districts: The Governance of the Global Value Chain*. London: Routledge, 2009.

Borzaga, Carlo, and Jacques Defourny, ed. *The Emergence of Social Enterprise*. London: Routledge, 2001.

Borzaga, Carlo, and Alberto Ianes. *L'economia della solidarietà. Storia e prospettive della cooperazione sociale*. Rome: Donzelli, 2006.

Borzaga, Carlo, Sara Depedri, and Ermanno C. Tortia. *The Role of Cooperative and Social Enterprises: A Multifaceted Approach for an Economic Pluralism*. University of Trento; European Research Institute on Cooperative & Social Enterprises (EURICSE) Working Paper no. 000/09, 2009.

Boscia, Vittorio, Alessandro Carretta, and Paola Schwizer. *Cooperative Banking in Europe. Case Studies*. Basingstoke: Palgrave Macmillan, 2010.

Chandler, Alfred. *The Visible Hand. The Managerial Revolution in American Business*. Cambridge, MA: Harvard University Press, 1980.

Chandler, Alfred. *Scale and Scope. The Dynamics of Industrial Capitalism*. Cambridge, MA: Harvard University Press, 1990.

Chloupková, Jarka. *European Cooperative Movement. Background and Common Denominators*. Working paper 24204 from the Royal Veterinary and Agricultural University. Copenhagen: Department of Economics and Natural Resources, 2002.

Curl, John. "The Co-operative Movement in Century 21." *Affinities: A Journal of Radical Theory, Culture and Action* 4, no. 1 (2010): 12–29.

Das, Banishree, Nirod K. Palai, and Kumar Das. *Problems and Prospects of the Cooperative Movement in India Under the Globalization Regime*. Helsinki: XIV International Economic History Congress, Session 72, 2006.

Ekberg, Espen. *Consumer Co-operatives and the Transformation of Modern Food Retailing. A Comparative Study of Norwegian and British Consumer Co-operatives, 1950–2002*. Oslo: University of Oslo Publications, 2008.

European Union. *Towards World Class Clusters in the European Union*. SEC 2637. Brussels, 2008.

Fonteyne, Wim. *Cooperative Banks in Europe. Policy Issues*. IMF Working Paper/07/159, 2007.

Furlough, Ellen, and Carl Strickwerda, eds. *Consumers against Capitalism? Consumer Co-operation in Europe, North America and Japan, 1840–1990*. Maryland: Rowman & Littlefield, 1999.

Granovetter, Mark. "Coase Revisited: Business Groups in the Modern Economy." *Industrial and Corporate Change* 4, no. 1 (1995): 93–130. https://doi.org/10.1093/icc/4.1.93.

Gui, Benedetto, and Robert Sugden, ed. *Economics and Social Interaction: Accounting for Interpersonal Relations*. Cambridge: Cambridge University Press, 2005.

Harada, Yutaka. *Can Japanese Farming Survive Liberalization?* 2012. www.tokyo-foundation.org/en/articles.

Jones, Marian V., Pavlos Dimitratos, Margaret Fletcher, and Stephen Young, ed. *Internationalization, Entrepreneurship and the Smaller Firm: Evidence from around the World.* Cheltenham: Elgar, 2009.

Juliá, Igual J. F., and Elena Meliá-Marti. "Social Economy and the Cooperative Movement in Europe: Contributions to a New Vision of Agriculture and Rural Development in the Europe of the 27." *Ciriec-España*, special issue, no. 62 (2008): 148–72.

Kazuito, Yamashita. *The Agricultural Cooperatives and Farming Reform in Japan.* Tokyo: The Tokyo Foundation for Policy Research, 2009. www.tokyofoundation .org/en/articles.

Kruse, Douglas L., Richard B. Freeman, and Joseph R. Blasi. *Shared Capitalism at Work. Employee Ownership, Profit and Gain Sharing and Broad Based Stock Options.* NBER Conference, University of Chicago Press, 2010.

Lamoreaux, Naomi R., Daniel M. G. Raff, and Peter Temin. "Beyond Markets and Hierarchies: Toward a New Synthesis of American Business History." *American History Review* 108, no. 2 (2003): 404–33.

MacLeod, Greg, and Darryl Reed. "Mondragon's Response to the Challenges of Globalization: A Multi-localization Strategy." In *Co-operatives in a Global Economy: The Challenges of Co-operation Across Borders*, edited by Darryl Reed and J. J. McMurtry, 111–40, Newcastle-upon-Tyne: Cambridge Scholars Publishing, 2009.

McPherson, Ian. *A Century of Cooperation.* Ottawa: Canadian Cooperative Association, 2009.

Menzani, Tito, and Vera Zamagni. "Cooperative Networks in the Italian Economy." *Enterprise and Society* XI, no. 1 (2010): 98–127.

Morikawa, Hidemasa. *A History of Top Management in Japan. Managerial Enterprises and Family Enterprises.* Oxford: Oxford University Press, 2001.

Ostrom, Elinor. *Governing the Commons. The Evolution of Institutions for Collective Action*, Cambridge: Cambridge University Press, 1990.

Ostrom, Elinor. *Understanding Institutional Diversity.* Princeton: Princeton University Press, 2005.

Rajaratne, Anura R. "Roles and Effectiveness of Agricultural Cooperatives in Japan, with Special Emphasis on Organized Farm Activities." *Journal of Developments in Sustainable Agriculture* 2, no. 2 (2007): 192–98.

Restakis, John. *Humanizing the Economy. Cooperatives in the Age of Capital.* Gabriola Island (Canada): New Society Publishers, 2010.

Sabel, Charles F., and Jonathan Zeitlin. *World of Possibilities. Flexibility and Mass Production in Western Industries.* Cambridge: Cambridge University Press, 1997.

Schneiberg, Marc, Marissa King, and Thomas Smith. "Social Movements and Organizational Form: Cooperative Alternatives to Corporations in the American Insurance, Dairy and Grain Industries." *American Sociological Review* 73, no. 4 (2008): 635–67.

Scranton, Phillip. *Endless Novelty. Production and American Industrialization 1865–1925*. Princeton: Princeton University Press, 1997.
Shaffer, Jack. *Historical Dictionary of the Cooperative Movement*. London: Scarecrow Press, 1999.
Toninelli, Pier A. T*he Rise and Fall of State-owned Enterprises in the Western World*. Cambridge: Cambridge University Press, 2000.
Williams, Richard C. *The Cooperative Movement. Globalization from Below*. Aldershot: Ashgate, 2007.
Yamashita, Kazuhito. *The Agricultural Cooperatives and Farming Reform in Japan,*2009. www.tokyofoundation.org/en/articles.
Yutaka, Harada. *Can Japanese Farming Survive Liberalization?* Tokyo: The Tokyo Foundation for Policy Research, 2012. www.tokyofoundation.org/en/articles.
Zamagni, Stefano, and Vera Zamagni. *Cooperative Enterprise. Facing the Challenge of Globalization*. Cheltenham: Elgar, 2010.
Zamagni, Vera, ed. *Camst: ristorazione e socialità*. Bologna: Il Mulino, 2002.
Zamagni, Vera. "Granovetter and Enterprises Networks." *Business History Review* 80, no. 1 (2006): 159–61.
Zamagni, Vera. *Finmeccanica. Competenze che vengono da lontano*. Bologna: Il Mulino, 2009.
Zamagni, Vera. "A World of Variations: Sectors and Forms." In *The Cooperative Business Movement, 1950 to the Present*, edited by P. Battilani and H. Schroter, 63–82. Cambridge: Cambridge University Press, 2012.
Zamagni, Vera. *Perché l'Europa ha cambiato il*. Bologna: Il Mulino, 2015.
Zamagni, Vera, Patrizia Battilani, and Antonio Casali. *La cooperazione di consumo in Italia. Centocinquant'anni della coop consumatori: dal primo spaccio a leader della moderna distribuzione*. Bologna: Il Mulino, 2004.
Zeitlin, Jonathan. "The Historical Alternatives Approach." In *The Oxford Handbook of Business History*, edited by Geoffrey G. Jones and Jonathan Zeitlin, 120–40. Oxford: Oxford University Press, 2008.'

Chapter 2

Moral Commitment as a Driver for Successful Business Development: The Cooperative Way

Greg MacLeod

HISTORICAL CONTEXT

Human beings have a long history, and all their structures, including economic ones, evolve. Before trying to change the present economic system, we must begin with a brief historical review. It seems obvious that, in early history, economic development was based on natural resources such as animals and plants. People developed the resources in the places where they lived. Economic development was local. After 1500, however, new patterns began to develop. In the southern parts of North America, the Spanish and Portuguese reaped gold and silver for their kingdoms. In the northern parts of the American continent, the French and English led in reaping fish and furs for Europe. As resources got exhausted, the adventurers would move to other places such as Africa. Of course, people had traded internationally for thousands of years, but this new kind of trade was on a nation-to-nation basis, with political and economic forces merging. This was a radical departure from traditional economic development. Thus, began the large-scale process of delocalization of economic development with approximately 250 large global corporations controlling most of the world's economy by the year 2000. The headquarters are mainly located in the United States, Japan, and Germany.

Many of the problems we face today are rooted in that strategy of seeking resources at a long distance away. Today, the investors from the United States, Canada, Russia, and China are in Africa and Asia, not out of love for Africans and Asians, but in the hope of making profit through the development of Asian and African natural resources. In this process of delocalization, wealth is created in one location, but this same wealth is transferred to another location. Locally, the benefits are minimized and, at a distant control center, the benefits are maximized. In those regions which have thus become branch plants or branch regions, the consequences are often negative from the economic and the environmental points of view. However, the owners in distant places usually do not accept responsibility for the consequences.

For any thinking person with a sense of social justice, this model is wrong. It involves wealthy people in distant places owning, controlling, and profiting from wealth-producing entities in distant places. Whether they are kings, queens, emperors, or stock investors, it comes down to the same thing. Money and power are the means to exploit people in other places. It is true that, through government controls and labor unions, the benefits of work have been spread more evenly through the trickle-down effect. But the dynamic is the same. These large global corporations have great political influence and promote unfettered free market systems. In the United States, it costs several hundred million dollars to run a presidential campaign. Billionaires and large business corporations supply a good percentage of this money. A recent book by a highly regarded French economist pointed out with statistics that the rich are really getting richer and the poor are not moving up (Piketty 2014). During the twentieth century, the big debate had been whether state socialism inspired by Marx, or capitalism inspired by Adam Smith could solve the problems. With the fall of the Berlin Wall in 1988, many thought that capitalism had won and that corporate capital would solve the problems of poverty and unemployment in the world. However, the recession of 2008 showed that corporate capital was not working for the common good. Besides Marx, there were other reformers who were moderate. They saw the need for new, less radical models. Robert Owen floated the idea of creating a new moral world based on mutual help and cooperation replacing the old immoral world based on competition and exploitation. He believed that as much as it was necessary for business owners to earn profits, workers should also be equally provided with benefits and treated in a just manner. Thus, with his socialist ideas, he was credited to transform England during the Industrial Revolution. Similarly, Charles Fourier who is often referred to a "Utopian Socialist," opposed the principle of laissez-faire capitalism and supported the idea of cooperation in communities that work toward a common goal, rather than competing against each other. To him, the creation of relatively small communities would be self-contained based on the principle of cooperation that leads to improving the lives of all people in the society.

For over 150 years, the cooperative movement has made an important contribution to counteract the growing power of the large corporate business system, but it is not enough. The intentions were correct, but the cooperative sector in business is relatively small across the world. Governments have become extremely bureaucratic. They are capable of making regulations to control the market system, but it is not likely that they will come up with significant change in the free market system. Technology has made bureaucratic systems all the more resistant to change from outside (Habermas 1990). Because of all this, I would like to suggest that we must put a great deal of effort in finding new forms and new structures so that community groups will be able to exert greater influence in our economic system.

Basing ourselves on the history of the cooperative movement, I suggest that we must experiment a great deal more. I use the word "experiment," because we are never certain what will work best in solving the deep-rooted problems of poverty and unemployment. When we transform a solution into an "ism" such as capitalism, communism or even cooperativism, we make our systems sacrosanct and resistant to change. We must try new forms of organization and, if they don't work, we must modify them and try new experiments in socioeconomic re-construction. These should be place-based local structures and community controlled.

For the present, I wish to focus on nonmetropolitan areas because the highest unemployment is usually found there. Marx spoke of the "idiocy of the countryside," and a number of years ago, a Ford Foundation study called for the merciful death of small-town America. Especially from a cultural point of view, I think that nonmetropolitan areas are extremely important for world civilization. Such areas are more difficult to absorb into technocratic systems. I believe that smaller decentralized societies are more resistant to conformity and uniformity. Large global corporations depend upon uniformity. Whether a Ford or Honda automobile is made in any part of the world, they are all the same.

I have been fascinated by several examples of successful socioeconomic development which do not fit the global pattern of delocalization. These are Mondragon in the Pyrenees Mountains of Spain, Trentino in the Alpine border areas of northern Italy, and Hansalim in rural South Korea. In Cape Breton, Canada, we have New Dawn Enterprises along with the BCA Group, and there are significant cooperative innovations in Quebec, which have their roots back in the 1880s and mainly in the dairy industry (*Aidons-nous les uns les autres, la cooperation est la cle du succès*). I am sure there are many more, but I focus on the larger international cases.

The traditional cooperative movement is understood as either consumer or producer controlled. Throughout the world, the vast majority of cooperative business organizations are grocery stores and credit unions and are consumer owned and controlled. Farmers often form marketing cooperatives controlled by farmers.

Henry Mintzberg is a widely published international authority on business management. He suggests that we forget about the opposition between private enterprise and government enterprise and that we focus on the balance between individual needs versus community needs (Mintzberg 2015). He calls for new models based on balance and harmony among conflicting needs and desires. I suggest that the following examples help respond to the need outlined by Mintzberg. In discussing the following cases, I offer a more detailed description of the Mondragon Cooperative Corporation (MCC) since I know it best. Then I will give brief overviews of the other cases. These cases are very different on the surface, but if we examine them closely, we will find a common thread that is of the moral order, but which is very powerful.

Mondragon

Today, the MCC in northern Spain is a huge industrial complex with over 75,000 workers and over $20 billion in sales. They produce foodstuffs, automobile parts, refrigerators, furniture, and so on, and have a university. For communities suffering from high unemployment and low wages, it is a very powerful model and looks impossible to replicate. But it was not always that way. Hence, it is more useful to go back sixty-five years to their beginning. It is not necessary to copy Mondragon, but the principles used can be useful.

In 1939, the civil war between the Republicans and Royalists in Spain was terminated and Franco, the anti-republican, became the dictator of Spain. The Basque people were ancient people living in northern Spain. The Basques had favored the Republicans and the result was that Franco refused to support development in that area. During the 1940s, the Basque area suffered from high unemployment and a high rate of emigration. They used a very ancient language which Franco forbade but, they had very strong social cohesion. The Basques number approximately four million and are the oldest ethnic group in Europe. To explain the development of Mondragon, we will provide a historical sequence.

Stage One: Development of Motivation, 1944–1955

During these times, a local religious leader, Don Jose Maria Arizmendiarrieta, began teaching young people to take responsibility for change in their community. In 1943, Don Jose Maria developed a sports center for young people. He also organized a new school of apprenticeship, using a rented building. In the first year, in spite of their humble and scant facilities, twenty-one students graduated. It became known as "the school of the poor." Don Jose Maria continually reminded the students of social responsibility. Also, he insisted on preservation of their ancient language and culture. He helped some of them to become qualified for university study.

Don Jose Maria encouraged them to study engineering, since technology would become extremely important in the future economy. In the history of Mondragon, this period of preparation and motivation is considered the first stage of development.

Stage Two: Initial Business Phase, 1956–1973

In 1955, five of these students returned as young engineers to their native village of Mondragon which had a population of approximately 800. These young men began a factory to produce small paraffin stoves. Don Jose Maria supported them in their new business. As they hired more people, they agreed to follow the principles of social justice. They made a rule that each worker would be a shareholder in their cooperative and that no person would earn more than four times the wages of the lowest paid. They also made a rule that all profits would be shared by workers in proportion to their salaries. Their business soon became successful but, they did not stop there. They believed that unemployment was the greatest problem in the Basque area, so they sought new ways to create jobs for the unemployed.

In 1958, they had their first expansion which was the creation of a consumer food cooperative. It would eventually evolve into the giant supermarket chain called Eroski. It was different from the typical consumer cooperative because both the customers and the workers became shareholders with the right to elect the board of directors.

In 1959, as they tried to expand, they had the problem of raising money. Don Jose Maria promoted the creation of a cooperative bank or credit union (Caja Laboral). He told the young entrepreneurs that they could not rely on the big banks for investment. The main purpose of their community bank would be to raise money for job creation. He also told them to locate their cooperative bank in the communities where they lived so that people would know what their money was being used for. In addition to the usual functions, their bank would eventually provide insurance and various social-security systems (Lagun Aro). A motto was posted on each cooperative bank. It read "Saving Books or Suitcases" (Tarjeta o Maleta). The idea was that money placed in large banks would go to development in prosperous areas but money placed in the local cooperative bank would be used to develop business and jobs for their children. Without local investment, the young people would leave, sometimes for other countries.

In 1966, they built a polytechnic school to prepare future workers. They realized that science and technology would be key to business success in the future, so a highly trained workforce would be essential.

Each cooperative business had its own board of directors elected by the worker-shareholders and the board chose the manager. The financial plan was quite unique. To obtain a job, the candidate was required to purchase a share. The worker would spend a year on probation. During that time, the worker would be evaluated from two points of view. The manager would evaluate the technical ability to do the job and the fellow workers would evaluate the applicant in social terms. If the worker was difficult to work with, he or she would not be hired. They also made it possible for the worker to borrow money to purchase the share which could be paid back through wages.

At first, each enterprise operated independently although they considered themselves to be a family of companies. But as they grew in size, the leadership decided that they should form groupings. At first, the groupings were geographic. Enterprises in the same valley formed a conglomerate, sharing certain resources. Later, the groupings were changed so that all the enterprises connected with food production formed one conglomerate and the enterprises connected with machine parts formed another grouping. This is called sectoral grouping rather than geographic grouping.

By this time, their bank had set up an entrepreneurial division to help launch new businesses, so the bank became the glue holding the different enterprises together. The bank was a kind of internal consulting company. Each of the individual enterprises contributed to a central fund, which would be used for the development of new businesses.

In 1968, the industrial student cooperative Alecop was created, where students work half a day and study half a day. Don Jose Maria wanted to make sure that even the poorest could earn money to pursue their education. Continuing education soon became a part of the Mondragon corporate culture. Approximately, 4 percent of profit was devoted to worker education of various kinds.

They also created the industrial cooperative Auzo-Lagun to introduce women to industrial work. In Spain at that time, it was unusual for women to work in industry. Don Jose Maria claimed that, once children were in school, it did not make much sense for women to stay at home keeping house. He said that modern appliances such as washers and dryers liberate women from traditional housework. He knew that men could cook very well. In fact, the Basque area was famous for gastronomical clubs where men met with friends at least once a week to cook marvelous meals. Women were not allowed membership. So, Don Jose Maria concluded that women should not be chained to a stove at home waiting to feed their men (Joxe 1984).

Stage Three: The Mature Organization, 1973 to the Present

In 1974, the technological research center Ikerlan was created. It specializes in electronics and mechanics. Visiting groups are always impressed when they see the technicians at Ikerlan constructing robots for use in their factories. The leadership recognized that technology is always changing and that businesses that fall behind in technology will not survive.

In 1976, the first foreign offices were created in France, Germany, and Great Britain. This occurred after the death of Franco, the dictator who bitterly opposed the Basques. At this time Spanish trade barriers were dropped and the Mondragon leaders saw new opportunities in Europe.

In 1986, the first subsidiary factory was built in Southeast Asia (Thailand).

In 1987, the second research center, Ideko, was created. It specializes in machine-tools.

In 1989, the first Mondragon Cooperative Congress was organized. It was the first time that all the individual producer cooperatives were represented under one umbrella structure. This facilitated higher levels of joint-venturing and collaboration.

In 1992, the headquarters for the MCC was created as part of the new Congress structure. The entrepreneurial division of their bank was absorbed into the central offices and the bank became limited to finance. The corporation then became composed of four divisions: knowledge, finance, retail, and industrial.

In 1997, Mondragon University was established as the first university to be approved by the new Basque provincial parliament. It comprised three centers located in the Mondragon valley: the polytechnic school in Mondragon, the business faculty in Oñati, and the faculty of humanities in Eskoriatza.

In 2003, the Garaia Innovation Research Center was created. It groups many of the innovation and research centers in one location.

In 2007, they built their first industrial park in Southeast Asia, in Kunshan, China.

Reasons for the Initial Success

It is a rule in economics that the important thing is to build a platform as a launching pad for a new business. The aeronautical metaphor suggests that with sufficient force a rocket can overcome gravity and take off. Once in orbit, through the balance of gravitational forces, the rocket can function with very little fuel. Launching a new business is similar. It takes great effort and resources to start a new business but, once launched it requires little effort—if done with appropriate planning and capitalization.

In the early history of the Mondragon, complex several factors helped create a launching pad for new business. Some were external to the businesses themselves, and some were internal to the businesses. We could say there were two external and two internal factors.

External Factors

The most important external factor was leadership from Don Jose Maria. His charismatic personality motivated people to do things. For fifteen years, he imbued in young people a sense of the values that he was himself a living example of. When he succeeded in finding enough followers who agreed with his message, he would say, "Let's get going!" He was an extraordinary inventor of structures, an excellent promoter, and a fine teacher. But he always insisted on hard work and action.

The second external cause was the ease with which at that time a company could be created in Spain. After the civil war, Spain needed a wide variety of goods. It was relatively simple to create companies and take advantage of a growing market. A wall of tariffs kept the competition out of the internal Spanish market. People with basic mechanical abilities and ambition could build factories and produce things. Armed with engineering degrees and imbued with commitment to local development, the founders of Mondragon were especially well situated to launch a new manufacturing business.

Internal Factors

Among the internal factors was a very demanding ethical code that included a strong sense of social responsibility. The personal convictions of the founders became a decisive element in the dynamic growth that eventually led to the creation of a launching pad for new businesses. Later, other questions would arise about structure and technology. Without any doubt, however, the basis of the Mondragon experiment launched by Don Jose Maria is a very demanding ethical code and a rigorous work ethic. One of the biggest tests occurred in 2008. This was the biggest economic crisis since the Great Depression of 1929. Many businesses around the world went bankrupt. Mondragon was in difficulty, but the workers gave their full support by accepting lower wages. In the retail chain, the workers worked without pay for one week per year.

The overarching aim of the Mondragon leaders was to promote development of the community as well as the persons within it. This kind of cooperativism was not aimed at creating rich individuals. Rather, *it sought to create rich communities* in which individuals could have a reasonable standard of living, opportunities to develop, and well-ordered personal and social lives. This basic social doctrine would always be part of the debate when the problem of excessive individualism arose. Guided by this code, the founders worked to form an enterprise whose priority was the workers. Basic to their conception was the need to humanize all production systems. This entailed emphasizing education and recognizing the value of work and discipline. Discipline involves respect for institutional rules and good order in the manufacturing processes.

The second internal factor was the innovative structure of the complex. Technology is not simply about machines but also about business organization and corporate architecture. The Mondragon corporate architecture with its mutually supporting divisions and systems of inter-cooperation promotes high efficiency. The framework and structures were developed through a system of complex norms and statutes. The statutes, based on their basic corporate and cooperative principles, and shaped by the internal life of the institution, impose both limitations and increased capacity on each individual enterprise in the system. Good statutes do not make a good company, but a company without good statutes will not be good.

The cooperative enterprises are now grouped into four divisions: finance, industrial, retail, and knowledge. They work independently within a common strategy coordinated by the central headquarters. Approximately, fifty executives are responsible for managing the corporate headquarters. The elected board of directors of the umbrella Congress controls the headquarters. The industrial division comprises twelve sectoral subdivisions. At the global level, the same basic principles are used even though the affiliates are not legally cooperatives.

There are four levels of organization in the Mondragon system. First, there are the individual enterprises controlled by the individual member shareholders such as Fagor. Second, there are the groupings of individual enterprises around a sector such as automobile parts. Third, there are four divisions: industrial, retail, finance, and headquarters. Fourth, there is the Mondragon General Congress, the highest authority of all, which comprises 650 delegates chosen by individual cooperatives. Their decisions affect all the participating cooperative enterprises. They approve or refuse the strategies and plans presented by the central headquarters.

The benefits of grouping under one umbrella system are as follows:

1. Economies of Scale: Several enterprises can collaborate in group buying.
2. Marketing: Instead of each enterprise having a foreign office, one marketing company can serve several enterprises.
3. Shared insurance and pension systems.
4. Shared Research Faculties: Modern businesses depend on up-to-date research. What one enterprise cannot afford, the group can.
5. Common rules: For instance, if a worker is made redundant in one enterprise, he or she has the right to transfer to another enterprise in the system, under certain conditions.
6. Financial systems are similar. In each enterprise, profits are shared, but the worker can only withdraw profits on retirement or when leaving the system. This is of great importance in cash flow.

The preceding is some of the benefits of cooperation among Mondragon cooperative enterprises. However, whether they are cooperative or not, there are obvious benefits from grouping business enterprises in a collaborative system (Porter).

In their annual statement, they list four pillars as the basis of their success:

1. Cooperation
2. Participation
3. Social responsibility
4. Innovation

The lesson from Mondragon is that moral commitment can result in tremendous economic success if coupled with collaborating structures and participation of workers in both capital and management.

Grameen

Bangladesh is one of the poorer countries in the world with enormous economic problems. In that environment, the creation of a successful business is a great challenge for any kind of entrepreneur according to anyone's definition. Dr. Muhammad Yunus, former Fulbright scholar at Vanderbilt University, became head of the Economics Department at Chittagong University in 1972. When he left the university every day, he saw poverty all around him. Such suffering disturbed him and, especially, he noticed the plight of the rickshaw pullers. According to local custom, a rich person would buy rickshaws and lease them to the drivers. The interest rates were such that the drivers had hardly enough left over to pay for food. Many became sick and died. Using his own money, he helped some but, soon came to the old Confucian conclusion: "Give a person a fish and you feed him for a day, teach him to fish and you feed him for life." He saw that a long-term sustainable solution was required.

In 1974, he embarked on an experiment with the help of his MBA students. "I kept trying to bring the academic world and the village together by championing a university project called the Chittagong University Rural Development Project or simply CURP" (Yunus 1999, 37). Recognizing the high level of social capital among the poor, he decided to take advantage of their sense of mutual aid and they embarked on a kind of "action research" project. One of their early experiments was in Jobra, a very poor village. He noted that women were especially exploited. Many of them depended on usurious moneylenders. They met a woman named Sufiya Begum who made bamboo stools for sale but she was heavily in debt to the lenders. This woman would later become a leader.

Through student research, they found that forty-two poor people had borrowed a combined total of $27 dollars at a high interest rate. The borrowers used the money to produce goods for sale, such as buying material to make stools or for weaving cloth. The products would be sold in the local market. Effectively, poor people became indentured slaves. To break the circle of debt, Yunus provided $27 dollars from his own pocket to liberate the group. Thus, they began a kind of action-research project. It was obvious that some kind of friendly lending institution was required to lift these people out of poverty.

The university became an important launching pad for Yunus to develop a wide array of new business innovations to benefit the poor. He saw it as a place of privilege, knowledge, and power. For him, the question would be how that power would be used. With his small student team from the Master's program, he organized an experiment, called the Grameen (village) experiment.

Yunus tried to get a government bank called Janata to provide funds for such low-income people who wanted to do business. They finally agreed after much argument, but Yunus himself had to guarantee each loan. Using the facilities of the Janata bank, they set up a micro-loan business targeting poor people who had no collateral for bank loans. Recognizing the high level of social capital among the poor, he decided to take advantage of their sense of mutual aid. His student team organized loan circles of five or six people around each applicant who wanted a small loan. The circle was made up of friends and neighbors. Loan defaults of an individual became the responsibility of the group. Only when two borrowers from the group had repaid their loans could the other members become eligible for loans. Instead of a mortgage on property as collateral, peer pressure and personal reputation became the collateral for loans. Loan defaults of an individual became the responsibility of the group. Also, 5 percent of each loan was donated to a group fund to provide security. Social capital instead of personal property and cash became the foundation of the system. The experiment worked very well. The number of borrowers grew rapidly so that by 1979 Yunus was overloaded and decided to take a two-year unpaid leave from Chittagong University.

Within three years, the experiment made loans to over 500 people with great success. The borrowers were much better off than before: divorce rates dropped, birth rates dropped, and women were treated with more respect by their husbands. Also, since the majority of the clients were women, the primary beneficiaries of the loans were children. The repayment rate was also much higher in the Grameen Bank (village bank) than in traditional banks.

After this initial success and further lobbying, Yunus convinced the Central Bank to adopt his experiment in December 1979. The Grameen Bank grew quickly under the umbrella of the Central Bank. By 1983, it had 59,000 clients and 87 branches. At that time, the Grameen Project was transformed into an independent bank, and Yunus left the university to manage it. As an independent bank, Grameen has grown even faster. By 2001, it had 2.38 million members in 1,170 branches. It has spawned replicas on all continents. Grameen is owned by its clients (90 percent) and by the government (10 percent).

While the banking function of Grameen is well known, there is less discussion about the other entrepreneurial aspects of this commercial complex. As the bank developed a net worth and a strong equity base, the leaders saw that diversification was possible and important. Eventually, Grameen grew larger and began to look like a modern corporate business complex. The difference is that it was driven by the needs of the people and not simply by the needs of shareholders for more profit.

In the late 1980s, Grameen started to diversify to improve the rural economic base. They developed fishing ponds and irrigation projects. By 1989, these various enterprises had developed into two separate groups. One was Grameen Motsho ("Grameen Fisheries Foundation") and the irrigation project became Grameen Krishi ("Grameen Agriculture Foundation").

By 1999, Grameen Bank was making over 7.5 million loans and 97 percent of these members are women. Easy, friendly finance has been a key tool for lifting these women out of poverty. It is estimated that 68 percent of the families of Grameen Bank borrowers have crossed the poverty line. The record of repayment has been outstanding, currently running at 98.4 percent. The bank has been profitable in every year of its existence except 1983, 1991, and 1992.

One of the more innovative business developments was in the telephone communications area. Poor people in villages could not afford telephones so the Grameen leadership set up a village phone project. Telephone ladies in villages were provided with mobile cell phones. Local residents were charged a small fee to make a telephone call. This provided a locally needed service and created jobs for the telephone ladies. Since 1996, there have been 260,000 people who operated this telephone service in 50,000 villages. This was a significant improvement in the life of the village poor.

The leaders saw that investment was fundamental for business development and job creation. This triggered the creation of financial institutions such as Grameen Trust and Grameen Fund. These investment funds helped launch new businesses such as Grameen Software Limited, Grameen CyberNet Limited, and Grameen Knitwear Limited.

The Grameen model has become famous all over the world and has been adopted by 100 developing countries. The biggest beneficiaries tend to be women, and the motive is always service first and job creation with profit as a means. It is worthwhile noting that in Grameen as well as Mondragon the university and research played important roles. The Nobel Peace Prize

2006 was awarded jointly to Muhammad Yunus and Grameen Bank for their efforts to create economic and social development from below.

Hansalim, South Korea

Hansalim is the oldest cooperative with the largest membership in South Korea. Korea is particularly interesting since it is sandwiched between China in the west, the largest communist nation in the world, and Japan in the east, the third-strongest capitalist county in the world. It must be remembered that after the Korean War (1950–1953), the political tradition was mostly authoritarian and military. In the 1980s, there was great interest in change. Various movements to promote human rights and social justice arose in South Korea. The Hansalim cooperative organization grew out of these movements for change. Today, it is an overwhelming success doing business in the hundreds of millions, but in the beginning, it was simple and motivated by great visions and moral commitment.

The original organizers were supported by such movements as Amnesty International. In the 1980s such social activists became concerned with rural life. A huge problem in South Korea is that the capital city, Seoul, is rapidly expanding to over 15 million people. Seoul is very modern and some of the largest business corporations in the world are located there such as Samsung and Hyundai. However, an increasing number of South Korean leaders have become very concerned about the preservation of their culture. As Seoul grows larger, small villages tend to disappear. Traditional culture is often confined to smaller places, so the fear is that the domination of the large cities will lead to the disappearance of the traditional cultures. Along with globalization and large cities came pollution and contaminated food. For some, this was seen as destructive of human life in the cities. The harmony of nature, including of humans, was basic to their world view.

Hansalim was led by three activists, Daniel Hak Soon Ji, Il Soon Jan, a schoolteacher, and Jae Il Park, a student activist. Daniel Hak Soon Ji, a Korean Catholic priest, was president of Amnesty International in Korea. The other members were Buddhist. They formed Hansalim into a legal organization in 1986. One of their early actions was the development of a Public Manifesto to promote the preservation of rural life and culture. One important campaign they led resulted in the preservation of the traditional strain of Korean wheat. They opposed the genetic modification of crops for fear that it would reduce the variety of strains available (contrary to global Monsanto's policy). Genetic modification also tends to benefit very large food corporations. In 1996, Hansalim set up the Korean Federation of Sustainable Agricultural Organizations. They have carried out a variety of "solidarity" projects such as providing food for North Korea as well as for refugee camps in Afghanistan and sending aid to the Philippines.

Their motto is "Save Our Food Table, Save Our Agriculture, Save Our Life And Our Earth." "Han" and "Salim" are native Korean words. "Han" means great, one, whole, and together. It also refers to all living things on Earth. "Salim" has two meanings. It is the domestic work that takes care of the houses, families, and children, and also means to revive and to give life. "Hansalim" as a compound of these two words, means "Save all living things."

In seeking to find harmony in all things, the most obvious challenge is economic. In modern nations, the poor are getting poorer and the rich are getting richer. According to an Oxfam report, eighty billionaires in countries such as the United States, Japan, and Saudi Arabia possess more wealth than 50 percent of the world's population. The gap between the rich and the poor is growing (*Guardian*, January 19, 2015). In their analysis, the Hansalim leaders came to the conclusion that a key area of conflict was the opposition between producers and consumers: producers want to earn higher prices for their products, and consumers want to pay less for the products they buy. This engenders conflict. One side will gain and the other side will lose. Hansalim is based on harmony, so they organized a system to avoid this conflict.

Traditionally, in the West, cooperatives tend to be oriented to the consumer. Mondragon is an exception since it is a producer cooperative or worker based. In the typical consumer cooperative, the customers choose the board of directors and the board chooses the management and workers. Usually, the consumer cooperative will buy products that are the cheapest so as to benefit the consumer. They have little or no contact with producers. Especially in small villages the farm producers have little choice and have great difficulty in selling the produce for enough money to live on. It is especially difficult when they must compete against large international food corporations which can produce more cheaply through genetic engineering and fertilizers.

For Hansalim, the formula for economic harmony is simple. Bring the producers and consumers together. However, their goal was not simply economic but also environmental. They saw that it would be pointless to achieve economic success if public health were to deteriorate because of contaminated food. Most consumers do not know where the food comes from and do not have the means to test for contamination. Globalization is bringing more and more cheap food from around the world. Besides damaging health, another result is that local farmers cannot compete with the foreign products. The result is that city dwellers become less healthy and farm dwellers become poor and unemployed. It has now become an international trend to establish mega-cites and to close down rural/small-town life. Many oriental cultures consider ancestral villages to be sacred to the memories of their ancestors.

Against this mega-trend which is based on economic centralization, Hansalim has been seeking new forms of economic development.

Thus, the two pillars of their approach are good economy and good health. To achieve this, on the producer side, they organized 2,000 small farmers who agreed to produce only eco-friendly food that would provide good health for their customers. On the consumer side, in the cities, they organized retail cooperative stores. Once a year they bring together the cooperative organization of consumers and the cooperative organization of farmers for a special meeting. They negotiate a price for food that guarantees a living wage for the farmer and healthy food for the consumer.

In 2012, Hansalim had three divisions: (1) 2,000 farmer producers, (2) 195 retail consumer stores, and (3) support organizations. These three divisions make up the Hansalim Federation. The support organizations include a publishing company as well as a research center. Their research has been successful in preserving traditional food strains of rice and wheat. They have resisted large international companies such as Monsanto which provide genetically modified seeds all over the world. Through their efforts, the production of Korean wheat has increased dramatically. Their research has made significant contributions in environmentally friendly agricultural methods and eco-friendly fertilizers.

Hansalim has three main goals:

1. to save life through a healthy diet
2. to save agriculture
3. to save Life and Earth.

They are very strong in public advocacy for the rules for healthy living. Hansalim has influenced many progressive movements for peace, protection of the environment, human rights movements, and religious freedom. They are active in advocating changes in public policy. In 1995, they set up the Korean Federation of Sustainable Agriculture Organizations and have received many awards for their promotion of environmentalism.

Hansalim is also an excellent example of place-based economic development. They favor food that was produced in Korea. Hence, they do not sell coffee. Place-based development means that we choose a defined geographical area and establish linkages of solidarity that will create jobs and a good living for the people who live in that area. This approach favors local ownership and control in contrast to global corporations which are owned by stock markets around the world.

Excerpt from Hansalim Annual Report for 2013:

> Over the past year, the average of 175 families became the new member of Hansalim each day. So now we have: 420 thousand families as consumer

> members, 2,048 households as producer members and 300 million USD in total sales.
>
> Hansalim has protected Korean rice and mixed grains through eco-friendly farming, meanwhile tried to raise self-sufficiency on feed. Hansalim is continually trying to maintain Korean agriculture with raising food self-sufficiency and to save our Earth and consumers' health through steady efforts.
>
> Especially, in 2013, the new distribution center was built in Anseong, Geonggi in order to narrow the distance between producer and consumer. This center of 19,040㎡ size has various facilities such as Reuse Bottle Washing Factory and Recycle Facility for packing box and food by-products. And these facilities reduce 1,653 thousand tons of greenhouse gas every.
>
> It left much to be desired, but I hope it would become a stepping stone for 2014 Life-Saving activities. I look forward to have abundant report in 2014 with wider, deeper and more energetic activities from rural field to urban kitchen and table interacting with all the lives. I'm suggesting all the Hansalim members to pleasantly fill up these activities again in this year (Annual Report for 2014 Federation President, Kwak Keum Soon, p. 5).

Hansalim has been very strong in translating visions into action. But the action was not simply enthusiastic energy. It was based on serious research as it was in the case of Mondragon. For instance, this community-based organization now has a photovoltaic power generating plant that can produce enough electricity for 200 families. They have also maintained a spirit of international solidarity, assisting refugees in Afghanistan and providing disaster relief for the Philippines.

To conclude this section, we may regard Hansalim as twofold:

1. A social movement dedicated to the creation of a new kind of civilization where the economy and nature can co-exist
2. A business structure such that both producers and consumers function in mutual trust and transparency

There are many other fascinating and successful cases around the world but we cannot discuss all of them. One is in northern Italy called Trentino. In contrast to Mondragon, this model is mainly agricultural. It all started way back in 1881, when Don Lorenzo Guetti, a local priest, began a campaign to support and promote the rural agricultural area. In 1890, they began forming cooperative retail stores to sell their produce. In 1892, they formed a cooperative bank to finance their development. In 1895, they formed a federation of cooperatives for the purpose of mutual support. This became an organized cluster of mutually supporting cooperative businesses. At the turn of the century in 1900, they had 170 cooperatives with 22,000 members. Today, the federation includes 545 cooperatives with over 200,000 members owning over two billion dollars in assets with 13,000 employees.

In Cape Breton, Canada, we have New Dawn Enterprises and the BCA Investment Development Group. These are projects with assets well under $100 million. They are small compared to the above, but they are signs of an emerging movement for new, innovative structures that answer community needs. New Dawn is not-for-profit with a multifunctional structure. The concept is that it has no shareholders and is owned by the community at large. They organize businesses that respond to community needs such as affordable housing, dental clinics, home care, and skill training. The BCA Group is a not-for-profit group. They simply raise money to invest in and advise small businesses in a job creation strategy. BCA has specialized in purchasing bankrupt companies and restarting them, usually as family businesses.

All of the cases mentioned above are at different stages of development and have differing structures. Trentino is 120 years old; Mondragon is 60 years old; New Dawn is 41 years old; and Hansalim is approximately 30 years old. It is impossible to give a fair description of these cases, but I would like to begin devising a set of criteria that we can use in developing a place-based, community-controlled kind of business structure. In business schools, they often use templates or scorecards to ascertain levels of excellence in various categories such as marketing, innovation, leadership, and so on. Examples are the Malcolm Balrige National Quality Award and the Kaplan Balanced Scorecard.

It would be useful to develop a scorecard to evaluate various kinds of cooperative community-based businesses. I use the term "community business" in a rather loose manner to include cooperatives, not-for-profits, and forms of worker-owned businesses. I am thinking mainly of nonmetropolitan areas but, many of these criteria apply to large cities as well.

It is assumed that the purpose is not simply of making profit, but that these successful enterprises were motivated by a moral concern for the good of the local community. I am using a system that I call reverse engineering. Normally, social activists begin with theories and principles and try to find real cases that are consistent with their theories. In reverse engineering, we do the opposite. We start with real-world cases that we consider to be worthy of imitation and which seem to match our value system. Then we analyze them to discover the principles and theories upon which they are based. In other words, we begin with the empirical.

I have picked some real-world cases which I admire. They are diverse with different cultures and different religions, but they have a lot in common. I am trying to analyze and unpack the principles upon which they are based, and this work is far from complete. Nevertheless, I hope that these chosen principles will help us determine the criteria for judging best practices.

1. Job Creation: All over the world, unemployment is a problem. Having a job is fundamental for personal development and should be considered a human right. Mondragon explicitly proposes job creation as a fundamental purpose in its planning and business strategies.
2. Sustainability: There are different kinds of sustainability. Key ones are financial and environmental. Community-based businesses that are not financially sound simply disappear. Of course, profit must be generated, but as a means to achieve more social goals and not as an end in itself. Trentino has stood the test of time so we can assume it is financially sustainable. Hansalim is outstanding for environmental sustainability.
3. Personal Development: Participation in any organization establishes relationships that can be positive or negative. In the nineteenth-century Industrial Revolution, the worker was a disposable tool. We consider two key tests of the relationship of the individual to the organization: (1) participation in capital and (2) participation in management. This requires transparency through an open-book policy. Worker shareholder cooperatives are the best structures to implement these principles.
4. Community Development: Members of a business organization often consider the purpose to be the benefit of the individuals in the structure, whether workers through unions or profit for shareholders. Some cooperatives also view their purpose solely in terms of benefit to members. I consider that benefit to the "community at large" must be a priority in a community-based business.
5. Multifunctional Integration: The majority of businesses in the cooperative tradition are organized around one function. It would be a grocery cooperative, a housing cooperative, a financial cooperative, and so on. Each was separate. The cases we looked at were multifunctional with an umbrella structure. The needs of society are complex, and they change over time. I think that a multifunctional type of business is much more capable of responding to the changing needs of society.
6. Localization: To what degree is the business tied to the local community? Can it be purchased by outside businesses? It is a fact in Canada and in Britain that some traditional cooperatives have been purchased by outside companies, and they have lost their ties to the local community. It is called "demutualization." This is usually contrary to the intention of the founders, but the legal structure was porous and allowed "takeovers." It is important that community businesses have a legal structure that prevents takeovers.
7. Technology: It seems obvious but is worth stating that the best of technology must be used. It may require less workers, but it will produce more income and more jobs in the long run. This is one of the reasons why it is always useful to be linked to a local university.

8. Leadership: The cases above demonstrate the importance of leadership. However, the leadership is not of the individualistic type. It is usually an elder who has gathered a handful of enlightened followers: Mondragon with five engineers, Grameen with five university students, Hansalim with three activists. It is not the leadership of one powerful individual alone.

The above are some of the criteria I am suggesting. But no one has designed a perfect structure yet. Every structure will have good points and bad points. But we contend that there is one common denominator in all of the successful cases we examined: that is "the moral commitment of the founders to serve the local community."

In this chapter, I have been criticizing the global corporate system, but I am not claiming that it can be replaced by community business structures. If we did not have such large corporations, we would not have such low-cost automobiles, airplanes, and computers which we all use. I believe that such large corporations are necessary, but they need more government regulation. Also, I claim that it is extremely important to develop alternative forms of business that we call "place-based community business." If 25 percent of the world's economy were controlled by such community businesses, then this would be an enormous corrective to our present system.

To make this happen, I think that we need to develop more comprehensive criteria, which can be a sort of building plan for community activists. This writing is only the beginning.

REFERENCES

Gower, Laurence C. B. *The Principles of Modern Company Law*. London: Stevens and Sons, 1969.

Habermas, Jurgen. *Moral Consciousness and Communicative Action*. Cambridge: Polity Press, 1990.

Hansalim Cooperative Organization. *Hansalim Annual Report for 2013*. Seoul, 2013. www.eng.hansalim.or.kr.

Hansalim Cooperative Organization. *Annual Report for 2014 Federation President, Kwak Keum Soon*. Seoul, 2014. www.eng.hansalim.or.kr.

Joxe, Azurmendi. *El Hombre Cooperativo*. Pensamientos de Arizmendiarrieta. Caja Laboral: Mondragón, 1984.

Kaplan, Robert, S. and David Norton. "Using the Balanced Scorecard as a Strategic Management System." *Harvard Business Review* (January–February 1996): 75–85.

MacLeod, Greg. *From Mondragon to America: Experiments in Community Economic Development*. Sydney (NS): University College of Cape Breton Press, 1997.

MacLeod, Greg. *How to Start a Community Enterprise*. Sydney: Tompkins Institute, 2010.

Mintzberg, Henry. *Rebalancing Society: Radical Renewal Oakland*. Oakland: Berrett-Koehler Publishers, 2015.

Piketty, Thomas. *Capital in the Twenty-First Century*. Cambridge, MA: Harvard University Press, 2014.

The Guardian. *New Oxfam report says half of the global wealth held by the 1%*. January 19, 2015. Accessed September 28, 2020, https://www.theguardian.com/business/2015/jan/19/global-wealth-oxfam-inequality-davos-economic-summit-switzerland.

Yunus, Muhammad. *Banker to the Poor: Micro-lending and the Battle against World Poverty*. New York: Public Affairs, 1999.

Chapter 3

Cooperative Management in Emerging Markets

Satyendra Singh

Recently, cooperative management has received considerable attention. The United Nations General Assembly has declared the year 2012 as the International Year of Cooperatives to highlight the contribution of cooperatives to the socioeconomic development worldwide. Cooperatives are defined as community-based businesses set up to serve the needs of their members (i.e., owners) (Brown 1997). The cooperative business model differs from for-profit firms as their priority is not to generate revenue and profit, but rather to benefit its members (Hind 1997). One of the most distinctive features of a cooperative is that it fuses ownership and employment; most workers are shareholders, and most shareholders are workers (Craig and Pencavel 1992). Thus, members' participation and cooperation are required to achieve the intended goals (Freeman and Evan 1990; Gamble and Kelly 1996). Although cooperatives are flexible and adaptive institutions, reconciling different forces and interests may cause members to struggle between focusing on achieving their economic incentives and their social goals (Fairbairn 2002). Forces such as social benefits, profit, community participation, and environmental benefits all receive equal weight and may, therefore, cause conflicting ideologies in a cooperative (Reid and Griffith 2006).

Cooperatives are more efficient than other forms of business (Bontems and Fulton 2009). Unlike for-profit firms, where the ultimate decision-making power is held by the investors who receive the profits, management power in cooperatives lies in the hands of the users and beneficiaries of the organization (Clemente et al. 2012). Cooperatives help businesses perform functions more efficiently, promote a pro-market ideology by letting supply-and-demand guide the price for producers, and provide members a means of maintaining competition. A traditional cooperative model is characterized by unallocated equity, collective decision-making, equal treatment, and other cooperative principles (Golovina and Nilsson 2011).

Cooperatives provide a mechanism for promoting and fostering social entrepreneurship ideologies. Cooperatives have social welfare rooted in the principles of their existence, as it is driven by a mission, and not by wealth creation. A cooperative can be a potential breeding ground for social entrepreneurship and social innovation. Cooperatives seize opportunities better than for-profit organizations, as the concept of social innovation is not a manageable administrative process but a self-sustaining one (Novkovic 2008). By directing efforts to achieve social goals, cooperatives help foster a creative and unified goal, which, in turn, develops a favorable environment for social entrepreneurs. An analysis of economic and social entrepreneurship reveals that an individualistic general view of entrepreneurship and the collective nature of social entrepreneurship is prominent in cooperatives (Spear 2006).

Usually, cooperatives are run by social entrepreneurs who assume the role of change agents in the social sector by creating and fostering social value, continuously pursuing innovative opportunities and engaging in learning, and act as risk-takers (Dees 1998). The motivations of social entrepreneurs——who run the businesses and organizations, who study them, and who support them——vary considerably. However, the motivation has conflicting perspectives: for example, the horizon problem may occur when an owner's claim on net cash flow generated by an asset is shorter than the productive life of the asset. Thus, if a cooperative can successfully address the issue of employee ownership, it should be able to retain high member commitment and remain a successful entity (Porter and Scully 1987). Theoretically, several factors, as discussed above, may contribute to the success of a cooperative; however, their relative contribution to the success is not clear. This chapter is designed to fill this in the literature.

Therefore, the purpose of the chapter is to identify the factors that impact the performance of cooperatives in emerging markets. To maintain parsimony, we identify the three most important factors: government policies, membership commitment, and organizational structure and corporate culture. We begin the chapter by defining cooperatives and social entrepreneurship in the context of developing countries and emerging markets, followed by a discussion on the pros and cons of each factor and their impact on cooperative performance. We conclude with managerial insights. Figure 3.1 depicts the graphical representation of the factors and their linkages.

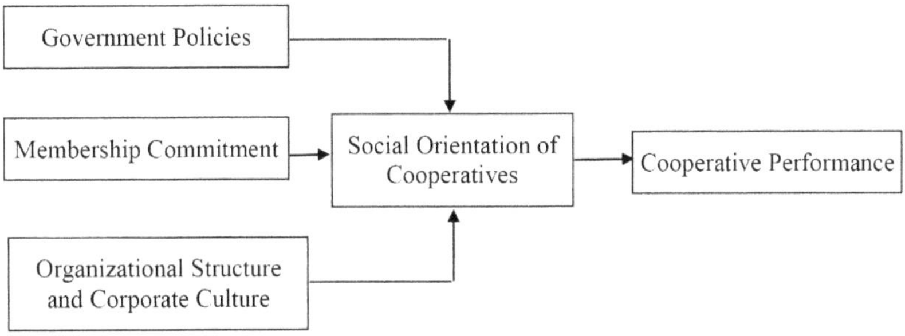

Figure 3.1 Link Between Government Policies, Membership Commitment, Organizational Structure and Corporate Culture, and Cooperative Performance
Source: Author.

DEFINITION OF SOCIAL ENTREPRENEURSHIP

Social entrepreneurship is defined as a practice that integrates economic and social value creation and as a process that catalyzes social change and addresses important social needs in a way that is not dominated by direct financial benefits for the entrepreneurs (Mair and Marti 2004). Social entrepreneurship is emerging as an innovative approach for dealing with complex social needs (Johnson 2000), as social entrepreneurs are better equipped to handle several different interests of stakeholders that exist within cooperatives; they excel at recognizing and taking advantage of opportunities to deliver a superior social value (Peredo and McLean 2006).

A social entrepreneur pursues opportunities to follow the social mission and engages in continuous innovation (Weerawardena and Mort 2012). They (agents) create a kingdom (act) by establishing a company (agency) in the market to make a profit and contribute to growth (purpose). They put emphasis on initiatives and endeavors that create social change and develop our society (Berglund and Wigren 2012). Social entrepreneurs look for sustainable ways to address social problems. They are focused on social problems and, they create innovative initiatives, build new social arrangements, and mobilize resources in response to those problems rather than the dictates of the market or commercial criteria (Alvord, Brown and Letts 2002). Thus, cooperatives can act as a primary place for social entrepreneurs to develop innovative ideas to reach cooperative goals.

ROLE OF COOPERATIVES IN EMERGING MARKETS

Cooperatives play an important role in developing countries and emerging markets (Stiglitz 2004). Cooperatives serve the community and strive to maintain non-opportunistic behavior and, are sustained by repeated interactions among the participants (Banerjee et al. 1994). Further, cooperatives are meant to increase the income of their members, improve their working and living conditions, and promote grassroots development. Cooperatives such as waste pickers are meant to operate in Third World cities where they need to focus on improving waste management systems. This is caused by the realization that developing and developed countries are subject to extremely differing conditions; for example, technology commonly used in developed countries often fails in Third World cities (Medina 2010). Furthermore, cooperatives can touch the lives of millions (e.g., Bangladesh) by providing them with small loans for the development of new enterprises (Stiglitz 2004).

However, cooperatives need to be formally recognized by the local governments for their economic and social contributions to the communities. The vast majority of communities in developing countries and emerging markets lack understanding of the cooperative model and its use, which leads to failures (Taimni 1994). Membership commitment is also an issue that cooperatives now face due to structural changes and globalization (Fulton 1999).

Successful social entrepreneurs look for ways to find solutions to problems such as poverty, hunger, and diseases; for example, building local capacity by creating groups that can solve local problems and provide services to support local development, or building local movements by empowering individuals through education in an attempt to address a specific social problem and to break the cycle (Alvord, Brown and Lett 2002). When social entrepreneurs are innovative in finding strategies and ways of attempting to implement programs and development tools, the cooperative can be effective in achieving their mission. Such possibilities exist for cooperatives to assist emerging markets by aiding the provision of employment opportunities and capital creation. In fact, the impact of cooperatives on poverty reduction in Africa is generally positive, including the positive impacts in terms of linking smallholder farmers to international markets. The increasing cooperative presence in developing countries and emerging markets can assist in providing employment opportunities, purchasing power in the international market, and affordable services for their members.

GOVERNMENT POLICIES AND COOPERATIVES

Governments play a significant role in promoting activities of cooperatives. Without government support, cooperatives may fail as they may not be able to achieve the required economies of scale and economies of scope. Developed countries have established the importance of cooperatives and their roles in the communities; hence, governments tend to subsidize and loan capital to emerging cooperatives in developed countries. For example, the government under the 1976 Industrial Common Ownership Act established a revolving loan fund for cooperatives and gave a capital sum of £250,000 to Industrial Common Ownership Finance (Jefferis and Mason 1990). Indeed, for cooperatives to succeed, governments need to first understand and acknowledge the fact that cooperatives are needed.

Governments provide policies to guide and facilitate cooperatives. The greatest impediment to growth and development of a cooperative may be the lack of an appropriate legal and regulatory framework (Theron 2010). For example, SACCO, a cooperative bank in Kenya, was defaulting on payment of loans for its members. The political and administrative campaign for the establishment of cooperatives failed because the government decision-makers had limited and incorrect knowledge about the conditions of agricultural producers (Golovina and Nilsson 2011).

Appropriate government laws and regulations can help cooperatives achieve their goals. A genuine cooperative activity needs lighter regulation if it is to succeed. It needs a grading system that acknowledges good governance with the freedom to develop (Birchall and Simmons 2010). Although continuous attempts for cooperatives to eliminate cost layers at every stage to remain effective and competitive is desirable, it should create a climate that is conducive to the development of self-reliant, members-driven, and autonomous cooperatives, free from all undue external influence and interference (Taimni 1994).

Governments also provide policies to regulate cooperatives to prevent abuse by cooperative managements and to protect the interests of members of cooperatives and the public. Weak cooperatives in developing countries have been found to be correlated with corruption and mismanagement. For example, the multipurpose society proved to be a disappointment in Sri Lanka. They were not really multipurpose: retail sales were inadequate, and there was inefficient and dishonest management (Birchall and Simmons 2010). Another example is Malaysia where, in 1986, deposit-taking cooperatives suddenly mushroomed, collecting millions of dollars from the public. This indicates how cooperatives can take advantage of the country's bank regulations, which actually prevents nonbanking companies from accepting deposits from the public. There was alleged mismanagement and misappropriation of the funds by the directors and bank management, resulting in the Central Bank of Malaysia clamping down on all the deposit-taking cooperatives (Othman and Kari 2008). Clearly, government policies are needed for cooperatives, even though they are essentially self-help organizations set up to help communities.

MEMBERSHIP COMMITMENT AND COOPERATIVE PERFORMANCE

Member commitment is a critical factor for the success of cooperatives. For-profit firms can credit their success to the development of unique products and be able to differentiate themselves from their competitors. As a result, they are able to raise prices without the fear of losing their customer base, because they offer a niche product. However, cooperatives with higher member commitment have become themselves a niche product; members are prepared to pay more for this product because of the uniqueness and desirability of the cooperatives, and thus contributing to the effectiveness and success of cooperatives (Fulton 1999).

To increase and maintain membership within a cooperative, trust among members must be present. Trust refers to the extent to which one believes that others will not act to exploit one's vulnerabilities. If cooperatives are able to maintain truthful relationships, group cohesion should occur, because members feel more positive about one another and feel a higher sense of belonging to the group (Hansen et al. 2002). Cohesion refers to an individual's sense of belonging to a particular group and their feelings of morale associated with membership in the group (Bollen and Hoyle 1990).

Two issues have been identified for weak member commitment in cooperatives: the appearance of the horizon problem, and the free-rider effect (Novkovic 2008). The horizon problem arises when a member's residual claim on an asset is shorter than the life of that asset, so the members have no incentive to invest in their cooperative because they cannot withdraw its full value upon departure. This problem is caused by joint asset ownership, as members of the cooperatives do not bear the full costs of their actions, preventing members from feeling any ownership within the cooperatives, hence, low membership commitment. The free-rider problem arises when members of the cooperative behave more opportunistically.

Too-high member commitment may be detrimental to cooperatives too. High member commitment allows cooperatives to have considerable market share. Cooperatives may appear to be operating effectively, which in reality may be significantly underperforming. Thus, member commitment can disguise poor management (Fulton 1999). Another side effect of high member commitment is that it enables cooperative managers to pursue their own interests while still being able to retain profits in the cooperative. High member commitment makes it difficult to supervise the actions of managers. Further, managers of cooperatives feel less pressure to perform, as high member commitment may camouflage the managers' underperformance records.

ORGANIZATIONAL STRUCTURE AND CORPORATE CULTURE

Cooperatives face financial difficulties and investment constraints due to the organizational structure and nontransferable ownership rights, and due to proportional distribution by usage rather than by members' investments. By relaxing some of these restrictions on ownership rights, nontraditional cooperatives may provide incentives for member and nonmember investment in organization-specific assets, thereby ameliorating perceived financial constraints (Chaddad and Cook 2004). The organizational structure of cooperatives has been criticized because of the potential loss of profit maximization as compared to for-profit organizations.

However, recent studies have shown that the growth of cooperatives is, in fact, comparable to profit-driven companies. In a study conducted between 2005 and 2010, the cooperatives that were analyzed maintained a similar growth rate compared to for-profit firms in terms of market share. In fact, cooperatives outperformed publicly listed companies on market share gains, underperformed on portfolio momentum, and were roughly on par with mergers and acquisitions (McKinsey & Company 2012). Cooperatives encompass a better understanding of their markets, and are devoted to a well-founded set of social values that favor their members. Perhaps cooperatives excelled in market share because they are driven by members' needs.

Corporate culture consists of beliefs, norms, attitudes, and relationships of the individuals within a cooperative. These factors influence the day-to-day activities of cooperatives and form two kinds of corporate culture: strong and weak performance culture. Strong cultures are fully developed and have direct influence and the ability to either increase or decrease performance, whereas weak cultures have little or no influence on performance (Byles, Aupperle, and Arogyaswamy 1991). For a strong performance culture to exist, it is imperative that the members within the cooperative share the same beliefs and norms. A strong corporate culture builds trust and should exist both within the members of the cooperative and its allies.

Members of the cooperative should share the same beliefs, norms, and values to build trusting relationships. Trust is essential for the success of a cooperative, as a cooperative is a manifestation of trust. Violated trust leads to noncooperation, and rectification requires both parties to be willing to cooperate again (Harris and Dibben 1999). Trust can explain the behavior of members (Valérie, Henninger, and Akremi 2012). Team meetings, peer reviews, and social events are just a few ways in which managers can establish a strong cooperative culture and build trust (Lawless and Reynolds 2004). A strong corporate culture helps build a foundation that makes a cooperative arrangement beneficial. A strong culture may lead to a productive and effective cooperative. Thus, a strong corporate culture is preferred to a weak culture to ensure ethical standards and trust among employees. It is shown that strong culture is based on values of self-help, self-responsibility, democracy, equality, equity, and solidarity. Cooperatives cover a wide range of activities including agriculture, financial services, manufacturing, transport, utilities, health care, and funerals (DFID 2010). Trust has a positive impact on the performance of cooperatives, as it increases commitment and strengthens business relationships.

PERFORMANCE MEASUREMENT OF COOPERATIVES

Social entrepreneurship can lead to increased performance and effectiveness of a cooperative. The goals of cooperatives differ from those of for-profit firms. Return on investment is not the main goal of a cooperative; rather, it is to achieve the mission of its members, gain social benefits, and create a positive environmental outcome. Thus, any profit generated is used for sustainability and is reinvested in the cooperative (Cornelius et al. 2008). Cooperatives are sustained by their members because they trust that doing so will be in their own interest and the interest of other members. Therefore, members within a cooperative are more likely to exhibit trust when they perceive cooperatives as an effective agent for themselves (Fairbairn 2006). Members of cooperative are also stakeholders; therefore, they have a stake in the overall success of an organization (Meadowcroft 1999). Member commitment also impacts the ability of cooperatives to establish a positive reputation with their members. The foundation of a cooperative rests on a group of people with a common need which they undertake to satisfy by making a commitment to act together in a united way (Laidlaw 1980). Membership commitment should lead to positive cooperative performance. In fact, member ownership in itself is a unique form of direct investment (Kyriakopoulos et al. 2004). Thus, a cooperative can attribute its success to a high level of membership commitment.

However, measuring the success of social entrepreneurs may be ambiguous and may be a difficult task even though cooperatives achieve social goals and maintain commitment to their members and their communities. While cooperative principles are consistent with the goals of social entrepreneurs and provide an environment to achieve these, they lack the ability to measure their impact. Social entrepreneurs cannot capture the value they create in an economic form; rather, they aim to create change, innovation, and opportunities in the social sector (Dees 2001). For example, cooperatives create jobs and develop the institutions and infrastructure for development, and, therefore, can be the engine of economic and social development on a global scale (Zahra et al. 2008). In fact, innovation and new knowledge created by cooperatives is estimated to contribute between 50 percent and 80 percent of economic growth (Mulgan 2006).

Social entrepreneurship and social innovation are part of the solution, as they both explicitly aim to provide innovative solutions to unsolved social problems by putting social value creation at the heart of their mission to improve the lives of individuals and communities and increase their well-being (OECD 2010). Yet, funding, capital investment, and technical assistance are not readily available to social entrepreneurs (Basterretxea and Martinez 2012). Surprisingly, social innovations are strangled at birth in several societies where power is tightly monopolized, and where free communication is inhibited, and where there are no independent sources of money (Mulgan 2006). Thus, cooperatives could face a challenge in retaining managers and social entrepreneurs, as they are unable to provide salaries comparable to the market average. This could lead to unshared values among cooperative members and lower levels of social entrepreneurship and decreased cooperative performance.

CONCLUSION

Government support for cooperatives is needed more now than has been in the past because developing countries and emerging markets have developed dramatically over the past few years by the forces of globalization, competition policy, liberalization, and privatization (Trewin 2004). Now, cooperatives occupy firm positions in many business sectors (Nilsson 2001). Thus, government policies should foster promotion of activities of cooperatives, as without government assistance, cooperatives cannot become properly established (Gill and Mustafa 1999). Cooperatives depend on government policies that govern and regulate the acceptance of cooperatives in developing countries and emerging markets. Further, governments can educate society on the value of becoming a member of a cooperative, which will lead to their success. Although cooperatives are member-controlled autonomous organizations, governments should promote the growth and viability of cooperatives by facilitating access to investment finance, credit, and should enter into partnerships with cooperatives where appropriate.

Member commitment is a debated topic in cooperative management as employee ownership has implications for the overall level of its success. A cooperative is an organization in which the owners are also the users of the products and services supplied by the organization; this complicates the management and employee relationship (Giannakas and Fulton 2005). Members are the statutory (but not exclusive) beneficiaries of the goods and services produced. In other words, the members of the cooperative find value in being part of the cooperative, as they see it as providing them with a greater advantage or saving that they would receive without its existence (Thomas 2004). A cooperatives' need to maintain employee or member commitment is essential to its success, and to the achievement of organizational goals. Employee ownership may be used as a method of providing incentives for greater employee efficiency (Paul et al. 1987). Although the aim of social entrepreneurs is to create social value, cooperatives face a challenge in that they need to be able to attract social entrepreneurs and retain them as members. Therefore, it is important to examine how membership commitment impacts the performance and effectiveness of cooperatives.

The fact that a cooperative is sustainable and continues to serve society does not necessarily measure its effectiveness and social value. Social entrepreneurs may find innovative ways to fulfill their mission and vision and increase their performance and effectiveness. However, they face higher levels of uncertainty and risk, which could lead to decreased performance of the cooperative. Social entrepreneurs may, rather, choose a business structure that creates social value that is quantifiable through a measurable profit generation.

Measuring the social impact of a cooperative in terms of monetary profit can be challenging, though profits and revenue are good indicators of value. Social entrepreneurs should use their innovations in combination with organizations such as cooperatives. This allows both the social entrepreneurs and the cooperatives to thrive and achieve the intended social, environmental, and cultural goals. These can at times be evaluated by examining social cohesion, trust, and equity among members of society (Alvord, Brown, and Letts 2002).

REFERENCES

Alvord, Sarah, David Brown, and Christine W. Letts. *Social Entrepreneurship and Social Transformation: An Exploratory Study*. No. 15, 2002. (November 2002). Available at SSRN: https://ssrn.com/abstract=354082 (Accessed on Oct 26, 2020).

Banerjee, V. Abhijit, Timothy Besley, and Timothy W. Guinnane. "Thy Neighbor's Keeper: The Design of a Credit Cooperative with Theory and a Test." *Quarterly Journal of Economies* 109, no. 2 (1994): 491–515.

Basterretxea, Imanol, and Ricardo Martinez. "Impact of Management and Innovation Capabilities on Performance: Are Cooperatives Different?" *Annals of Public and Cooperative Economics* 83, no. 3 (2012): 357–381.

Berglund, Karin, and Caroline Wigren. "Soci(et)al Entrepreneurship: The Shaping of a Different Story of Entrepreneurship." *Journal for Critical Postmodern Organization Science* 10, no. 1/2 (2012): 9–22.

Birchall, Johnston, and Richard Simmons. "The Co-operative Reform Process in Tanzania and Sri Lanka." *Annals of Public and Cooperative Economics* 81, no. 3 (2010): 467–500.

Bollen, Kenneth A., and Rick H. Hoyle. "Perceived Cohesions: A Conceptual and Empirical Examination." *Social Forces* 69, no. 2 (1990): 479–504.

Bontems, Philippe, and Murray Fulton. "Organizational Structure, Redistribution and the Endogeneity of Cost: Cooperatives, Investor-Owned Firms and the Cost of Procurement." *Journal of Economic Behavior and Organization* 72, no. 1 (2009): 322–343.

Brown, Leslie H. "Organizations for the 21st Century? Co-operatives and 'New' Forms of Organization." *Canadian Journal of Sociology* 22, no. 1 (1997): 65–93.

Byles, Charles M., Kenneth E. Aupperle, and Bernard Arogyaswamy. "Organizational Culture and Performance." *Journal of Managerial Issues* 3, no. 4 (1991): 512–527.

Chaddad, Fabio. R., and Michael. L. Cook. "Understanding New Cooperative Models: An Ownership-Control Rights Typology." *Review of Agricultural Economics* 26, no. 3 (2004): 348–360.

Clemente, Jesús, Millán Diaz-Foncea, Carmen Marcuello, and Marcos Sanso-Navarro. "The Wage Gap Between Cooperative and Capitalist Firms: Evidence from Spain." *Annals of Public and Cooperative Economics* 83, no. 3 (2012): 337–356.

Cornelius, Nelarine, Mathew Todres, Shaheena Jivraj, Adrian Woods, and James Wallace. "Corporate Social Responsibility and the Social Enterprise." *Journal of Business Ethics,* 81, no. 2 (2008): 355–370.

Craig, Ben, and John Pencavel. "The Behaviour of Worker Cooperatives: The Plywood Companies of the Pacific Northwest." *American Economic Review* 82, no. 5 (1992): 1083–1105.

Dees, Gregory J. *The Meaning of 'Social Entrepreneurship.'* Centre for the Advancement of Social Entrepreneurship. City: Duke University, 2001.

Dees, Gregory. J. *The Meaning of Social Entrepreneurship.* Comments and Suggestions Contributed from the Social Entrepreneurship Funders Working Group, 1998.

DFID. *Working with Co-operatives for Poverty Reduction.* Department for International Development (2010): 1–19.

Fairbairn, Brett. "How 'Social' are Co-Ops? Tensions, Transitions, and the Social Economy of Co-Operatives in Canada." *Économie et solidarités, Revue du CIRIEC-Canada* 33, no. 1 (2002): 47–56.

Fairbairn, Brett. *Cohesion, Adhesion, and Identities in Co-operatives.* Saskatoon (Canada): Centre for the Study of Co-operatives, 2006.

Freeman, Edward. R., and William M. Evan. "Corporate Governance: A Stakeholder Interpretation." *Journal of Behavioural Economics* 19, no. 4 (1990): 337–359.

Fulton, Murray. *Co-operatives and Member Commitment.* Center for the Study of Co-operatives, University of Saskatchewan, 1999.

Gamble, Andrew, and Gavin Kelly, "Stakeholder Capitalism and One Nation Socialism." *Renewal: A Journal of Social Democracy* 4, no. 1 (1996): 23–32.

Giannakas, Konstantinos, and Murray Fulton. "Organizational Commitment in a Mixed Oligopoly: Agricultural Cooperatives and Investor-Owned Firms." *American Journal of Agricultural Economics* 83, no. 5 (2001): 1258–1265.

Gill, Zulfigar A., and Khalid Mustafa. "Cooperatives and Development: Lessons from the Punjab Experience." *Pakistan Development Review* 37, no. 4 (1999): 1017–1030.

Golovina, Svetlana, and Jerker Nilsson. "The Russian Top-Down Organized Co-operatives: Reasons Behind the Failure." *Post-Communist Economies* 23, no. 1 (2011): 55–67.

Hansen, Mark H., Morrow, J. L., and Juan C. Batista. "The Impact of Trust on Cooperative Membership Retention, Performance, and Satisfaction: An Exploratory Study." *International Food and Agribusiness Management Review* 5, no. 1 (2002): 41–59.

Harris, Simon, and Mark Dibben. "Trust and Co-operation in Business Relationship Development: Exploring the Influence of National Values." *Journal of Marketing Management* 15, no. 6 (1999): 463–483.

Hind, Abigail M. "The Changing Values of the Cooperative and its Business Focus." *American Journal of Agricultural Economics* 79, no. 4 (1997): 1077–1082.

Jefferis, Keith, and Nigel Mason. "The Financing of Worker Co-operatives in the UK." *Annals of Public & Cooperative Economics* 61, nos. 2/3 (1990): 213–232.

Johnson, Jean L., John B. Cullen, Tomoaki Sakano, and Hideyuki Takenouchi "Setting the Stage for Trust and Strategic Integration in Japanese–U.S. Cooperative Alliances." *Journal of International Business Studies* 27, no. 5 (1996): 981–1004.

Johnson, Sherrill. *Literature Review on Social Entrepreneurship.* Canadian Centre for Social Entrepreneurship, 2000.

Kyriakopoulos, Kyriakos, Matthew Meulenberg, and Jerker Nilsson. "The Impact of Cooperative Structure and Firm Culture on Market Orientation and Performance." *Agribusiness* 20, no. 4 (2004): 379–396.

Laidlaw, Alexander F. *Co-operatives in the Year 2000. International Cooperative Alliance*, 1980. https://trove.nla.gov.au/work/17342087 (Accessed on Oct 26, 2020).

Lawless, Greg, and Anne Reynolds. *Worker Cooperatives: Case Studies, Key Criteria & Best Practices.* UCWW Staff Paper from the World Council of Credit Unions, No. 3, 2004.

Mair, Johanna, and Ignasi Marti. "Social Entrepreneurship Research: A Source of Explanation, Prediction, and Delight." *Journal of World Business* 41, no. 1 (2004): 36–44.

McKinsey & Company. *McKinsey on Cooperatives.* McKinsey & Company Industry Publications, 2012, 1–76.

Meadowcroft, James. "Cooperative Management Regimes: Collaborative Problem Solving to Implement Sustainable Development." *International Negotiations* 4, no. 2 (1999): 225–254.

Medina, Martin. *Waste Picker Cooperatives in Developing Countries*. https://www.researchgate.net/publication/23777707_Waste_Picker_Cooperatives_in_Developing_Countries (Accessed on Oct 26, 2020).

Mulgan, Geoff, Simon Tucker, Rushanara Ali, and Ben Sanders. *Social Innovation: What It Is, Why It Matters and How It Can Be Accelerated*. Skoll Centre For Social Entrepreneurship, Oxford Said Business School, 2006.

Nilsson, Jerker. "Organizational Principles for Co-operative Firms." *Scandinavian Journal of Management* 17, no. 3 (2001): 329–356.

Novkovic, Sonja. "Defining the Co-operative Difference." Journal of Socio-Economics 37, no. 6 (2008): 2168–2177.

OECD. *Social Entrepreneurship and Social Innovation. SMEs, Entrepreneurship and Innovation*. Paris: OECD Publishing, 2010, 185–213.

Othman, Azmah, and Fatimah Kari. *Enhancing Co-operative Movements to Achieve Malaysia's Development Goals: The Role of Co-operatives in Sustaining Development and Fostering Social Responsibility*. ICA Research Conference, 2008.

Paul, Robert J., Yar M. Ebadi, and David A. Dilts. "Commitment in Employee-Owned Firms: Involvement or Entrapment?" *Journal of Business and Economics* 26, no. 4 (1987): 81–99.

Peredo, Ana M., and Murdith McLean. "Social Entrepreneurship: A Critical Review of the Concept." *Journal of World Business* 41, no. 1 (2006): 56–65.

Porter, Phillip K., and Gerald W. Scully. "Economic Efficiency in Cooperatives." *Journal of Law and Economics* 30, no. 2 (1987): 489–512.

Reid, Kirsten, and Jon Griffith. "Social Enterprise Mythology: Critiquing some Assumptions." *Social Enterprise Journal* 2, no. 1 (2006): 1–10.

Spear, Roger. "Social Entrepreneurship: A Different Model?" *International Journal of Social Economics* 33, no. 5 (2006): 399–410.

Sitglitz, Joseph. *The Role of Cooperatives in Globalisation*. The Culture of Development, Globalisation and Cooperative Enterprise, Working Paper No. 9 (2004).

Taimni, Krishan. K. "Asia's Rural Cooperatives: Origin, Evolution and Emerging Challenges." *Annals of Public and Cooperative Economics* 65, no. 3 (1994): 469–488.

Theron, Jan. *Cooperative Policy and Law in East and Southern Africa: A Review*. Cooperative Facility for Africa, Working Paper No. 18 (2010): 11–32.

Thomas, Antonio. "The Rise of Social Cooperatives in Italy." *International Journal of Voluntary and Nonprofit Organizations* 15, no. 3 (2004): 243–263.

Trewin, Ray. *Cooperatives: Issues and Trends in Developing Countries*. Australian Centre for International Agricultural Research, ACIAR Technical Report No. 53 (2004): 1–88.

Valérie, Barraud-Didier, Marie-Christine Henninger, and Assâad El Akremi. "The Relationship Between Members' Trust and Participation in the Governance of

Cooperatives: The Role of Organizational Commitment." *International Food and Agribusiness Management Review* 15, no. 1 (2012): 1–24.

Weerawardena, Jay, and Gillian S. Mort. "Competitive Strategy in Socially Entrepreneurial Nonprofit Organizations: Innovation and Differentiation." *Journal of Public Policy & Marketing* 31, no. 1 (2012): 91–101.

Zahra, Shaker. A., Hans N. Rawhouser, Nachiket Bhawe, Donald O. Neubaum, and James C. Hayton. "Globalization of Social Entrepreneurship Opportunities." *Strategic Entrepreneurship Journal* 2, no. 2 (2008): 117–131.

Part II

COOPERATIVE AS A VIABLE BUSINESS MODEL

PERFORMANCES, POTENTIALITIES, AND CHALLENGES

Chapter 4

Agricultural Cooperatives and Their Role in Poverty Reduction in Tanzania

John Sumelius, Stefan Bäckman, and Faustine K. Bee

Poverty is a complex phenomenon, which often requires actions to be taken by the poor to improve their situations. There have been a number of different initiatives that have brought about varied results in different areas and with different groups within populations. Successful cooperatives that function well and strive for effective, surplus-driven businesses may offer one route for the poor to increase their incomes. Cooperatives that are people-centered, democratic business organizations, may offer one approach to address poverty in the world, especially in developing countries.

Cooperatives have been used as a form of business entity worldwide. This is particularly the case in the agricultural sector, whereby cooperatives process farm produce and facilitate the marketing of agricultural products. Several examples of cooperatives that have provided good opportunities to enable their members to improve their incomes exist. What are the features of successful, efficient cooperatives? What concrete examples of such cooperatives exist? What are the factors that contribute to the success of these cooperatives, and what are the obstacles to such success? Which measures work and which do not? How could cooperatives in Tanzania be promoted in a sustainable way? These are some of the central questions this chapter tries to answer in the context of cooperatives in the United Republic of Tanzania.

Cooperative enterprises are self-help organizations that play a significant role in enabling and enhancing the socioeconomic situations of their members and the communities to which they belong. Ideally, cooperative organizations operate as people-centered businesses and also serve as catalysts for social organization and cohesion. Although cooperatives are a form of business entity, they are quite different from classic profit-maximizing firms. Cooperatives are associations of owner members that usually have divergent objectives, some of which are contrary to one another. According to the definition given by the International Cooperative Alliance (ICA), "a cooperative is an autonomous association of persons united voluntarily to meet their common economic, social, and cultural needs and aspirations through a jointly-owned and democratically-controlled enterprise." This definition emphasizes that cooperatives are independent of governments and are not exclusively owned by anyone other than the members. It is worth noting in this context that experiences with government-controlled cooperatives in Sub-Saharan Africa in the 1960s and 1970s were not always successful (World Bank 2008).

Development partners and other stakeholders have supported the promotion of cooperatives at various times with controversial results for various reasons. The new focus on promoting a competitive cooperative business model generates the need to study, analyze, and recommend an appropriate policy of support for cooperatives, particularly in the agricultural and food sectors of many African countries, including Tanzania. Additionally, it is vital to establish a model as a basis for analyzing and understanding why cooperative movements have not fully succeeded in their operations in Tanzania and identifying the factors that drive successful cooperatives. The research is especially useful for Tanzania at the present stage of its development. Cooperatives in Tanzania are recognized to be vehicles that can promote sustainable development, including environmentally sound practices and, are tools for poverty alleviation. Based on the above arguments, the objectives of the study are:

1. To identify efficient successful cooperatives in Tanzania that strive for poverty reduction through a people-centered business approach.
2. To provide concrete examples that exist for effective, surplus-driven businesses that also improve the situation for the poor in Tanzania, and identify and describe the success factors and obstacles that affect these.
3. To recommend how managers of food and agribusiness cooperatives could promote businesses and create opportunities for rural actors to improve their living conditions.
4. To establish a typology of cooperatives in Tanzania with regard to their strengths, weaknesses, opportunities, and threats.

The structure of the chapter is as follows. First, we review the theoretical background for cooperative formation and the principles behind cooperatives. Second, we review published studies and give specific examples of how cooperatives improved the livelihoods of their members. Third, we provide a framework of how cooperatives can improve the livelihoods of their members based on the literature review. Fourth, we select and briefly describe some cooperatives in Tanzania. Fifth, we present the methods and data generated from these cooperatives. Finally, we draw conclusions and give recommendations.

THEORETICAL BACKGROUND

Formation and Principles of Cooperatives

The cooperative offers a different organizational route to profit from those used by investor-oriented firms or joint-stock companies (corporations), common in many parts of the industrialized world. Profit for a cooperative is a term that is commonly referred to as surpluses. In a joint-stock company the votes are divided into shares in proportion to the levels of the investments of the shareholders. A cooperative is owned by its members who each have only one vote. The voting rights and the property structure in a cooperative are, therefore, different from those of the joint-stock company. For this reason, there is a fundamental difference between the two organizational forms. Each of them has their own benefits and weaknesses. The management approach based on the one-man, one-vote principle is different from the joint-stock company (Liu and Sumelius 2010). Certain practices of cooperatives have been criticized by Hendrikse and Veerman (2001), who claim that a marketing cooperative is neither an efficient organizational form for final-product markets nor for market-differentiated products that require sizable funds for investment at the downstream stage of production.

Cooperatives in many African countries have a very important function as marketing channels for agricultural surpluses for small- and medium-sized producers and smallholders. The cooperative business also offers one way for smallholdings and intermediate-size farms to organize the collection, processing, and marketing of their agricultural produce.

The benefits of forming cooperatives for entrepreneurs and members are derived from economies of scale in production, by selling products with added value, and buying inputs cheaper. Other benefits are achieved through a greater diversification by making the value chain longer and by the reduction of transaction costs. However, only when the benefits from lower production costs outweigh the increased organizational cost of the cooperatives will the entrepreneurial cooperative be successful (Göler von Ravensburg 2010, 55–56).

The disadvantages of cooperatives are the high administrative costs, unclear property rights, management inefficiencies, and high agency costs (Porter and Scully 1987; Vitaliano 1983; Hackman and Cook 1997).

The use of cooperatives as a system of organizing production and raising the productive forces of the peasantry is not new. Cooperatives have been used historically by most of the northern and western European countries. Traditional societies in Africa have used different forms of cooperative movements. There are examples of cooperative movements and associations to improve the economic performance of societies in indigenous African culture (ILO 2007).

However, cooperatives have inherent contradictions as they serve both social and economic objectives. This duality of purpose has to be looked at in greater detail to enable cooperatives to be as efficient and effective as possible while satisfying social and economic objectives. Birchall and Simmons (2010) argue that before cooperatives in Tanzania can maximize their potential for reducing poverty, the prevailing policy environment they work in has to be adequate and that all vested interests including those at the highest level need to be scrutinized.

The espoused cooperative principles must be put into practice. According to the ICA (1995), these principles include: (1) voluntary and open membership; (2) democratic control; (3) economic participation of members; (4) autonomy and independence; (5) education, training, and information; (6) cooperation among cooperatives; and (7) concern for the community.

According to Hannan (2014), good governance of cooperatives is a key and prerequisite component of their contribution to poverty reduction. Understanding what good governance is can support cooperative development. In addition to the seven principles above, she mentions six values that are recognized internationally.[1] Good governance could include transparent, accountable, and responsive interactions between those that run the cooperative and the membership they serve. According to this reasoning, it is essential to understand exactly *how* cooperatives are able to reduce poverty. Hannan's findings suggest that the extent of the impacts of cooperatives in reducing poverty varies in accordance with the quality of their governance. In this case, governance includes the relationships between the internal actors and the external stakeholders, which in turn has a bearing on how cooperatives carry out their activities. A number of policy implications are evident; therefore, greater acceptance of the roles cooperatives can play in helping villagers to define and direct the development of these policies is imperative. If cooperatives are considered an important vehicle for poverty reduction, then directors and staff could be effectively trained to undertake facilitating roles in achieving policy outcomes. Hannan (2014) concluded that development agencies can play an important role in supporting cooperatives. This role would require development agencies to work with cooperatives as partners and realize that the involvement of cooperative members at all levels in the decision-making is at the core of the cooperative contribution to poverty reduction.

The Finnish Development Policy Program, 2012 (Ministry of Foreign Affairs of Finland 2012) pursues a human-rights-based approach to development that focuses on poverty reduction and on ensuring that poor people know their rights. In executing this policy, the following specific measures and principles apply: (1) democratic ownership and accountability, (2) effectiveness and impact, (3) openness, (4) policy coherence for development, the operation of cooperatives should be coherent and consistent with other forms of development policies followed by Finland, (5) focus on the least developed countries such as Tanzania, (6) promote gender equality, and (7) reduce or eliminate inequality. The effective alleviation of poverty should include and adhere to all of these principles.

The Second National Strategy for Growth and Reduction of Poverty of the United Republic of Tanzania (2010) (NSGRP II or MKUKUTA II, its Kiswahili acronym) emphasizes some central principles. We particularly mention a sharper focus on the following interventions: strengthening evidence-based planning; scaling-up the role and participation of the private sector in priority areas of growth and poverty reduction; and improving human resource capacity in terms of skills, knowledge, and efficient employment. MKUKUTA II states three interrelated outcome clusters, which should be reached: (1) "Growth for Reduction in Income Poverty," (2) "Improvement of Quality of Life and Well-Being," and (3) "Good Governance and Accountability" to ensure that the poor have access and control of natural resources for productive purposes.

The principles mentioned above are taken as a starting point for proposing recommendations vis-à-vis Tanzanian cooperatives.

Research on How Cooperatives Have Improved the Livelihood of Their Members

The literature provides several examples that describe how cooperatives have made it possible for members to increase their earnings and improve their livelihoods. The question of whether cooperatives or private enterprises offer better opportunities for farmers to increase their incomes cannot be answered unequivocally since that depends upon the background setting. We reviewed the relevant studies below.

Kwapong and Hanisch (2013) carried out a literature review on empirical research on the potential of cooperatives to reduce poverty. They found substantial evidence to support the claim that cooperatives can indeed reduce poverty. Four research perspectives on this topic were identified by them in their review: one group of researchers argued that cooperatives have a tendency to automatically reduce poverty. This view was, however, challenged by advocates of a moderate perspective, which opined that members of cooperatives have certain chances of benefiting from the activities of their cooperatives, although there is nothing automatic in the process. A third group of researchers represented a more balanced perspective, by arguing that cooperatives have the potential to reduce poverty when their values and principles are respected and certain preconditions are met. The fourth group argued that cooperatives are the only group of institutions that have the potential to meet all the millennium development goals. A combination of all four views suggests that cooperatives have the ability to reduce poverty, but *certain preconditions need to be met.* Cooperatives provide the opportunity for the poor to work themselves out of poverty.

Conolly (2014) pointed out that Africa needs to transform from relying upon extractive industries such as mining and timber to industries that add value and that agribusiness could help effect such a transformation. Three-quarters of the African population relies upon agriculture and agribusiness and over 30 percent of national income is derived from agro-industries. Agribusiness can play a role in harvesting, storage, and postharvest storage. However, small holders have difficulties accessing markets for inputs and for marketing their food (Conolly 2014).

Hill et al. (2007) described the Ngolowindo Horticultural Cooperative Society Limited as a successful example of a cooperative that has improved food security and reduced poverty at household level through the generation of income. The goals had been achieved by upgrading the technical and human resources (training), encouraging crop diversification, and improving market access for members. The cooperative has been successful in terms of incomes, production, irrigation, and its accountancy system and marketing. Members can reach markets, have access to transport, and can afford to pay school fees for their children. Employment has increased and several new associated jobs have arisen as a spin-off of the project (Hill et al. 2007).

Vandeplas et al. (2013) studied household data that had been obtained from the state of Punjab in India and found that farmers that supplied informal channels made lower profits per dairy animal and were less efficient than cooperative members and farmers that supplied the cooperative and the multinational sectors. Farmers who supplied the multinational sector were more efficient than their counterparts who supplied the cooperatives but made the same profits. The same group of authors concluded that supplying the cooperative channel was no more beneficial for local dairy farmers than it was for supplying the multinational sector. The multinational and cooperative channels are better than informal channels at creating an environment that facilitates the offering of incentives, developing technologies, and providing support programs for commercial dairy producers. Singh et al. (2001) used a stochastic frontier analysis approach and found that cooperative dairy plants in India were more efficient than the private plants, although the difference was not significant at the 5 percent level. That group's study suggested that efforts to encourage more private firms into Indian dairy processing may not bring any benefits.

The question as to whether smallholder farmer groups in Tanzania facilitate collective action initiatives to improve group marketing performance has been investigated by Barham and Chitemi (2009). These authors basically found that even well-organized farmer groups will have little likelihood in succeeding without a core of natural assets. Groups that are endowed with favorable agro-ecological factors, such as a reliable water source, good land and soils, and crops with inherent market potential are more likely to improve on these marketing alternatives. Creating a culture of entrepreneurship, training farmers to become more business minded, and to get farmers to think of their crops as commodities are at the heart of improving marketing performance. The organization of group activities as business enterprises and also for the farmers' groups to become less risk-averse are two other requirements for poverty alleviation and economic improvement through better marketing.

Lie et al. (2012) assessed the potential of local dairy value chains by examining a small dairy goat cooperative in Tanzania that attempted to improve smallholder livelihoods through commercialization of goat milk yogurt. They concluded that producing yogurt from raw milk added considerable value to the basic milk product, which has increased the market for milk in general. However, the marketed volumes were not large enough to involve all local goat owners although the potential for scaling-up production also existed. More aggressive marketing in local villages would have required the establishment of a mini milk-collection center and also the development of new distribution channels. The participatory farmer-led cooperative mode of organization and the cooperative governance was, in the judgment of those authors, crucial for the distribution of value and local development of the chain.

Newman and Newman (2014) report positive impacts from the decentralization of livestock cooperatives on livestock markets, which made them more profitable for producers. These authors also noted other positive impacts along the value chain that resulted from decentralization. The new decentralization law in Benin shifted responsibility from national to local government authorities.

Meskela and Teshome (2014) reported that the Oromia Coffee Farmers' Cooperative Union (OCFCU) in Ethiopia was able to expand by specializing in export markets under the fair-trade and organic coffee schemes/label/sector. Smallholder farmers in OCFCU were able to participate in these specialty export markets and reap the benefits of economies of scale with regard to the collection, processing, and marketing of coffee provided by OCFCU.

Bernard et al. (2008) found that cooperatives in Ethiopia obtained higher prices for their members collectively than what members received individually. However, cooperatives did not obtain a significant increase in the overall share of cereal production sold commercially by their members. In particular, they found that smaller farmers tended to reduce their marketed output as a result of higher prices, whereas the opposite was true for the larger farmers. According to Holloway et al. (2000), milk groups in Ethiopia are an example of a simple agro-industrialization innovation, which appears to be a necessary first step in the process of developing more sophisticated producer-oriented cooperative organizations. Wollni and Zeller (2007) and also Valkila and Nygren (2010) found that coffee producer cooperatives in Nicaragua seem to improve price stability and lessen some of the hardships brought on by low prices in the conventional coffee sector, although they did not generally pay higher prices than the conventional private sector. Murekezi et al. (2012) compared cooperatives with private processors in Rwanda using the instrumental variable method and also evaluated which type of organizational form had benefited producers most. They found no indication that farmers who sold to cooperative factories received more benefits than those who sold to private processing plants. Milford (2014) found in a study in Chiapas in Mexico that one important reason for producers not choosing cooperatives is production requirements that follow organic production.

Verhofstadt and Maertens (2014) found that cooperative membership of rural agricultural households in Rwanda led to a change in the use of inputs, the adoption of intensification, commercialization of farm produce, higher revenues, higher labor productivity, and increased farm incomes. These authors also found that cooperatives can be important institutions that can transform a smallholder farm sector into a commercial and intensified sector, for selling lower-value staple crops such as maize and higher-value horticultural products. Cooperatives should refrain from organizing agricultural production in a communal way but should instead focus upon cooperative marketing, input supply, and land acquisition with remunerations systems that are in line with individual farm-household systems.

Moustier et al. (2010) found that farmers' associations (cooperatives) in Vietnam were able to increase the profits per kilo of produce for their members compared to traditional supply chains through supplying supermarkets directly with produce. Farmer organizations have become the preferred route for the direct supply of farm produce to supermarkets, unlike the traditional commodity chains. Retailers who are supplied by the traditional commodity chains are supplied by a chain of wholesalers and collectors that deal with farmers who sell on an individual basis. Therefore, farmers who belonged to farmer groups received a better price from supermarkets than did individual farmers for three reasons, because: of economies of scale (amounts collected, lower transaction costs, guaranteed delivery, lower cost of contracts); farmers have been trained in quality improvement; and the farmers' group made joint investments in quality improvement, labeling, and certification possible. Public and international support for food quality improvement was decisively critical for changing farmers' organizations in this beneficial direction.

These studies when taken as a whole provide many concrete examples of cooperatives that have been able to offer their members the opportunities to improve their livelihoods and incomes. A framework for what makes this process possible is presented in figure 4.1.

The following intervening variables determine the conditions whether cooperatives provide the means for its members to improve their livelihoods:

1. Good governance
2. Adherence to cooperative principles
3. Adequate policies
4. Favorable agro-ecological endowments
5. Culture of entrepreneurship

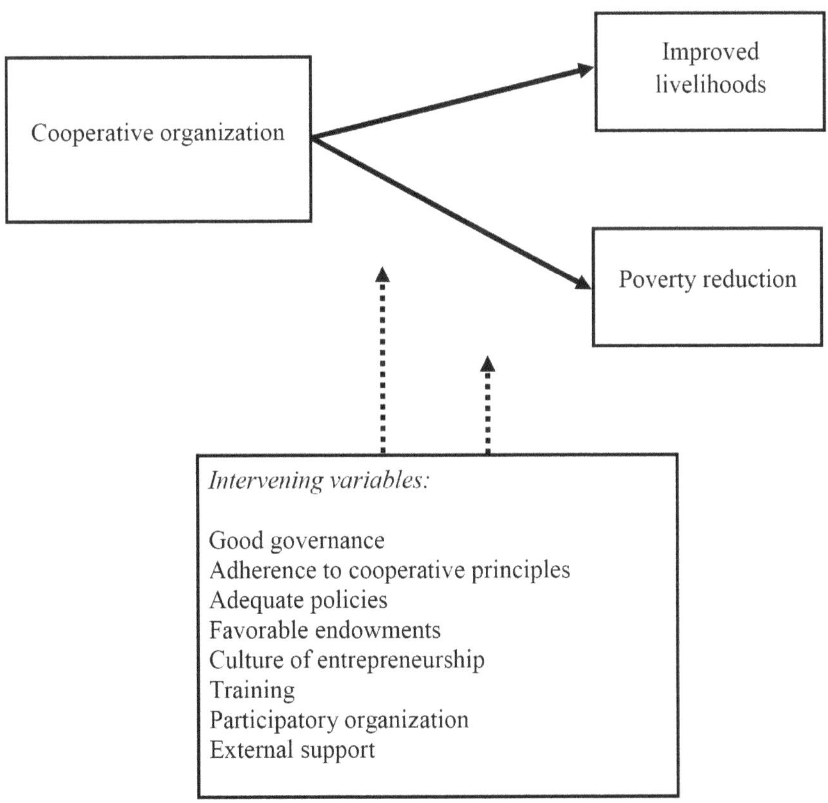

Figure 4.1 Framework Describing How Cooperatives Improve the Livelihoods of their Members
Source: Authors.

6. Training
7. Participatory farmer-led organization
8. Initial support from government or external agents such as development agencies and NGOs

We conclude from the literature review that the factors listed above affect the ability of cooperatives to offer improved livelihoods (and in some cases reduced poverty) for their members.

DESCRIPTION OF THE COOPERATIVES OF TANZANIA

A study was carried out in Tanzania from March to October 2013. It involved cooperative development partners in Tanzania: the selected cooperative societies/unions, the Tanzania Federation of Cooperatives (TFC) and the Government of Tanzania through the Department of Cooperative Development. Other stakeholders included the Finnish Embassy in Dar-es Salaam, the ILO Office in Dar-es Salaam, and the Dunduliza company owned by Savings and Credit Cooperative Societies (SACCOs).

Tanzania comprises an area of 945,203 square kilometers. The country had a population of 44,929,002 in 2012. The majority of the country's population (75.9 percent) depends on agriculture (including hunting and fishing), and agriculture accounts for about 26.5 percent of the gross domestic product of mainland Tanzania (URT 2013). The drivers of economic growth in Tanzania recently have been mining, construction, communications, and financial services, whereas agriculture has been in decline (World Bank 2012). Coffee, sisal, tea, cashew nuts, and cotton constitute the main agricultural export-earning crops.

Cooperative organizations are among the important economic and social actors in Tanzania. Although traditional forms of cooperation existed even before the colonial times, the modern forms of agricultural cooperatives were established in many countries during the colonial period. After independence was achieved, cooperatives were promoted vigorously by the national government with support from various development partners, especially the Nordic and Scandinavian countries of Finland, Norway, Sweden, and Denmark. The government policies changed from market-oriented policies to state-controlled economy. The performances of cooperatives declined. Tanzania also had some experiments in forced "villagization," which were directed by the Ujamaa cooperatives in the 1960s and 1970s (Mhando 2011; Birchall and Simmons 2009, 33). In contrast, there are some recent success stories of rural entrepreneurs who successfully formed cooperatives on a voluntary basis.

In the wake of the trade liberalization of the 1990s, cooperatives were caught unprepared due to the failure of their policies to compete with multinational companies that were allowed to do business in the country. Unfortunately, the free-market economic policies, despite increasing the aggregated economic, indicators have widened the poverty gap between rich and poor, which made living conditions worse for the majority of the people.

Currently, there are several forms of cooperatives that operate in the country, which include financial, agricultural marketing, dairy and livestock, fisheries, mining, housing, irrigation, and industrial cooperatives. Table 4.1 provides a summary of forms of cooperatives in Tanzania.

The financial cooperatives (especially the SACCOs) are the dominant form of cooperatives in Tanzania and they account for 56 percent of the total members, followed by Agricultural Marketing Cooperatives (AMCOs) (36 percent), and the remaining forms of cooperatives account for 8 percent. Financial cooperatives in Tanzania include the SACCOs and two regional unit cooperative banks (Kilimanjaro Cooperative Bank or KCB, and the Kagera Farmers' Cooperative Bank or KFCB). In terms of membership, in December 2012, the total national cooperative membership stood at 1,628,457. However, cooperatives in effect serve more people. If a typical rural household size of five people is assumed, then the estimated number of people that benefit from cooperative services could actually be around 8,142,285 individuals. In addition, there are nonmembers who also use cooperative services.

Threats to the operations of most cooperatives in Tanzania include fierce competition from local processors and imported brands. The imported brands

Table 4.1 The Status of Cooperatives in Tanzania, December 2012

Type of Cooperatives	*Membership*			*Shares (in Tanzanian Shillings)*
	Men	*Women*	*Total*	
SACCOS	537,121	369,325	906,446	33,291,211,825
AMCOs	482,986	111,241	594,227	3,468,815,495
Consumer	22,184	3,338	25,522	209,326,972
Irrigation	17,912	7,631	25,543	308,973,360
Livestock	9,665	4,371	14,036	287,025,089
Industrial	4,502	1,239	5,741	449,899,000
Housing	1,725	1,360	3,085	109,163,880
Mining	409	926	5,023	96,212,000
Fisheries	4,504	1,430	5,934	376,091,810
Others	26,458	16,442	42,900	663,333,399
Total	1,11,154	517,303	1,628,457	39,260,052,830

Note: USD = 1,600 TZS, June 2013.
Source: Tanzania Cooperative Development Commission, Ministry of Agriculture, Tanzania.

are a result of the activities of multinational companies and imports from neighboring countries. Other threats include the inaccessibility of services because of long distances and having few vehicles.

METHODS AND DATA

The present study relied on both primary and secondary data that were collected from various sources through a combination of techniques. The core of the study is based on case studies of cooperatives for which the data were obtained by semi-structured interviews in combination with a formal questionnaire. Stakes (1995) has discussed the methodology involved in the selection of cases in case study research and highlighted the differences in the quality of the data to those data obtained by sampling. Case study research is not random sampling of research and, sometimes an unusual case helps to illustrate a particular point. According to Stakes the first criterion for selecting cases should be to maximize what we can learn from each particular case. Other criteria included cases of good or optimum performance, cases of sub-optimal performance representative of selected sectors, and their accessibility. Using these same criteria enabled us to select a group of eleven cooperative organizations that represented three different regions (Kilimanjaro, Kagera, and Tanga) out of thirty existing regions in the United Republic of Tanzania. Three different categories of cooperatives were chosen (the number of cooperatives in each category is given in parentheses): dairy cooperatives (2), AMCOs (5), and financial cooperatives (4). The proper names of the cooperatives that were included in each category, the region and also the district to which they belong are listed below:

1. Dairy cooperatives (2): Tanga Dairy Cooperative Union in Tanga region, and Kalali Women Dairy Cooperative Society in Hai District in the Kilimanjaro region
2. AMCOs (5): two unions dealing in the export of coffee through the fair-trade scheme: the Kagera Cooperative Union, and the Group 32 Kilimanjaro New Cooperative Initiatives Joint Venture Enterprises Ltd (G32 KNCI_JVE Ltd); three primary AMCOs, Mwenyanjale Primary Society in the Kagera region; Karansi AMCOS (maize, soya beans) in Magadini village Siha District in Kilimanjaro region; and the MAMCS in Moshi rural district in the Kilimanjaro region
3. Financial cooperatives (4): KCB in Moshi; Mruwia SACCOS in Moshi Rural; Umoja SACCOS in Magadini; and KFCB in Kagera.

We conducted interviews with selected groups of interviewees and observed the activities undertaken by the cooperatives to obtain primary data.

Focus group discussions were used mainly for carrying out discussions with groups of members, nonmembers, and leaders of cooperatives.

The semi-structured interviews were based on a set of questions that were relevant to the research theme, and a formal questionnaire was also given to representatives of the cooperative organizations mentioned above to complete. The combined approach of interview and questionnaire accommodates the opinions and concerns expressed in the respondents' own words, which would not be the case if only a questionnaire was given.

The selected sample societies were interviewed over the June 11–20, 2013, period. The interviews were carried out by two teams of three researchers each, and this involved traveling to the regions of Kilimanjaro, Kagera, and the Tanga. Three formal questionnaires that were, respectively, appropriate for ordinary members, board members, and nonmembers were prepared in advance. A checklist of issues and topics for these interviews was also prepared. The interviews with members of the primary societies at village level were conducted in the Swahili language, whereas interviews with the managers of the primary and secondary societies and also the cooperative banks were carried out in English.

A supplementary source of data was obtained from interviews with relevant organizations and institutions that took place mainly in the capital, Dar-es Salaam. These supplementary data were used as background formation in the initial phase June 5–7, 2013. During this period representatives of the TFC, the Department of Cooperative Development under the Ministry of Agriculture, Food Security and Cooperatives, the ILO Office for East Africa, the Managing Director of Dunduliza Company, the Embassy of Finland, and the Kepa office of Tanzania (Kepa is an umbrella organization for Finnish civil society organizations) were interviewed. Most of the interviews were recorded.

We used the framework presented in figure 4.1 to evaluate how the Tanzanian cooperatives that were studied have succeeded in improving the livelihood of their members. We grouped these cooperatives into four different categories, according to their common characteristic features, which were: (1) traditional cooperatives, (2) reforming cooperatives, (3) new cooperatives, and (4) innovative cooperatives. We described the features of each category and the success factors, failures or obstacles in creating the means and opportunities for cooperative members to increase their incomes with reference to the intervening variables of that framework (figure 4.1). We have further evaluated each category of cooperative with regard to their strengths, weaknesses, opportunities provided, and threats faced by using a SWOT analysis as the analytical tool, which is presented in table 4.2. Strengths and weaknesses represent attributes of internal origin, whereas opportunities, challenges, and threats represent attributes of external origin (Kotler et al. 2012, 112).

Table 4.2 Typology of Cooperatives in Tanzania and their Strengths, Weaknesses, Opportunities, and Threats

Type of cooperative	*Strengths*	*Weaknesses*	*Opportunities/ Challenges*	*Threats*
Traditional cooperatives	• Identity of people-owned business • "Democratic institution," one man, one vote • Organization of framework provides a voice for members • Original reason of foundation was sound: to remove exploitation by middlemen traders • Trusted by authorities • Would be able to mobilize some funds	• Conservative institutions that are not disposed to change or innovation • Failure to practice participatory democracy • Lack of transparency • High operational costs • Lack of sensitivity to members' needs • Pervasive business relations between union and primaries • Investing in projects that have no relation with primary societies • Attitude of dependency • Coffee producers do not get fair-trade premium paid directly in the prices but as collective projects • Delivery of education and training to the members • Ability to provide innovations and value-added products • Creating management of cost-effective services to primaries • Clear and transparent cost structure of both the primaries and the union	• Expanding demand on export market • Expanding relations with NGO fair-trade coffee	• Low remuneration and human resource policies and development • Slow speed of adaptation to advanced technology • Lack of integration with financial services, including cooperative insurance and pension funds • Unions control assets of the primaries

Reforming cooperatives	• Business is done at primary society level (member within close proximity, cost-effective business, immediate impact of innovation can be measured) • Secondary structure facilitates supporting the members more • Timely business decisions and payments • Opportunities to introduce innovations, both of products and finance • Freedom to exercise investment in project's autonomy and independence at level of primary society • Transparency, information on how much and from where • Dissemination of information to members is fast • The voice of the members is heard better • Secondary structure facilitating entry or exit • Secondary structure deals with knowledge-information management • Secondary structure provides opportunity for diversification • Managing business negotiations • Nurturing the growth of other cooperatives and other commodities • Encouraging women's participation by owning coffee • Health insurance schemes • Continuing transformation	• Low level of knowledge and education; AMCOs and SACCOs are not integrated as institutions • Youth participation is low	• Change is not easily accepted by government • Producers of fair-trade coffee obtain a premium paid in the prices for their product • Fair-trade coffee exports could increase	• Competition between primary societies will become stronger • Prices are volatile for coffee cooperatives • Funds for development are difficult to obtain • Acceptance of authorities that seem to have stronger ties to the traditional unions • The social marketing may be weak

(*Continued*)

Table 4.2 Typology of Cooperatives in Tanzania and their Strengths, Weaknesses, Opportunities, and Threats *(Continued)*

Type of cooperative	*Strengths*	*Weaknesses*	*Opportunities/ Challenges*	*Threats*
New cooperatives	• Business approach is partnership between local and foreign cooperatives • High demand of products • Expanding market • Inclusion of young producers and facilitating meeting their needs • Provision of equipment and establishment of collection centers • Efficient milk collection	• Weak enforcement of regulations • Capacity not fully utilized • Delay of audited accounts • Inadequate training in governance • Quality of milk difficult to maintain • Transport from farm to collection center problematical	• Extension services • Increasing market shares of new brand in major cities	• Cooperative union does not own a majority of shares so is dependent • Lack of capital for expansion and promotion
Innovative cooperatives	• Income generation sources • Diversification • Gender-based • Empowerment of women • Collectors are processors • Goodwill from society • Network of different associations • Diversification of financial products • High degree of commitment of board members • Environmental protection	• Limited geographical coverage • Limited capital for expansion and reinvestment • Lack of proper equipment, coolers, buildings, and electricity • In dairy cooperatives, poor quality of milk, inadequate hygienic handling, and poor packaging and storage • Transport facilities • Development of new products • Training in handling products and entrepreneurial skills • Extension services	• How to fulfill external demand for new products	• Lack of capital for expansion and promotion outside • Competition from local processors

Source: Authors.

RESULTS

Traditional Cooperatives

The evaluation of traditional cooperatives revealed that the *strength* of traditional unions is that they have an identity of a people-owned business, originally created to remove exploitation by middlemen traders. They are democratic institutions in the sense of one man, one vote and, they also provide a forum in which their members can express opinions and raise issues. Typically, this type of cooperative is found among the coffee unions.

Weaknesses

There are several weaknesses of the traditional cooperatives. They are conservative institutions that do not easily make innovative changes. They are generally characterized by a lack of good governance; in many cases, they fail to practice participatory democracy, lack transparency, and have high operational costs. It is highly questionable whether they follow the cooperative principles of democratic control, autonomy and independence, education training, and information.

One particular union the researchers visited had surprisingly little information available about its primary societies and could not readily produce basic data such as the number of female versus male members. One primary society of this union confirmed that services related to the provision and dissemination of information had been scrapped. This included the abolition of an information department, no dissemination of information about price changes, and no information about important decisions that were to be or had been taken. That union seemed not to follow the participatory farmer-led organization paradigm. Provision of the most important inputs had ceased and very little training seemed to be given. Services given to primary organizations seemed not to be cost-effective although collection and processing of products was taking place. The primaries could obtain a greater share of the final price paid by the buyer for processing their products. However, a large part of processing incomes generated by the processing plant seemed to stay at the union level, which is not in accordance with democratic principles of the community as a whole.

Although a certain union that handled a range of products could play a role in taking care of the processing and marketing of products, it is not clear how the primary producers of one product, coffee, would benefit from these activities. It appears that any added value accrued on coffee was for the benefit of the union, not the producers. It should be stated, however, that this union declared it had used fair-trade money from coffee sales to improve roads and offices, schools and subsidized school fees in the primary societies. We also note that adding value or the processing of products was not mentioned as a success either in the union or in the primary societies. We, therefore, conclude although the collection and processing is taken care of by the unions, it could be managed in a far more expansive and dynamic business-like way. The culture of entrepreneurship is lacking in such traditional cooperatives. In general, it seems to us that this type of union is quite common in the traditional secondary cooperatives (unions) in Tanzania.

Opportunities and Challenges

Traditional cooperatives have the opportunities or challenges to become more competitive to compete against world market prices and expand on them.

Threats

The threats relate to not being able to compete successfully against international companies. The speed of adapting advanced technology is faster outside the traditional cooperatives, that is, in the external world. The perspective of the primary societies was that the control of some of the assets by the unions effectively amounts to an external threat. One may conclude that traditional cooperatives do not comply with many of the intervening variables listed in the framework (figure 4.1).

Reforming Cooperatives

Reforming cooperatives are characterized by the fact that most of the intervening variables listed in the framework (figure 4.1) are realized in these cooperatives.

Strengths

The strengths of this category of cooperatives are that they offer good opportunities for their members to improve their living conditions. Reforming cooperatives are often primary societies that adhere closely to cooperative principles and practices of good governance by having efficient coordination mechanisms. A typical feature of these cooperatives is that they have a participatory farmer-led organization, which entails that most business activities are carried out at primary-society level. The financial services offered by credit cooperative societies, agricultural marketing services, cooperative banks, and cooperative insurance companies are close to the members of the primary society. The activities of the cooperative are cost-effective and the impact of innovation can be measured immediately.

The secondary structure is more active in supporting the members and also supports entrepreneurship. The business decisions and payments are timely. Training is included in the activities the cooperatives offer. There are opportunities to introduce innovations, such as new products and financial investment for this type of cooperative. There is non-exclusivity for producers to sell their products; thus, the primary cooperatives have the freedom to sell to other buyers rather than to the secondary structure alone. The cooperatives invest in a project's autonomy and independence at all levels of the primary society. The cooperatives are transparent, and freely provide information on prices, quantities of products, and their sources. Dissemination of information to the membership is fast. The opinions and viewpoints of the membership are taken into cognizance better than in the traditional cooperatives. The secondary structure facilitates entry or exit of primary societies, deals with knowledge management, and provides opportunities for diversification. It manages business negotiations, nurtures the growth of other cooperatives and the development of other commodities. Women's participation is encouraged through the ownership of their produce. In one particular case one-third of the coffee was sold as fair-trade coffee to Japan. The structure of these cooperatives allows the development of health insurance schemes for the primary member cooperatives in the villages. One particular opportunity for coffee-producing cooperatives is that producers of fair-trade coffee must obtain a premium paid directly for the coffee they produce and that fair-trade coffee exports could increase.

Weaknesses

The weaknesses of many of these reforming cooperatives include a low level of knowledge and/or education, shortage of funding, the AMCO and SACCO institutions are not yet integrated with the cooperatives, and youth participation is low.

Threats

One threat facing these cooperatives is how to be accepted by government authorities that are used to dealing with traditional cooperatives. Other threats include the competition from other more established cooperatives, volatile coffee prices, and weak social marketing. As a whole, this category of cooperatives possesses most of the features in the framework shown in figure 4.1.

New Cooperatives

New cooperatives are relatively recent developments.

Strengths

Some strengths of this category are that their business approach is their partnership between local and foreign cooperatives and that they meet high demands of products and operate in an expanding market. This cooperation seems to strengthen good governance, underpins cooperative principles, and creates a favorable atmosphere for entrepreneurship. Interestingly, these cooperatives have been able to include young producers and facilitate their needs. Thus, new cooperatives have been able to improve the employment situation in their localities. Members have been provided with equipment and collection centers for milk. New cooperatives face high demand for their products and also have expanding markets. They, therefore, conform to several of the features listed in our framework in figure 4.1.

Weaknesses

A few weaknesses are that the capacities of these new cooperatives are not fully used, regulation is weak, and the quality of dairy products may also be low because of inadequate training and poor transport to the collection centers.

Challenges and Opportunities

The challenges and opportunities facing new cooperatives include the provision of extension services and inadequate product development.

Threats

A major threat is that the cooperative union does not own a majority of shares so there is an overdependency on a foreign collaborator. Another threat is the lack of capital for expansion and promotion.

Innovative Cooperatives

Strengths

The strengths of innovative cooperatives are their gender-based category, that is, they empower women, they create income-generating sources and a diversification of products, and they protect the environment. The collectors are the processors, and they enjoy goodwill in the community. There is a network of different associations and a high degree of commitment to each cooperative from the members of its board, which enables the organization to be producer based.

Weaknesses

The weaknesses of innovative cooperatives are that they are restricted by limited geographical coverage, they have limited capital for expansion, have low levels of reinvestment, and lack proper equipment, coolers, buildings, and electricity. They also lack training, and the packaging, storage and hygiene (of milk) is currently poor.

Challenges and Opportunities

External challenges and opportunities are how to deal with and meet the demands of producing or processing new products.

Threats

Threats include a lack of external funds for development and strong competition from local processors and imported brands.

Innovative cooperatives have some desirable features such as a participatory farmer-led organization and support from external agencies but lack others such as proper governance and training. Thus, only some of the items in figure 4.1 apply.

CONCLUSION

The cooperatives that deliver benefits to their members and provide opportunities that improve the incomes of members also seem to be the organizations that are successful in reducing poverty. We, therefore, conclude that the poverty-reducing cooperatives basically are those cooperatives that support their members in an adequate and effective way, that is, they function well and are efficiently run. It is important that managers of food and agribusiness firms both in Tanzania and also personnel from cooperatives from other countries that collaborate with Tanzanian cooperatives keep this conclusion in mind.

Efficient and successful cooperatives in Tanzania can be described as adhering to the principles of good governance of cooperatives. Some central features of these principles include the following: (1) The organizations are based on strong primary cooperative societies that work as the driving force of a culture of entrepreneurship, business promotion, job creation, and training, all of which provide the members an opportunity to improve their own living conditions and to raise their incomes. The members, thus, have control of their cooperative. (2) Appropriate financial services, that is, services offered by the various financial actors are close to the members of the primary society. (3)

Members receive adequate and transparent information; they have the freedom to exercise and know their rights, and know how to run a cooperative efficiently, while being able to maintain independence from external pressures. (4) The secondary-level organization (unions or similar) are light. Members are free to sell their products through other channels when it suits them. (5) The secondary structure carries out business negotiations with both foreign and domestic buyers. (6) When the cooperative is expanding and market oriented, it seems beneficial to collaborate with a foreign investor cooperative.

Concrete examples of effective, profit-driven businesses that offer opportunities for cooperative members to improve their situation can be found in the close cooperation between AMOCs and SACCOs. The primary societies market their coffee through an AMCO and obtain financial services from a SACCO. Members receive higher prices, more timely payments, and the transparency of the organization is better than the traditional union that works in that locality. A large part of the coffee is sold as fair-trade coffee directly overseas to Japan.

On the whole, the members of the village cooperatives seem to have been able to increase their incomes and to create a successful business concept. A decisive factor is that the members of a cooperative decide upon all critical business activities and take care of the physical production of a product in addition to the cash transactions. Another critical condition is that the secondary-level organizations should only have a few employees, whose tasks are mainly to facilitate entry or exit, deal with knowledge management, disseminate information, and manage business negotiations with buyers. Such model partnerships are in accordance with the principles stated in the Finnish Development Policy Program 2012 and the NSGRP II-MKUKUTA II. We wish to underline that the Finnish Development Policy Program principles can provide guidelines and examples of successful partnerships that promote competitive cooperative business models as part of the Finnish government's objective of assisting in the reduction of poverty in Tanzania.

Some cooperatives, specifically the coffee unions, do not seem to be able to create conditions that nurture good governance and accountability, nor have they created dynamic conditions for improving the livelihoods for their members. The procedures they follow do not completely correspond to those qualities espoused by the MKUKUTA II, cluster III first goal. Cluster III was designed to ensure systems and structures of governance, uphold the rule of law democratically, and be effective, accountable, predictable, transparent, inclusive, and corruption-free at all levels.

The Cooperative Societies Act, 2013, of the United Republic of Tanzania recognizes two structures only: the primary society at the local level and the federation at the national level. This allows greater flexibility and space for primary societies to exercise freedom and autonomy for making choices on business development for their members. The Act is clear. The existence of a policy implementation framework called the Cooperative Reform and

Modernization Programme allows cooperatives to pursue opportunities offered by the government for achieving their own business objectives.

RECOMMENDATIONS AND FURTHER RESEARCH

Managers of food and agribusiness cooperatives (including the secondary cooperatives) in Tanzania should promote businesses and create opportunities for rural actors to improve their living conditions in the following ways:

1. Ensure that primary societies have the freedom to meet and make decisions at the member level.
2. Develop cooperative actions at village level to empower farmers to seek other opportunities to address risks, gain access to financial services, encounter more economic opportunities, and improve the democratization processes.
3. Help the system that delivers and disseminates information to primary societies to make them more effective and informative for the members through empowerment measures and inclusivity.
4. Women and youth's participation in cooperatives should be encouraged and enhanced. The role of women as landowners should be emphasized when coffee is traded, that is, with appropriate regard to gender participation.
5. More professional management of cooperative businesses is needed (human capital in cooperative management) at all levels.
6. Primary societies should have reserve funds to stabilize product prices, especially coffee prices. The Government of Tanzania could support this objective by ensuring that the officials of the secondary structure work with cooperative banks or other banks to create stabilization funds for this purpose. Furthermore, the Government of Tanzania should also guarantee that these officials also have enough knowledge and competence for creating such stabilization funds.
7. Financial services points/branches should be in close proximity and easily available to the members of the cooperatives and to the cooperatives themselves. The Government of Tanzania should give more support to those independent and efficient/successful SACCOs that are characterized by good governance.
8. Professional management of cooperative businesses is needed (human capital in cooperative management). Managers in agribusiness may support this objective by providing training for managers of primary societies. Training of secondary cooperatives in management issues is another area that should be supported.

Further research could focus on how cooperatives in the agriculture and food sectors in Tanzania have been able to improve the livelihoods and incomes of their members. This aim could be realized by using more quantitative data than those presented in the current study. Research on how well the Cooperatives Act, 2013, has been implemented is also needed.

NOTE

1. Self-help, responsibility, democracy, equality, solidarity, and equity.

REFERENCES

Barham, James, and Clarence Chitemi. "Collective Action Initiatives to Improve Marketing Performance: Lessons from Farmer Groups in Tanzania." *Food Policy* 34, no. 1 (2009): 53–59.

Bernard, Tanguy, Alemayehu S. Taffesseb, and Eleni Gabre-Madhina. "Impact of Co-operatives on Smallholders' Commercialization Behavior: Evidence from Ethiopia." *Agricultural Economics* 39, no. 2 (2008): 147–61.

Birchall, Jonhston, and Richard Simmons. *Co-operatives and Poverty Reduction: Evidence from Sri Lanka and Tanzania.* Manchester: The Co-operative College, 2009.

Birchall, Johnston and Richard Simmons. *The Co-operative Reform Process in Tanzania and Sri Lanka.* Manchester: The Co-operative College, 2010.

Conolly, Aidan J. "A Glimpse into the Future. A Lens through which Considering Africa's Future." *International Food and Agribusiness Management Review* 17, special issue B (2014): 9–18.

Göler von Ravensburg, N. *Economic and Other Benefits of the Entrepreneurs' Co-operative as a Specific Form of Enterprise Cluster.* Dar es Salaam: International Labour Office, 2010.

Hackman, Deanne. L., and Michael L. Cook. "The Transition to New Cooperative Organizational Forms: Public Policy Issues." In *Cooperatives: Their Importance in the Future Food and Agricultural System*, edited by M. Cook et al., 105–12. Washington, DC: Food and Agricultural Marketing Consortium, 1997.

Hannan, Rowshan. "Good Co-operative Governance: The Elephant in the Room with Rural Poverty Reduction." *Journal of International Development* 26, no. 5 (2014): 701–12.

Hendrikse, George W. J., and Cees P. Veerman. "Marketing Cooperatives and Financial Structure: A Transaction Costs Economic Analysis." *Agricultural Economics* 26, no. 3 (2001): 205–16.

Hill, Trevor R., Etienne L. Nel, and Peter Illgner. "Partnership for Success: Community-Based Economic Development: A Case Study of Ngolowindo Cooperative, Malawi." *Environment and Planning C: Government and Policy* 200, no. 25 (2007): 573–90.

Holloway, Garth, Charles F. Nicholson, Chris Delgado, Steven J. Staal, and Simeon Ehui. "Agroindustrialization through Institutional Innovation Transaction Costs, Cooperatives and Milk-Market Development in the East-African Highlands." *Agricultural Economics* 23, no. 3 (2000): 279–88.

International Co-operative Alliance (ICA). *Cooperative Identity, Values and Principles*, 2015. http://ica.coop/en/what-co-op/co-operative-identity-values-princi ples.

International Labour Office. *Cooperatives & Rural Development.* COOP Sheet No. 1, 2007.

Kotler, Phillip, Kevin L. Keller, Malread Brady, Malcolm Goodman, and Torben Hansen. *Marketing Management*, 2nd ed. Essex: Pearson, 2012.

Kwapong, Nana A., and Markus Hanisch. "Cooperatives and Poverty Reduction: A Literature Review." *Journal of Rural Cooperation* 41, no. 2 (2013): 114–46.

Lie, Helen, Karl M. Rich, Lusato R. Kurwijila, and Anne M. Jervell. "Improving Smallholder Livelihoods through Local Value Chain Development: A Case Study of Goat Milk Yogurt in Tanzania." *International Food and Agribusiness Management Review* 15, no. 3 (2012): 55–85.

Liu, Y., and John Sumelius. "Analysis of the Factors of Farmers' Participation in Co-operative Management in Finland." *Journal of Rural Cooperation* 38, no. 2 (2010): 1534–54.

Meskela, Tadess, and Yalem Teshome. "From Economic Vulnerability to Sustainable Livelihood; the Case of Oromia Coffee Farmers Cooperatives Union (OCFCU) in Ethiopia." *International Food and Agribusiness Management Review* 17, special issue B (2014): 103–108.

Mhando, Lindah "Tanzania and the Geo-Politics of Rural Development: The Return of Neoliberalism." *Journal of Emerging Knowledge on Emerging Markets* 3, art. 26 (2011): 455–72.

Milford, Anna B. "Co-operative or Coyote? Producers' Choice between Intermediary Purchaser and Fairtrade and Organic Co-operatives in Chiapas." *Agriculture and Human Values* 31, no. 4 (2014): 577–91.

Ministry of Foreign Affairs of Finland. *Finnish Development Policy Programme, 2012.* Unit for Development Communications, 2012.

Moustier, Paule, Phan Thi Giac Tam, Dao The Anh, Vu Trong Binh, and Nguyen Thi Tan Loc. "The Role of Farmer Organizations in Supplying Supermarkets with Quality Food in Vietnam." *Food Policy* 35, no. 1 (2010): 69–78.

Murekezi, Abdoul, Songqing Jin, and Scott Loveridge. "Do Organisational Forms of the Coffee Supply Chain Matter in Poverty Reduction?" *Development in Practice* 22, no. 7 (Sept 7, 2012): 962–77.

Newman, Eric, and Mark Newman. "Building a Better Livestock Market in Benin and a Safer, More Reliable Food Supply." *International Food and Agribusiness Management Association* 17(B) (2014): 89–101.

Porter, Phillip K., and Gerald W. Scully. "Economic Efficiency in Cooperatives." *Journal of Law and Economics* 30, no. 2 (1987): 489–51.

Singh, Satbir, Tim Coelli, and Euan Flemming. "Performance of Dairy Plants in the Cooperative and Private Dairy Sectors in India." *Annals of Public and Cooperative Economics* 72, no. 4 (2001): 453–79.

Stakes, Robert E. *The Art of Case Study Research*. London: Sage Publications, 1995.

United Republic of Tanzania. *Cooperative Reform and Modernization Programme* (CRMP) (2005–2015). Dodoma, Tanzania, 2005.

United Republic of Tanzania. *Tanzania in Figures. National Bureau of Statistics*. Dar es Salaam: Ministry of Finance, June 2013.

United Republic of Tanzania. *Cooperative Societies Act, 2013*. Dar es Salaam: Tanzania Cooperative Development Commission, 2013.

United Republic of Tanzania. *Second National Strategy for Growth and Reduction of Poverty, NSGRP II, MKUTAI II*. Dar es Salaam: Ministry of Finance and Foreign Affairs, 2010.

Valkila, Joni, and Anja Nygren. "Impacts of Fair-Trade Certification on Coffee Farmers, Cooperatives and Laborers in Nicaragua." *Agriculture and Human Values* 27, no. 3 (2010): 321–33.

Vandeplas, Anneleen, Bart Minten, and Johan Swinnen. "Multinationals versus Cooperatives: The Income and Efficiency Effects of Supply Chain Governance in India." *Journal of Agricultural Economics* 64, no. 1 (2013): 217–44.

Verhofstadt, Ellen, and Miet Maertens (2014) "Smallholder Cooperatives and Agricultural Performance in Rwanda: Do Organizational Differences Matter?" *Agricultural Economics*. 45, no. S1 (November, 2014): 39–52.

Vitaliano, Peter. "Cooperative Enterprise: An Alternative Conceptual Basis for Analysing a Complex Institution." *American Journal of Agricultural Economics* 65, no. 5 (1983): 1078–83.

Wollni, Meike, and Manfred Zeller. "Do Farmers Benefit from Participating in Specialty Markets and Co-operatives? The Case of Coffee Marketing in Costa Rica." *Agricultural Economics* 37, no. 2 (2007): 243–48.

World Bank. *Agriculture for Development. World Development Report 2008*. Washington, DC: World Bank, 2008.

World Bank Poverty Reduction and Economic Management Unit Africa Region. *Tanzania Economic Update. Spreading the Wings: From Growth to Shared Prosperity*. Washington, DC: World Bank, 2012.

Xiang, L. Y., and John Sumelius. "Analysis of the Factors of Farmers' Participation in Co-operative Management in Finland." *Journal of Rural Cooperation* 38, no. 2 (2010): 1–22.

Chapter 5

Effectiveness of Farmers' Cooperatives in Agricultural Development: Evidence from the State of Assam, India

Niranjan Roy

The state of Assam in India comprises three physical divisions, namely the Brahmaputra Valley, the Barak Valley, and the Hill range. The Brahmaputra Valley, which forms the northern part, is the largest in size comprising 71.7 percent of the total geographical area of the state. The Barak Valley region, which forms the southern part, is comparatively smaller in size. The two valleys derived their names from the respective main rivers, the Brahmaputra and the Barak flowing East to West in the valleys. The hill regions formed by the Karbi-Anglong and the North Cachar Hills separate the two valleys in the middle (Bhattacherjee 1977). On October 9, 1958, the Government of Assam by an Extra Ordinary issue of the Assam Gazette published the resolution on the policy of Settlement of Agricultural Land and Re-Organization. It was stated, inter alia, that steps would be taken to organize the cultivators' field-wise by forming Field Management Committees (FMCs) as cooperative institutions. It was only in late 1980s that the Government of Assam took up the "Crash Programme" of revitalizing the FMCs. The Government of Assam introduced the scheme of Integrated Farming System on May 4, 1990, as a follow-up of clause 7 of the Assam Accord for micro-planning at the grass-root level and for development by involving farmers' organizations, including rural youths. The FMCs started to function on the basis of an Integrated Farming System on the models of a cooperative institution. The FMCs are supported with funds primarily from the various departmental programs. It has been decided by the government that all the activities of the agriculture department in a particular village will be channelized through the FMCs (Roy and Bezbaruah 2003).

The main objectives of the present study are to assess the role of FMCs toward development of the Integrated Farming System in the state of Assam. An assessment has also been made on the overall functioning of the FMCs in the state. The hypotheses taken up for testing in the course of the study are:

1. The FMCs failed to function effectively in farmer's field
2. The FMCs could make any significant contribution in agricultural development

DATABASE AND METHODOLOGY

The study is based on both secondary and primary data. The main source of secondary data has been the publications of government and semi-government agencies such as the Directorate of Economics and Statistics, Government of Assam; Agro-Economic Research Centre, Assam Agricultural University; Directorate of Agriculture, Irrigation, and so on.

The micro-level analysis has been based mainly on primary data collected by carrying out a field survey. The field survey for the study has been confined to the Barak Valley region of the state considering the paucity of time and resources. Moreover, the main objective of the study was to assess the efficiencies in functioning of the FMCs and not to find the aggregates only. Hence, it was decided to confine the field survey to the Barak Valley region.

The sample for this purpose has been selected through a process of multistage sampling. In the first stage, two Agricultural Development Officer (ADO) circles each have been selected from each agricultural subdivision in the district as the field study locations. There are six agricultural subdivisions in the three districts of the Barak Valley region. The district-wise subdivisions are the following: (1) Cachar District, three subdivisions; (2) Karimganj District, two subdivisions; and (3) Hailakandi District, one subdivision. Each subdivision has eight to nine ADO circles. A total of twelve ADO circles were selected for the sample study. The selection of two ADO circles from each subdivision was based on the criteria of highly developed and another less developed in agriculture on the basis of standard norms of agricultural development like higher productivity, practice of modern agricultural inputs, cropping intensity, and so on. Thus, the selected ADO circles represent all the subdivisions in respect of agricultural development. The selection at this stage was done in consultation with the District Agricultural Officers and the information available from their offices.

While choosing ADO circles, efforts were made to cover flood-prone areas as well as non-flood-prone areas. The circles so selected represent the different farming conditions within the region. In the second stage, three villages were selected at random from each of the selected ADO circles. Thus, in all thirty-six villages were selected for the sample study. From the selected villages, farming households have been divided into FMC member and non-FMC (if any). At least twenty and ten farmers, respectively, of FMC and non-FMC farms were chosen. This gives the sample size of 1,080 consisting of 720 FMC members and 360 non-FMC members. A separate schedule was used to collect information from the office bearers of each FMC consisting of 458 samples from Karimganj District, 627 from Cachar District, and 426 from Hailakandi District. The data thus collected were separated into FMC and non-FMC-member households.

To study the impact of FMCs in the agricultural development of Barak Valley, different agricultural performance indicators or indexes such as agricultural production, access to agro-capital, cropping intensity, and crop diversity were computed. All these performance indicators were compared between FMC farms and non-FMC farms using statistical techniques by formulating the hypothesis that there is no difference between agricultural performance between FMCs and non-FMCs.

The following are the two agricultural development indexes used for the analysis of the study.

Cropping Intensity

Cropping intensity refers to raising of a number of crops from the same field during one agriculture year. It can be expressed as:

$$\text{Cropping intensity} = (\text{Gross cropped area/Net sown area}) \times 100$$

Thus, higher cropping intensity means that a higher portion of the net area is being cropped more than once during one agricultural year. This also implies higher productivity per unit of arable land during one agricultural year.

Cropping Diversity

Cropping diversity means the share of different types of crops in a particular plot of land. If the plot of land is shared by more number of crops, it implies more crop diversity. In our study, we have used the Crop Diversity Index (CDI) formulated by Kshirsagar et al. (1997) as follows:

$$CDI_i = 1 - \sum_{j=1}^{n} \left[\frac{aij}{Ai} \right]^2$$

Where, $CDIi$ = crop diversity index
aij = area planted to the jth crop in the ith location
Ai = total area planted under all crops.

The index is zero for a crop area growing only one crop and, approaches unity as the level of diversity increases.

Profile of Sample Study Area

The Barak Valley region is situated between latitude 24° 8′ and 25° 8′ north and longitude 92° 15′ and 93° 15′ east, covering an area of 6,922 sq km. The valley constitutes 8.9 percent of the geographical area of the state, but contains 11.22 percent of the population as per the 2011 Census. The economy of the Barak Valley region is predominantly agricultural with 70 percent of the workforce being engaged in agriculture and other primary activities. Though the region is not devoid of manufacturing units, it is handicapped due to its relative geographical isolation for a program of large-scale industrialization. The prospect of economic development of the region, therefore, depends critically on the growth of agriculture and allied activities. Agriculture in Barak Valley, as it stands today, is predominated by small farms mainly growing paddy. There were about 209,875 agricultural holdings in the Barak Valley, 53.09 percent of which were in the size class of below one hectare. The average size of operational holding works out to be 1.62 hectares, which contains some amount of upward bias due to the large holdings of the tea estates. The paddy crops constituted 92.5 percent of the gross cropped area (GCA) (excluding the area under plantation and tree crops) of the region. The agriculture is almost entirely weather dependent, the irrigation cover being limited to only 2.43 percent of the GCA. Paddy is the major crop. Due to poor agricultural productivity, the income of the farmers of the valley is also very low (Roy and Bezbaruah 2003). A similar pattern of agriculture also exists in other parts of the state of Assam.

Formation of FMCs: Experience from Field Study

The formation of FMCs in a new form started in Barak Valley since 2009 along with other districts in the state. However, most of the FMCs of Barak Valley were formed during the year 2011–2012 and formation of new FMCs had been continuing during our survey. The agriculture officials failed to present any significant agricultural development schemes extended to those FMCs except support with a few seeds and fertilizers.

The responses received from the FMC as well as non-FMC members followed a dualistic pattern. There are 426 FMCs in Barak Valley region of Assam. A big rush among the agricultural landholders had been observed to enroll as members in FMCs. The field investigator faced the difficulty of finding the non-FMC members related to agricultural activities in many parts of the valley. Among the nonmembers, almost all are either very small holders or landless farmers. This represents the fact that there is an initial enthusiasm among the farmers to enroll in FMCs. When the nonmembers were asked whether they would like to join an FMC, almost 85 percent of them gave affirmative answers. What is the reason behind such enthusiasm? Two facts have been observed from the field study in this connection.

1. The state of farms and the economic status of most of those farmers were bad. They were eagerly looking for external support in terms of seeds, fertilizers, irrigation, warehousing, and so on.
2. A demonstration effect was working. They did not have any clear conception of collective farming. They were just pursuing the path of their co-farmers.

While the members of the FMCs were asked whether they had observed any benefits in joining an FMC, they responded with random answers. Most of the members supported FMCs in terms of mere delivery of seeds and a fraction of them for fertilizers. Again, the said facilities were not pertaining only to FMC members. Even nonmembers were having those meager facilities.

The level of agricultural infrastructure in Barak Valley is backward like that of the state of Assam as a whole. Irrigation facilities are almost absent. Apart from this, warehousing, cold storage, and so on are negligible compared to demand, and the role FMCs is reportedly passive in these respects. The notion of collective farming or taking farm decisions under the umbrella of FMCs was almost missing and, these were not systematic and organized.

ROLE OF FMCS IN MODERN AGRICULTURAL PRACTICES

Use of Agro-Capital and Agro-Technology

The terms agro-capital and agro-technology are used here to indicate the agricultural practices which help in enhancing performance or efficiency in agricultural practices. These are composed of three important stages of agricultural practices, namely, land preparation and plantation stage, plant growing stage, and harvesting stage. The use of agro-capital/technology by sample farmers is reported in table 5.1.

Table 5.1 Use of Agro-Capital/Technology in Sample Farms

Group	*Tilling/Sowing (%)*	*Watering, Weeding, Pest killing (%)*	*Harvesting*
FMC	7.0	26.5	–
Non-FMC	2.5	20.0	–

Source: Field Survey, 2013–2014.

It is seen that in the land preparation stage, modern agro-capital such as tractors, power tillers, and so on, are used to a very limited extent. Only 7 percent of FMC members have used such kinds of agro-capital. On the other hand, only 2.5 percent of non-FMC members have used agro-capital in tilling and planting activities. It has been reflected from the field study that farmers of the Barak Valley still rely on the traditional plough-bullock method of tilling. Moreover, from the field investigation, it has been found that sharing of agro-capital is also not taking place at the least cost. In fact, FMCs have not played any visible role in connection with sharing of agro-capital.

In the growing stage of plants, the important farm activities are watering the plants, removal of weeds, killing of pests, application of fertilizer, and so on. For performing these activities, there are many items of agro-capital such as pump sets, sprayer machines, and so on. From the field survey, it has been observed that only 26.5 percent of FMC members and 20 percent of non-FMC members have used such agro-capital and technology in this regard.

Even in the harvesting stage, no farmers were found using any kind of modern agro-capital or technology.

Agricultural Output

To examine the impact of FMCs in agricultural performance, all the principal crops which were widely cultivated in Barak Valley region have been taken. Based on the climatic conditions and availability of water, three seasonal varieties of paddy are cultivated in the region, like that of the rest of the state. These are summer paddy (*ahu*), autumn paddy (*sali*), and winter paddy (*boro*). Cultivation of *sali* paddy is very common throughout every part of this agro-climatic zone. Due to occurrence or threat of floods, meager or late rainfall, *ahu* cultivation is not that popular among the farmers. Regarding *boro* paddy, it is cultivated only in low-lying marshy lands or in *beels* [ponds] and in very few parts of Barak Valley. Table 5.2 presents the mean and standard deviation of the three types of seasonal paddy in Barak Valley.

The mean production of paddy in various seasons reflects that in the sample region summer paddy has the highest yield per hectare, followed by autumn paddy and winter paddy. However, due to the irrigation bottleneck

Table 5.2 Paddy Production in Sample Farms

Paddy	*Mean production (kg/hectare)*	*Standard deviation*
Summer Paddy (*Ahu*)	5,652.31	1,285.31
Autumn Paddy (*Sali*)	5,622.73	832.03
Winter Paddy (*Boro*)	3,868.81	3,328.11

Source: Field Survey, 2013–2014.

of the region winter paddy was cultivated only in a few areas. This is clearly reflected in the cropping pattern which shows that around 2 percent of the gross cultivated area is covered by the winter crop. Autumn paddy is mostly cultivated in different parts in the region.

The result of ANOVA of paddy between FMC and non-FMC farms in Barak Valley is shown in table 5.3.

The information in table 5.3 shows that the mean production of summer paddy in FMC-cultivated farms is 5,726.61 kg per hectare, while in non-FMC-cultivated farms, it is 5,625.09 kg. The difference in the mean production between FMC and non-FMC farms is highly insignificant as established by ANOVA. It is observed that the mean production of autumn paddy by FMC farms is 5,540.8 kg per hectare. In the case of non-FMC farms, the mean production is 5,425.2 kg. The result of ANOVA gives an insignificant F-value for autumn paddy. This shows that there is no significant difference in autumn paddy production between FMC and non-FMC farms. In other words, joining an FMC has not ensured any visible improvement in agricultural production on the assumption that non-FMC members were not solely enjoying any sort of extra institutional assistance. In the case of winter paddy also it was found that the mean difference was highly insignificant, which indicates that in Barak Valley there is no significant difference in farm production between FMC and non-FMC farms.

Due to lack of irrigation facilities, vegetables are not cultivated widely in the valley. However, depending on the rainfall, farmers grow different varieties of vegetables in very little quantities, as is shown in table 5.4.

In table 5.4, data relating to production of six principal winter vegetables are presented. The mean cauliflower production by FMC farmers is 13,028

Table 5.3 ANOVA of Paddy between FMC and Non-FMC Sample Farms

	Mean production (kg per hectare)		
Paddy	*FMC*	*Non-FMC*	*F-value (observed)*
Summer paddy	5,726 .61	5,625.09	1.12
Autumn paddy	5,540.80	5,425.20	3.68
Winter paddy	3,831.75	3,699.37	0.21

Source: Field Survey, 2013–2014.

Table 5.4 ANOVA of Vegetables in FMC and Non-FMC Sample Farms

	Mean production (kg per hectare)		
Vegetable	*FMC*	*Non-FMC*	*F-value (observed)*
Cauliflower	13,028.0	12,019.0	3.56
Cabbage	14,307.3	12,372.08	4.99*
Tomato	17,849.21	16,860.7	0.51
Potato	13,352.51	14,192.87	0.81
Radish	14,192.8	12,499.6	2.5
Brinjal	15,432.4	11,893.03	2.21

Source: Field Survey, 2013–2014.
*Indicates significant F-value.

kg per hectare, while the average production by non-FMC members is 12,019 kg. The nonsignificant F-value indicates that there is no significant difference between FMC and non-FMC farms in cauliflower production. In the case of production of cabbage, it is seen that the mean production by FMC farms is 14,307.3 kg per hectare, whereas the production of the non-FMC farms is 12,372.08 kg per hectare. The F-statistic is highly significant. This means that in the case of production of cabbage, FMC farms show more efficiency in contrast to non-FMC farms. In terms of other vegetables, the mean production of tomato, potato, radish, and brinjal are 17,849.21 kg, 13,352.51 kg, 14,192.8 kg, and 15,432.4 kg, respectively, by FMC farms. If we compare these mean production figures with the non-FMC farms, it is found that there is no significant difference in vegetable production. It can be concluded that FMCs have no extra impact on vegetable production.

Cropping Intensity

Cropping intensity, which is defined as the ratio of GCA to net sown area, is one of the agricultural development indices. The cropping intensities of FMC and non-FMC farms are presented in table 5.5.

In the fields of most of the farmers in the study area, at least two seasonal crops have been found to grow. However, there are some flood-prone cropping fields where farmers were compelled to practice mono-cropping. The crop cycle that was observed from the field investigation is mentioned below.

1. Summer paddy>autumn paddy>vegetables
2. Summer paddy>autumn paddy>fallow
3. Fallow>autumn paddy>vegetables
4. Fallow>autumn paddy>fallow>winter paddy
5. Fallow>autumn paddy>vegetables>winter paddy

Table 5.5 ANOVA of Cropping Intensity in FMC and Non-FMC Farms

Group	*Mean cropping intensity*	*F-value (observed)*
FMC	161.13	0.87
Non-FMC	166.57	

Source: Field Survey, 2013–2014.

Table 5.6 Cropping Intensity in Barak Valley, Assam, and All India, 2010–2011

Sl. no.	*District*	*Total cropped area*	*Net area sown*	*Cropping intensity*
1.	Cachar	160,728	115,386	139.30
2.	Hailakandi	73,246	50,294	145.64
3.	Karimgangj	103,474	76,035	136.09
4.	Barak Valley	337,448	241,715	139.61
Assam		4,159,525	2,810,597	147.99
India		197,323,000	141,559,000	139.39

Source: Directorate of Economics and Statistics, Assam.

Among these crop cycles, the first two have been found more extensively. However, just by observing the crop cycles, it will be wrong to assume that the total cultivable lands are used for multiple cropping. The mean value of cropping intensity for both FMC and non-FMC members is not encouraging. It is observed that the mean cropping intensity of FMC farms is 161.13, whereas for non-FMC members, it is 166.57. However, the insignificant F-value of ANOVA establishes that there is no significant difference between FMC and non-FMC farms in respect to cropping intensity.

It might be of some interest to note that the similarity of cropping intensity at the national (140.54), regional (147.99), and local (139.61) levels may not be interpreted as the similarity of agricultural environment in all these three tiers. At the national level, planned development of irrigation facilities plays an important role behind the multiple cropping that promotes higher cropping intensity. The availability of adequate surface water from the Brahmaputra–Barak river system and the occurrence of a high level of precipitation have made multiple cropping and higher cropping intensity possible. Thus, in no way does the similarity in cropping intensity indexes among national, regional, and local levels represent a situation of level playing fields for agriculture at these three levels (table 5.6).

Cropping Pattern

The observed cropping pattern of sample FMC, as well as non-FMC farms in the three districts of Barak Valley, is reported in table 5.7. It is seen that there is almost similar cropping pattern practiced by both FMC and non-FMC

Table 5.7 Cropping Pattern in Sample Farms (percentage)

	GCA (percentage)		
Crops	*FMC*	*Non-FMC*	*All farms*
Summer paddy	33.41	34.74	34.08
Autumn paddy	58.26	57.61	57.94
Winter paddy	7.58	6.73	7.16
Vegetables	0.75	0.91	0.84

Source: Field Survey, 2013–2014.

Table 5.8 Cropping Diversity between FMC and Non-FMC in Sample Farms

Group	*Mean*	*F-value*
FMC	0.45	6.84*
Non-FMC	0.48	

Source: Field Survey, 2013–2014.
*Indicates significant F-value.

farms. In all cases, summer and autumn paddy shares the major fraction of GCA. They together capture more than 90 percent of GCA for all farms. Share of winter paddy is near 2 percent for all farms. Vegetables are produced only in 0.84 percent of GCA in sample farms. There is no major difference observed between FMC and non-FMC farms in the Barak Valley.

Cropping Diversity

Cropping diversity indicates how an agricultural farm distributes its land among different types of crops. Table 5.8 shows the CDI of sample farms. It is observed that the mean CDI of sample FMC farms is 0.45, whereas for non-FMC farm, it is 0.48. The F-value of ANOVA is highly significant. This indicates that there is a significant mean difference in CDI between FMC and non-FMC farms. The result is somewhat surprising, as it was expected that FMC farms would enjoy a superior position. One reason may be that non-FMC farms have small holdings and the percentage of vegetable production to the GCA of non-FMC farms is more than that of FMC farms.

CONCLUSIONS

The various agricultural performance indicators of farms under FMC and non-FMCs of Barak Valley have been analyzed. The study finds that there is initial enthusiasm among farmers to enroll themselves in FMCs. However, the notion of working of FMCs or the concepts such as collective farming is found to be almost absent among the farmers. The result of ANOVA establishes that FMCs have no special impact on the agricultural performance of the farms. The FMCs of Barak Valley were newly formed during the period 2009–2014. Most of the FMCs are new in this sense. Only a few schemes have been granted to these FMCs. The Government of Assam asserted that in all agricultural developmental schemes FMC members would be given preference and these would be channelized to the farmers through FMCs. Some of the important findings of the study are as follows.

1. Agriculture in the state of Assam is still completely rain-fed. There are tube-wells, especially shallow ones, only in a few areas. However, these are too few in proportion to the needs. Irrigation facilities will certainly increase the cropping intensity and crop diversity in the state. Moreover, flood control measures should be adopted in flood-prone areas.
2. Proper knowledge is not available to the farmers regarding application of fertilizers. No soil testing facilities are available in the sample locations. For developing scientific methods of cultivation and farm mechanization, farmers' training programs should be arranged at regular intervals to teach modern agricultural practices like preparation of the land, selection of seeds, weeding, use of specific items and doses of soil nutrients, to harvesting, integrated pest management techniques, and so on.
3. Farmers in general are not aware of the benefits of cooperative farming. The concept of collective or cooperative farming should be popularized among the farmers. Every FMC member should work with a complementary approach so that the total agricultural performance improves under the cluster of FMCs.

The author is grateful to the Indian Council of Social Science Research, New Delhi, India, for funding the research project entitled "Impact of Field Management Committees (FMCs) towards Agricultural Development in the Barak Valley Region of Assam" during 2013–2015.

REFERENCES

Bhattacherjee, Jayanta B. *Cachar Under British Rule*. New Delhi: Radiant Publishers, 1977.

Kshirsagar, K. G., Sujeet Pandey, and Mauricio R. Bellon. *Farmer Perceptions, Varietal Characteristics and Technology Adoption: The Case of Rainfed Paddy in a Village in Eastern India*. Social Sciences Discussion Paper 5/97. Makati City, Philippines: International Paddy Research Institute, 1997.

Roy, Niranjan, and Madhurjya. P. Bezbaruah. *Agricultural Growth and Regional Economic Development*. New Delhi: Mittal Publications, 2003.

Chapter 6

Cooperatives as Organizational Choice: Past and Present Developments in the Post-Yugoslav Space

Franci Avsec

Cooperatives in the post-Yugoslav space (as the territory of the former Socialist Federative Republic of Yugoslavia) have a long and rich, but rather discontinuous history that had begun in the nineteenth century, several decades before the emergence of the South Slavic state after World War I.

The first cooperatives emerged during the nineteenth century to solve the most acute problems caused by the expansion of the capitalistic market economy in the prevalently agrarian societies. In the first period, credit cooperatives provided farmers and other small producers with access to credit, eradicated usury, and lowered transaction costs (due to business in the national language, low non-performance of loans because of good assessment of borrowers' credit capability, etc.). Credit cooperatives also paved the way for the establishment and successful operation of other cooperatives.

The Constitution of the Kingdom of Serbs, Croats, and Slovenes (Ustavotvorna Skupština Kraljevine Srba, Hrvata i Slovenaca 1921) provided for state support for cooperatives and foresaw the unification of cooperative law. That aim was achieved in 1937 when the state, then renamed as the Kingdom of Yugoslavia, adopted the Act on economic cooperatives (Zakon o gospodarskih zadrugah 1937).

Credit cooperatives were severely affected by the world economic depression in the 1930s when the Kingdom of Yugoslavia had to intervene with restructuring of farmers' debts so that credit cooperatives and other financial institutions transferred 25 percent of their claims toward farmers on the Privileged Agrarian Bank (PAB) in return for bonds and wrote off a further 25 percent). Before World War II, the cooperative movement become more diversified, the credit cooperatives, recovering from the crisis and still having the greatest economic importance, were outnumbered by other types of cooperatives.

After World War II, the socioeconomic system changed radically: the state property (property of the nation or of all the people) became the prevailing ownership form, while the cooperative property (property of cooperative organizations) was introduced as a lower form of collective property, but the private property on means of production was limited (viz., through agrarian means). The prewar credit cooperatives and their central organizations that had been the backbone of the previous cooperative system were, to great extent wound up through administrative measures, their property being nationalized.

The General Act on Cooperatives (1946) defined cooperatives "as voluntary economic associations of working people aiming at organization and promotion of agriculture and small trade and developing the initiative of the broadest people's masses in towns and on the countryside regarding the organization of production, supply and distribution of goods." The Act explicitly listed several traditional classes of cooperatives (marketing and supply, consumer, producer, processing, credit, housing, and health cooperatives) and introduced also a new type, namely, farmers' working cooperatives (for joint agricultural production) following the Soviet model of kolchoses. The concept of farmers' working cooperatives was elaborated more in detail by a special Basic Act on agricultural cooperatives (1949), which marks the beginning of a longer period when special cooperative legislation was adopted for certain types of cooperatives. In spite of various pressures infringing the principle of voluntariness, the overwhelming majority of farmers did not want to join working cooperatives. The campaign failed in 1953, when the land and other assets invested in these cooperatives were returned to farmers, but additional restrictions for private ownership of agricultural land were introduced at the same time. Nevertheless, the major part of agricultural land and forests remained as private property. From then on, cooperatives in

Table 6.1 Cooperatives in the Kingdom of Serbs, Croats, and Slovenes (1925), and in the Kingdom of Yugoslavia (1939)

Number of cooperatives or members/year	*1925*	*1939*
Local credit cooperatives	2,414	5,022
Local supply cooperatives	973	2,711
Other local cooperatives	556	3,494
All local cooperatives	3,943	11,227
Central cooperatives	n.a.	45
Auditing cooperative unions	29	37
Total members of all cooperatives	n.a.	1,609,176

Sources: Kraljevina Jugoslavija 1932, 304–405; 1941, 315–20.

agriculture and other sectors provided members with marketing, supply, and similar services.

The failure of working cooperatives of farmers was one of the main drivers for the replacement of the administrative planning system and state property with the so-called self-management system and social ownership. The regulation about agricultural cooperatives of 1954 (Uredba o kmetijskih zadrugah 1954) stipulated that "the property of [a] cooperative is social ownership and may in no case be evicted from the cooperative." The liberalization which followed stimulated the successful business operation of numerous multipurpose ("general") agricultural cooperatives supplying farmers and marketing their products. However, further development of social ownership as non-ownership resulted in strengthening of the governance influence of employees. This development was backed by the tendency to regulate cooperatives as much as possible in the same way as socially owned enterprises. In the 1960s, a lot of agricultural cooperatives merged with noncooperative enterprises. The legislation about enterprises explicitly stipulated that farmers and other private producers cooperating with enterprises had also certain governance rights relating to this cooperation. The number of cooperatives decreased.

In the beginning of the 1970s, the constitutional changes tried to curb the power of technostructure in enterprises and to reaffirm the governance position of workers through introduction of the so-called basic organizations. In a similar way as basic organizations of associated labor were organized within enterprises with the aim of enhancing governance rights of workers, farmer members alone or with employees could organize basic cooperative organizations within a cooperative. In addition, farmers as cooperators of enterprises could organize basic organizations of cooperators that in many cases later organized themselves as self-standing agricultural cooperatives.

The severe economic and political crisis at the end of the 1980s led to legislative changes that, inter alia, provided for wider options of organizing

Table 6.2 Number of Cooperative Organizations in Yugoslavia, 1954–1983

Type of cooperative organization	*1954*	*1959*	*1968*	*1969*	*1979*	*1983*
Agricultural cooperatives	6,715	4,086	1,371	1,278	471	585
Craft cooperatives	177	516	n.a.	n.a.	313	463
Other cooperatives					91	243
Basic cooperatives organizations					158	2,153
Organizations of cooperators					543	895

Source: Savezni Zavod za Statistiku, 1954–1984.

Table 6.3 Cooperative Entities in Yugoslavia, December 31, 1990 (According to the Yugoslav Federal Act on Cooperatives from 1990, minimum number of members is three)

Newly established or re-registered cooperatives	*1,908*
Cooperative entities according to the previous legislation on associated labor	
Agricultural cooperatives	818
Craft cooperatives	704
Other cooperatives	825
Basic cooperative organizations	120
Organizations of cooperators	238

Source: Savezni Zavod za Statistiku, 1991.

cooperatives in various sectors, while the constitutional amendments reintroduced cooperative property aiming at making the socioeconomic system more diversified and flexible through plurality of ownership forms. The federal Act on cooperatives (Zakon o zadrugah 1990) tried to regulate cooperatives in general as member-oriented organizations with different forms of ownership and also provided for partial transformation of social ownership into cooperative ownership. Further, systemic changes toward the system of a market economy without social ownership were completed in the newly emerged states.

This chapter outlines the present regulative framework of cooperatives and the recent development of cooperatives within the newly established legal system. The survey was made on the basis of data gathered from institutions responsible for registration of cooperatives, for statistics about business subjects and annual reports, as well as from competent ministries. Since cooperatives began their history before the emergence of the Yugoslav state, the beginnings of cooperative movement are briefly mentioned initially in the survey for each country.

A SURVEY ACROSS COUNTRIES

Bosnia and Herzegovina

The first cooperatives registered according to the Commercial code for Bosnia and Herzegovina from 1883 were credit cooperatives established in Sarajevo in 1900 and 1903. In 1912, there were twenty-one cooperatives registered in various towns across the country (Pajkić 2014).

Today, Bosnia and Herzegovina consist according to its Constitution, of two Entities, the Federation of Bosnia and Herzegovina, and the Republika Srpska. The Constitution of Bosnia and Herzegovina guarantees full freedom of movement of persons, goods, services, and capital throughout Bosnia and Herzegovina. The Constitution was amended in 2009 with a provision guaranteeing a special position to the Brčko District, which is a self-governing unit under the sovereignty of Bosnia and Herzegovina.

The General Act on cooperatives of Bosnia and Herzegovina (2003) takes over the definition of cooperatives and the cooperative principles following the Statement of Identity of the International Cooperative Alliance adopted in 1995. The Act stresses the principle that the business of a cooperative should provide benefits to its members and that a cooperative may conclude transactions of the same type as with its members, with nonmembers only if its statutes allow such business with nonmembers, if the cooperative auditing is performed regularly and if the business with nonmembers is the object of a separate accounting, the net income originating from these transactions being invested in the cooperative.

A cooperative may be founded by at least five members who may be natural or legal persons. The governance bodies of a cooperative are a general meeting (consisting of all members each of whom has one vote, while cooperatives with more than 300 members may replace a general meeting of all members with the meeting of at least thirty representatives elected from and by the members), an administrative committee (not obligatory in cooperatives with less than twenty-five members), a supervisory board, and (not obligatorily) a professional manager.

The capital of the cooperative is formed by the contributions of the members. On the paid-in contributions, a cooperative may not pay dividend, but interest, provided that its financial result is positive. After termination of membership, the contribution is reimbursed to a former member or her successors.

The surplus of income over expenses is used for obligatory reserves (in an amount not lower than 5 percent of members' contribution until these reserves achieve the highest value of capital attained after the founding of the cooperative), for voluntary reserves and distribution among members. The funds that a cooperative acquires after its establishment may not be used to increase the contributions of the members.

The winding up of a cooperative is rendered more difficult with a procedural provision that at least the minimum number of members as is required for the establishment of a cooperative may block the resolution about the voluntary liquidation. The Act specially regulates the indivisibility of a certain part of the property the cooperative acquired before its enforcement, so that in the case of winding up, the property a cooperative with the registered office in Republika Srpska had acquired before the General Act on cooperatives from 2003 entered into force, as well as the property acquired by a cooperative with the registered office in the Federation of Bosnia and

Herzegovina before the Act on cooperatives adopted by this Federation in 1997 entered into force, may not be distributed among the members. The other property of a liquidated cooperative, however, may be divided among the members.

The Act also provides for cooperative auditing that is performed by the cooperative unions of entities, while the rules pertaining to the application of cooperative principles, cooperative auditing, and the registration of cooperatives are issued by the Cooperative union of Bosnia and Herzegovina.

Besides the general legislation on cooperatives on the state level, the Republika Srpska and the Brčko District adopted their own legislation on agricultural cooperatives. On the other hand, within the Federation of Bosnia and Herzegovina several cantons also adopted special legislation on pupils, housing and other cooperatives.

According to Pajkić (2014, 186), 196 cooperatives were affiliated to the cooperative unions of both entities: these cooperatives were owned by 9,457 members, employed 864 persons, and collaborated with 15,465 cooperators. However, since the affiliation of cooperatives to cooperative unions is voluntary, the figures mentioned do not represent the total number of cooperatives.

On March 13, 2016, the register of business entities in the Federation of Bosnia and Herzegovina contained 302 entries about registered cooperatives (Registar poslovnih subjekata Federacije BiH 2016), while the similar register in the Republika Srpska disclosed data for 262 registered cooperatives (APIF 2016).

The cooperative movement in Bosnia and Herzegovina is faced with several challenges. The legislation about cooperatives on the state, entities' and cantons' level is sometimes inconsistent and causes divergent interpretation and disputes, especially regarding the ownership transformation and property rights of cooperatives. Cooperatives are too small to be able to separately implement their own marketing strategy, while cooperative unions with voluntary membership do not gather enough means to efficiently carry out their representing, supportive, and auditing tasks (Pajkić 2014).

The banking legislation in Bosnia and Herzegovina does not allow cooperatives to carry out financial services. However, some types of financial organizations regulated by the banking legislation, although not termed as cooperatives, are similar to cooperatives either due to organizational features (the so-called savings and loan organizations in Republika Srpska), or due to their purpose to satisfy the financial needs of individuals (microcredit organizations, regulated both in the Federation of Bosnia and Herzegovina and in the Republika Srpska).

At the end of 2014, there were nineteen microcredit organizations active in the entire state of Bosnia and Herzegovina, fifteen of which were microcredit foundations and four microcredit companies, while in Republika Srpska no savings and loan organization has been established yet (Centralna banka Bosne i Hercegovine 2015, 49).

Croatia

The first modern cooperative in Croatia was the Mutual Loan Society established in 1864 on the Dalmatian island of Korčula (Mataga 2009, 21). After the Austrian Act on cooperatives from 1873 (applicable in Istria and Dalmatia) and the Hungarian Commercial code from 1875 (also regulating cooperatives and applicable to the other territory of the Croatia of today) had been adopted, cooperatives and their unions were established in all Croatian regions (Kovačević 1956, 370–89; Mataga 2009, 23–27).

Cooperatives in Croatia are nowadays regulated by the Act on cooperatives (Zakon o zadrugama 2011) that defines a cooperative as "a voluntary, open, self-standing and independent society governed by its members who, through their work, use of services or other activities, on the basis of community and self-help, promote and protect their individual and common economic, social, educational, cultural and other needs and interests." The Act also refers to internationally recognized cooperative principles.

A cooperative may be founded by at least seven individuals or legal entities if not otherwise provided by the Act (e.g., a secondary cooperative may be founded by at least two cooperatives). The distinctive feature of a cooperative as a legal entity is the direct participation of its members in the activity of a cooperative.

The highest body of a cooperative is a general meeting, which elects a supervisory committee and a manager. In principle, the general meeting consists of all members. However, in cooperatives with at least sixty members, the general meeting may consist of at least twenty representatives elected by members. Each member or representative has only one vote in a general meeting. The supervisory committee consists of elected members of a cooperative and at most one person who is not a member of a cooperative. The manager, with a five-year term of office, represents the cooperative and manages its day-to-day business.

The capital of a cooperative is formed through basic and additional contributions. The amount of basic contributions that are obligatory for all members is set by the general meeting but may not be lower than HRK 1,000. The amount of additional, that is, voluntary contributions, is also set by the general meeting uniformly for all members. The cash contributions may also be paid by nonmember investors whose rights and liabilities are regulated by the contract concluded with the cooperative. The statutes may foresee that investors elect a representative to inform the general meeting of members about the opinion of investors regarding the business of the cooperative and the proposed resolutions if they could have an impact on the security and liquidity of the nonmembers' investments.

At least 20 percent of the net profit of a cooperative (reduced by the amount used to cover any loss brought forward) must be allocated for the development of the cooperative, and at least 5 percent must be earmarked for reserves until they achieve the sum of members' contributions. The remaining part may be used for distribution among members (either in additional shares or in cash), investors, and employees. A cooperative established exclusively to satisfy the needs of members (social, consumer, housing cooperative, or cooperative of local communities) without a profit-gaining purpose, is not allowed to distribute profits and has to bring forward the entire surplus of income over expenses after the losses from previous years have been covered.

Members are not liable for the debts of their cooperative except in cases when the exclusion of liability is misused (for instance, if members dispose of the cooperative's property as if it was their personal property).

The resolution about voluntary liquidation may be blocked by the written counter-vote of at least a minimum number of members required for the founding of a cooperative. If the resolution about winding up is, nevertheless, adopted, the assets that remain after the cooperative in liquidation has paid all debts and reimbursed members' contributions are transferred to the local community, which is obliged to assign the property to the existing or newly established cooperative or, subsidiarily, for the promotion of cooperation.

The Act also contains some special provisions for agricultural workers, fishing, housing, construction, and social cooperatives. The most innovative are social cooperatives, the purpose of which is to provide social services and to include individuals from vulnerable groups into work. Members of a social cooperative may be its beneficiaries, service providers, and employees.

In 2014, the Act was amended with a provision that transformed the Croatian union of cooperatives with obligatory membership of all cooperatives and cooperative unions into the Croatian center for cooperative entrepreneurship, having the status of a public foundation. The center promotes the interests of cooperatives and provides support services to cooperatives and their unions.

According to the data published by the chief officer of the Croatian center for cooperative entrepreneurship, on December 31, 2014, there were 1,247 cooperatives in Croatia that had 21,622 members and employed 2,730 workers (Stanojević 2014, 53).

The Croatian center for cooperative entrepreneurship also maintains a central register of cooperatives and cooperative unions where, as of March 15, 2016, there were 1,301 cooperatives and seven cooperative unions registered (three branch cooperative unions at the state level, for agriculture, fishing,

Table 6.4 Number, Members, Employees, and Turnover of Croatian Cooperatives, December 31, 2014

	Cooperatives		*Members*		*Employees*		*Turnover in 2014*	
Sector of activity	*No.*	*Share (%)*	*No.*	*Share (%)*	*No.*	*Share (%)*	*Value (HRK)*	*Share (%)*
Agriculture and forestry	509	40.8	7,925	39.2	1,263	46.5	935,454,133	55.3
Fishing	41	3.3	640	3.2	150	5.5	230,118,489	13.6
Manufacture	215	17.2	2,994	14.8	406	14.9	174,349,359	10.3
Construction	84	6.7	1,277	6.3	122	4.5	83,155,314	4.9
Trade	124	9.9	2,252	11.2	365	13.4	138,727,575	8.2
Accommodation and food service activities	75	6.0	634	3.1	91	3.4	22,329,304	1.3
Others	199	16.0	4,470	22.1	319	11.7	108,194,033	6.4
Total	1,247	100.0	20,192	100.0	2,716	100.0	1,692,328,207	100.0

Source: Hrvatski Centar za Zadružno Poduzetništvo, 2015.

and craft industry; and four regional cooperative unions—for Dalmatia, Istria, Zadar županija, and the Zagreb region).

The most numerous cooperatives are agricultural cooperatives, which could be explained with the long tradition of this type of cooperative in the country. On the other hand, fishery cooperatives realized the greatest turnover per cooperative in 2014, which is attributable to the public support for the concentration of supply through fishing cooperatives as producer organizations. There were forty-one fishing cooperatives at the end of 2014, of which fourteen were recognized as producer organizations. These fourteen cooperatives achieved 97 percent of the total turnover of all fishing cooperatives (Stanojević 2014, 53).

As a specific challenge facing the development of cooperatives in Croatia is the relatively low level of activity of cooperatives. About 58 percent of all cooperatives do not employ any person, while the remaining 42 percent employing one or more workers achieve 95 percent of the total turnover of all cooperatives. Experts also remark that cooperatives, especially with respect to obligatory profit allocations for reserves, are not treated adequately by the tax system (Stanojević 2014, 55).

Savings and credit cooperatives had been regulated by the general and special cooperative legislation until 2007, when the Act on credit unions (Zakon o kreditnim unijama 2007) prescribed that the general assembly of an existing savings and credit cooperative had to decide either to continue its operation as a credit union according to this Act, to transform itself into a savings bank according to the Banking Act, or to wind up and initiate liquidation proceedings.

A credit union is defined as a credit institution with its registered office in the Republic of Croatia that obtained the license for its operation from the Croatian national bank and is composed of members with a common bond

Table 6.5 Basic Data about Credit Unions in Croatia

Year	*2009*	*2010*	*2011*	*2012*	*2013*	*2014*
Number of credit unions	33	33	22	26	26	26
Balance sheet of credit unions (million HRK)	515	530	569	602	660	709

Source: Hrvatska Narodna Banka, 2014.

(relating to employment, profession, or residence), with paid-up capital at least in the amount of HRK 500,000. The activity of a credit union is, in principle, limited to financial transactions with members. Although the regulation of the governance of the credit union is similar to that of cooperatives (for instance, each member has only one vote in the general meeting), the credit union is not regarded as a cooperative.

The Croatian association of credit unions elaborated some proposals for the removal of some restrictions, advocating the extension of permitted services and membership of the credit unions as well as a similar regime for the insurance of deposits in credit unions and banks (Hrvatska Udruga Kreditnih Unija 2012).

While in 2007, when the new legislation entered into force, there were 124 savings and credit cooperatives in Croatia (Hrvatska udruga kreditnih unija 2012), there were twenty-five credit unions registered in Croatia as of December 31, 2015, that had 0.1 percent market share in 2014 (Hrvatska narodna banka 2016).

Kosovo

Cooperatives in Kosovo emerged in the period between the two world wars, when the colonists who held the land on lease, not being owners of immovables, formed cooperatives and other associations that were financially supported by the state (Gnjatović 2011, 18).

The present legislation on farmers' cooperatives was adopted during the operation of the United Nations Interim Administration Mission in Kosovo (UNMIK). According to the UNMIK Regulation on the Constitutional Framework for the Provisional Institutions of Self-Government in Kosovo, the Assembly of Kosovo adopted Act No. 2003/9 on farmers' cooperatives on May 15, 2003.

The Act defines a farmers' cooperative as a legal entity created by natural and legal persons. Members must be farmers. A farmers' cooperative does not make profit for itself and must derive at least 75 percent of its total turnover from activities with farmer members (for instance, acquiring agricultural outputs from members for sale or processing, supplying inputs, performing services for members, buying machinery for joint use of members, etc.). A member has the right to use the cooperative's services and an obligation to undertake specific agreed-upon activities exclusively with a cooperative for at least three consecutive years in accordance with the statutes of the cooperative.

A farmers' cooperative must have at least ten members and must not be established without capital. The capital is formed through members' contributions either in cash or in kind. After the membership is terminated, a former member is entitled to obtain the nominal value of her shares.

The main bodies of a farmers' cooperative are a general meeting consisting of all members, a steering committee that may nominate the director of the cooperative, external auditors, and a manager who is in charge of the day-to-day management.

The Act lays down detailed provisions about the allocation of net annual income. At least 5 percent of the net annual income has to be allocated to a compulsory reserve fund, a further 5 percent to a reserve fund for reimbursement of shares to existing members. Other allocations to reserves take place if so, required by the statutes. The remaining part of the net annual income may be used for interest on the paid-up capital of members, distribution among members in proportion to their activity with the cooperative, and increase of accumulated surplus or other reserves.

If a cooperative is wound up, net assets remaining after payment of all creditors and the reimbursement of members' contributions may not be allocated to members and have to be transferred to another cooperative, to a union of farmers' cooperatives, or to another legal organization of farmers' cooperatives.

Two or more farmers' cooperatives may establish a union of farmers' cooperatives for carrying out activities of common interest. The Act foresees also a federation of farmers' cooperatives as a voluntary interest representing and supporting association.

In 2015, there were eighty-three registered farmers' cooperatives in Kosovo (Pllashniku 2015, 93). Although the detailed data about the economic importance of farmers' cooperatives are not available, the establishment and operation of cooperatives proved to be successful not only for the economic recovery and development of the country but also to restore inter-ethnic trust and cooperation. Not only international organizations, foreign countries, and other public actors but also numerous cooperatives from all over the world have helped farmers in Kosovo to set up cooperative structures and provided funds (also through micro-financial organizations) for economic development, above all of micro and small enterprises. In this connection, a success story of Kooperativa Krusha, a pepper-producing cooperative of 100 percent women-run and staffed agricultural cooperative deserves to be mentioned.

Montenegro

The first cooperative in the Principality of Montenegro was a farmers' credit cooperative established in 1902 in Kamenari village (Četković 1956).

The cooperatives in Montenegro are regulated by the Act on cooperatives adopted by the Parliament of the Federal Republic of Yugoslavia in 1996. However, after the Republic of Montenegro gained independence in 2003, the Montenegrinian Parliament adopted two special Acts containing special provisions for housing cooperatives and later for (agricultural) cooperatives.

The Act on housing cooperatives (Zakon o stambenim zadrugama 2010) defines a housing cooperative as an association of natural and legal persons the purpose of which is to solve, according to cooperative principles, housing problems of its members or of employees employed by a member that is a legal entity. The activities of the housing cooperative may encompass construction of houses, apartments and business premises; obtaining and elaborating investment and other documentation; purchase and storage of construction material; maintenance of apartments and business premises; collecting financial assets of members for construction or purchase of apartments and business premises; and other tasks.

A housing cooperative may be founded by at least one legal person and fifteen individuals or at least by thirty individuals. In the general meeting of housing cooperatives, each member has one vote, with the exception of the legal entity that may have a number of votes proportional to the number of employees for whom the legal entity has paid contribution. The general meeting elects the administrative and the supervisory committees, while the administrative committee nominates the manager entrusted with the daily business. The capital of the housing cooperative is formed by members' contributions (a legal entity as a member of a housing cooperative pays a contribution for each one of its employees for whom it solves the housing problem). While the contributions are redeemable to members after termination of the membership, members are also obliged to pay a subscription fee that is not reimbursable. After contributions are paid, a housing cooperative must form reserves for which at least 5 percent of the annual profit must be allocated until the value of this reserve fund achieves half of the capital. The property that remains after the winding up of a housing cooperative is transferred to the local community, which is obliged to earmark it for the "needs of housing development."

The Act also foresees a union of housing cooperatives as a voluntary association of housing cooperatives with the aim of representing the interests of its members and to support the affiliated housing cooperatives.

The Act on cooperatives (Zakon o kooperativama 2015) regulates rural cooperatives encompassing quite a wide range of agricultural cooperatives, including beekeeping cooperatives, cooperatives for processing agricultural products, fishing cooperatives, rural tourism and cottage industry cooperatives, forest products and herbal plants collecting cooperatives, wood processing cooperatives and "other cooperatives in the area of agriculture." The notion of these cooperatives that are nevertheless limited to rural sector (and not to all economic activities) is termed with the general loan word "kooperativa" instead of the established general term "zadruga," without any specifying attribute. Although by introducing this terminological change, the legislator probably intended to improve the image of the newly organized cooperatives in the eyes of the population, the terminology nevertheless seems to be inconsistent. Also, the Act on housing cooperatives permits two terms in the registered name of housing cooperatives: "stambena zadruga" or "stambena kooperativa."

A cooperative may not be a founder of another legal entity (which is quite a restrictive provision) and may not transform itself into another legal entity. The minimum number of founders who may be individuals and/or legal entities is five. The minimum amount of a member's contribution is 200 euros. Besides the general meeting, a cooperative with fifteen or more members must have an administrative and a supervisory committee (in smaller cooperatives the functions of these committees may be performed by the general meeting), while a manager is obligatory in all cooperatives and is nominated by the general meeting on the proposal of the administrative committee.

The assets remaining after a voluntary liquidation of a cooperative are distributed equally among the members, while the property remaining after the bankruptcy proceedings of a cooperative is transferred to the local community that may grant use of these assets to newly established cooperatives.

The computation and analysis of registered cooperatives in the database of the Agency for Business Registers of the Republic of Montenegro (Centralni registar privrednih subjekata 2016) found 108 registered cooperatives in Montenegro on February 25, 2016. Most of them are agricultural farmers' cooperatives.

Table 6.6 Sectoral Distribution of Cooperatives in Montenegro, February 26, 2016

Sector of activity	*Number*
Agricultural and forestry cooperatives	65
Youth and student cooperatives	25
Housing cooperatives	6
Craft cooperatives	1
Fishery cooperatives	1
Pupils' cooperatives	1
Other cooperatives	7
Cooperative associations	2
Total number of cooperatives and cooperative unions	108

Source: Centralni Registar Privrednih Subjekata, 2016.

North Macedonia

The first initiatives for credit and other cooperatives in the today North Macedonia emerged in the beginning of the twentieth century when three supply and marketing cooperatives were established first in Robovo (1908) and later in Kreševo and in Dojran. A large number of cooperatives began to develop after World War II (Usepjanov 1956).

Cooperatives in North Macedonia are regulated by the general Act on cooperatives from 2002 and a special Act on agricultural cooperatives from 2013.

The Act on cooperatives (2002) defines a cooperative as an association of natural or legal persons aiming at "promotion or protection of a limited number of precisely defined economic interests in all activities except banking, insurance and other activities that the legislation does not allow to be performed by cooperatives."

A cooperative may be established by at least three members (individuals or legal entities), who assume either unlimited or limited liability for the debts of the cooperative. A member has the right to be treated equally as other members, to obtain information about the cooperative, to vote in the general meeting, and to obtain a part of the annual profit. Following the example of Swiss cooperative legislation, the North Macedonian Act provides that if a cooperative issues share certificates, each member must obtain at least one share.

At least 5 percent of the annual profit must be allocated for obligatory reserves (either at least for twenty successive years or, if the share certificates were issued, until the obligatory reserves achieve the amount of capital). The rights of former members relating to the property of the cooperative are regulated by the statutes.

The highest body of a cooperative is a general meeting of all members that elects an administrative committee and supervisors. The administrative committee, which must be predominantly composed of members of the cooperative, prepares and executes resolutions of the general meeting. The general meeting or, if so, provided by the statutes, the administrative committee may nominate one or more managers who manage the daily business and represent the cooperative. Managers are supervised by the administrative committee. The annual reports must be verified by authorized auditors or an auditing company.

The assets that remain after the liquidation of a cooperative may be distributed among members only if it is so provided by the statutes. The Act, however, does not determine the purpose of the remaining property in cases where the statutes do not regulate this issue.

Three or more cooperatives may voluntarily set up a cooperative union.

The Act on agricultural cooperatives (2013) contains some specific provisions about organization, stimulative measures, and supervision of agricultural cooperatives.

The notion of an agricultural cooperative is broader than the definition of a cooperative in general legislation. The Act stipulates that agricultural holdings satisfy, through membership in an agricultural cooperative, not only their economic but also social, cultural, and other interests and needs originating from the carrying out of agricultural activity. The Act refers also to the internationally recognized cooperative principles. Also, the contractual relationships between the members and their agricultural cooperative are defined very broadly and may include marketing and processing of agricultural products, supply of inputs, machinery, administrative, and similar services. Agricultural cooperatives that are founded according to the Act and registered by the Ministry of Agriculture are entitled to financial support.

The support for farmers' cooperatives is foreseen in the Strategy for agriculture and rural development for 2014–2020 that forecasts the removal of legal and administrative barriers, training, consulting, and financial support for the establishment and management of farmers' cooperatives that may contribute substantially to the concentration of fragmented supply (Ministerstvo za zemjodelstvo, šumarstvo i vodostopanstvo 2014). According to the Farm Structure Survey data from 2013, there were 170,885 agricultural holdings in the Republic of Macedonia. The average agricultural holding used 1.85 ha of agricultural area and bred 2.14 LSU (livestock size units), while around 58 percent of individual agricultural holdings used up to 1 ha of agricultural area and around 55 percent of the individual agricultural holdings used more than half of their production for their own consumption (Deržaven zavod na statistika na makedonija 2013).

The data about active cooperatives disclose that in 2016 only one active Macedonian cooperative was medium sized, and all others were either micro or small cooperatives.

Table 6.7 Number of Active Cooperatives in Macedonia (as of February 2016)

Number of micro cooperatives	71
Number of small cooperatives	19
Number of medium-sized cooperatives	1
Total number of cooperatives	92

Source: Central Registry of the Republic of Macedonia (February 2016).

The general North Macedonian Act on cooperatives explicitly excludes cooperatives from carrying out banking activity. The Banking Act of 2007 permits savings houses existing at the time of its enforcement to continue their activity, but does not provide for the establishment of new savings houses. There are three active savings houses supervised by the Central bank of the Republic of North Macedonia, among them also the FULM Saving House. (The name FULM is the abbreviation in the Macedonian language for Financial Services for the People of Macedonia.) This savings house wants to be, according to its mission statement, "an efficient member owned and member governed cooperative financial institution . . . providing members with safe and quality financial services . . . rendered more effectively than those provided by other financial institutions in Macedonia" (Fulm Saving House 2016). According to the banking legislation, the savings house was established as a limited liability company by one shareholder, an association with the same name (FULM) with more than 8,000 individual members. Although not organized as a credit union or credit cooperative, the FULM Saving House is a member of the World Council of Credit Unions.

Serbia

The first cooperative in the territory of the Republic of Serbia of today was founded in 1846 in Bački Petrovac (Vojvodina). Agricultural credit cooperatives established the first cooperative union in the territory of the Kingdom of Serbia in 1894. This union, headed by Mihailo Avramović (1864–1945), was one of the twelve founders of the International Cooperative Alliance in 1895 (Stojanović and Gnjatović 2015, 29). In 1898, the Kingdom of Serbia adopted the Act on agricultural and craft cooperatives. The oldest agricultural cooperative that is still active was founded in Azanja (near Belgrade).

The present Act on cooperatives (2015) defines a cooperative following the definition, cooperative values, and principles proclaimed by the International Cooperative Alliance.

The Act defines a cooperative as a special form of organization of individuals who realize that doing business on the basis of cooperative principles, their economic, social, cultural, and other interests governing and controlling the activities of the cooperative will benefit. The Act also permits a combined cooperative formed by at least two other cooperatives, while legal persons that are not cooperatives may not be members of a cooperative or of a cooperative union.

Members of a cooperative directly participate in the activities of the cooperative. On the other hand, a cooperative may conclude transactions with nonmembers if its purpose and cooperative principles are not questioned. The Act lists various kinds of cooperatives: agricultural (farmers'), housing, consumer, craft, workers, students and youth, social, health, and other kinds of cooperatives. Social cooperatives were introduced as a new type of cooperative aiming at social, economic, and working inclusion and satisfying other needs of individuals from vulnerable groups or at satisfying general interests of local communities.

A cooperative may be founded by at least five members, either with capital formed by contributions of members, or without capital, in which case members pay subscription fees. While contributions are redeemable, the subscription fees are not reimbursed to former members or their successors. The payment of contribution or of membership fee is a precondition to be admitted as a member.

The Act provides for four governing bodies of a cooperative. The highest body is the general meeting of all members. Each member has one vote in the general meeting. The general meeting in a cooperative with more than 100 members may consist of representatives who may not, except in student and youth and housing cooperatives with more than 50 members, adopt resolutions regarding reorganization and termination of the cooperative as well as about the disposal of the cooperative's property, that are reserved for the general meeting of all members. The general meeting elects an administrative committee, a supervisory committee, and a manager.

An administrative committee and a supervisory committee of a cooperative are obligatory in cooperatives with more than twenty members, while the functions of these committees in smaller cooperatives may be performed by the general meeting. According to the Act, a cooperative may, but is not bound to, form a reserve or a cooperative fund. The entire profit of a cooperative, the capital of which is formed by contributions, may be distributed among members (proportionally to contributions and business with the cooperative), while the profit of a cooperative financed by members' subscriptions is not distributable among members and has to be either brought forward or used for the development of the cooperative.

At least ten cooperatives may find a cooperative union, the task of which is the promotion of cooperatives and cooperative principles, providing professional support to cooperatives, and auditing of cooperatives.

The main purpose of cooperative auditing is to verify whether the cooperative's business, governance, and organization comply with cooperative principles and statutory provisions. The ordinary (biannual) or extraordinary cooperative auditing is performed by the cooperative union that obtained the license from the Ministry of Economy (auditing union). The number of cooperatives in Serbia dropped significantly around 2010, but in the past few years it has become more stable. The total turnover of cooperatives, however, is still shrinking according to the latest data available: it dropped from YUD 85.4 billion in 2013 to YUD 64.7 billion in 2014, while the financial results of cooperatives improved in the same period (Malešević 2016).

Agricultural cooperatives are the most numerous and also have the greatest economic importance. Their share in the total turnover of all cooperatives in 2014 amounted to 91 percent, while they employed 80.6 percent of the total number of employees in all cooperatives (Malešević 2016).

According to the strategy of agriculture and rural development of the Republic of Serbia for 2014, agricultural cooperatives are owned by approximately 31,000 members, being engaged in contractual cooperation with a further 100,000 other, nonmember farmers (Ministarstvo poljoprivrede i zaštite životne sredine republike Srbije 2014).

The Serbian cooperative sector has been rather neglected by systemic reforms that did not take into account specific features of cooperatives, especially in agriculture. The divergent views on unsolved property issues not only in politics but also in scientific circles (see, for instance, Njegovan 2011; Ševarlić 2014) also blocked faster development. Only the Act on cooperatives from 2015 addressed entirely the transformation of social ownership in

Table 6.8 Sectoral Distribution of Active and Non-Active Cooperatives in Serbia (October 2015)

Cooperatives by Sector	*Active Cooperatives*	*Canceled Cooperatives*	*Cooperatives in Liquidation Proceedings*	*Cooperatives in Bankruptcy Proceedings*	*Total Number of Cooperatives*
Agricultural cooperatives	1,466	1,072	74	79	2,691
Youth cooperatives	418	234	33	1	686
Housing cooperatives	113	182	12	5	312
Craft cooperatives	78	78	7	1	164
Consumer cooperatives	8	16	1	0	25
Other cooperatives	145	80	12	2	239
Total	2,228	1,662	139	88	4,117

Source: Skupština Republike Srbije, 2015.

cooperatives. Some researchers also draw attention to the so-called pseudo-cooperatives, that may be either old, "established" cooperatives where the employees and not farmer members have the main say (especially in cooperatives engaged in primary production), or newly established private cooperatives that are not open to new members and function like private companies owned by a closed circle of a small number of individuals (Stojanović and Gnjatović 2015). For the future sustainable development of cooperatives, the building of members' capacity and skills for democratic governance, investment in professional management, and general measures for reducing of the gray economy are needed.

Slovenia

The first Slovenian cooperative was the association for financial help to artisans and handicraftsmen in Ljubljana established in 1856 (Schauer 1945). In 1873, the Austrian Act on cooperatives was adopted and was applied in the major part of today's Slovenia. The first cooperative union of the Slovenian cooperatives was established in 1883 in Celje and began to perform voluntary auditing in affiliated cooperatives in 1888 (Schauer 1945).

The present Slovenian Act on cooperatives (Zakon o zadrugah 1992) defines a cooperative as an organization of an undefined number of members the purpose of which is to promote the economic interests of members and to develop their economic and social activities on the basis of voluntary adhesion and exit, cooperation based on equal rights, and governance by members. A cooperative may be established by at least three members. The highest body of a cooperative is the general meeting consisting of all members or representatives elected by members. The general meeting elects a management and a supervisory organ (a two-tier system) from its members. The management organ in a cooperative with at least ten members is an administrative committee, the president and other members of which are elected by the general meeting, while smaller cooperatives may have only a president. Also, the supervisory organ may be composed of more individuals (a supervisory committee) or of an individual (a supervisor). A professional manager is not obligatory but, may be nominated by the general meeting or, if the statutes so provide, by the administrative committee.

Each member is obliged to subscribe and pay at least one share and, from the surplus, at least 5 percent must be earmarked for the obligatory reserves each year.

The Act on cooperatives introduced some solutions from Regulation 1435/2003/EC about the statute of the European cooperative society also for domestic cooperatives as options (for instance, investor members, the minimum amount beyond which the capital of cooperative must not be reduced through redemption of shares, etc.), but these options seem to not have been used in practice. So far, no European cooperative society has been established with the registered office in Slovenia.

At the end of 2015, there were 387 cooperatives entered into the business register in Slovenia. According to the sectoral distribution, the most numerous are cooperatives dealing with trade and cooperatives in agriculture, forestry, and fishing. Among 332 active cooperatives [cooperatives that submitted their annual reports for 2014 to the competent authority—Agency of the Republic of Slovenia for Public Legal Records and Related Services (AJPES)], the most important are farmers' marketing and supply cooperatives that had a prevailing share in the total turnover (84 percent) and the total number of employees (85 percent; Zadružna zveza Slovenije 2015).

During the transition to a market economy, agricultural and forestry cooperatives could reaffirm their market position also due to their participation in the privatization process. The Slovenian Act on cooperatives entitled cooperatives and their unions to claim the restitution of their former property that had been nationalized after World War II and transferred without compensation to other users, just as former owners or their heirs could claim the restitution of the nationalized property (also from cooperatives, if the property nationalized to individuals had been transferred to cooperatives after nationalization). In this regard, the Slovenian cooperatives were better off than others in the post-Yugoslav space to which the restitution of the cooperative property was allowed only partly (the federal Act on cooperatives

Table 6.9 Sectoral Distribution and Economic Importance of Cooperatives in Slovenia (in 2015 and 2014)

Sector of Activity	*Number of Registered Cooperatives (December 31, 2015)*	*Number of Active Cooperatives (2014)*	*Total Turnover (2014)*	*Average Number of Employees (2014)*
Agriculture, forestry, and fishing	85	74	113,029	406
Manufacturing	34	29	31,423	232
Construction	16	13	4,539	16
Wholesale and retail trade, repair of motor vehicles and motorcycles	110	96	639,887	2,331
Real estate activities	38	34	2,470	29
Professional, scientific, and technical activities	35	27	5,941	53
Other activities	69	59	7,963	20
Total	387	332	805,252	3,087

Sources: AJPES 2015; AJPES, 2016.

from 1990 provided only for restitution of cooperative property transferred to other users after July 1, 1953). In addition, the Slovenian Act on cooperatives provided that cooperatives might be awarded up to a 45-percent share in the social capital of forty-five enterprises or their organizational units, mainly in the food processing industry, that were listed in the annex to the Act.

The property that was acquired as social ownership or being restituted during denationalization or awarded as a capital share to cooperatives has a status of indivisible cooperative property that may not be distributed among the members even in a case of winding up. In that case, the property is transferred to a cooperative union that is obliged to assign this property to a newly established cooperative in the same branch of activity and on the same territory or, if there is no such cooperative, to use the property for the promotion of cooperatives. Although the farmers' cooperatives have a large share in the marketing of products and supply of inputs, their share in processing is relatively small. As the farm structure is highly dispersed, the average size of the utilized agricultural areas per holding being half as small (6.6 ha) than in EU-28 (14.4 ha) and is improving only slowly, and cooperatives will have to further concentrate their supply due to the increasing market power of the processing industry and retail trade.

In the past few years, the public opinion and attitudes of policymakers toward cooperatives have been becoming more favorable, mainly due to cooperative initiatives to create new jobs and foster self-employment, to provide social and similar services, to maintain jobs through workers' buy-out, to transform some retail enterprises into cooperatives, and so on (although the most ambitious ideas have not been realized so far). In 2011, the Parliament adopted the Act on social entrepreneurship (Zakon o socialnem podjetništvu) according to which cooperatives, companies, foundations, and associations may obtain the status of a social enterprise if they comply with certain requirements that are very similar to cooperative principles and, in some aspects even stricter (for instance, limited divisibility of surplus and of assets). According to the Act, social enterprises must either employ a certain share of workers from vulnerable groups or carry out certain activities listed so that their operations are considered to be in public interest. As of February 29, 2016, there were 126 social enterprises in Slovenia, among them 30 cooperatives (Ministrstvo za gospodarski razvoj in tehnologijo 2016).

According to the previous legislation, cooperatives funded the so-called savings and loan services as well as their unions for certain banking services (collecting savings deposits and granting credits). Because the services were not allowed to carry out all banking services, the Slovenska zadružna kmetijska banka (Slovenian cooperative agricultural bank) was established by cooperatives in 1990. After the requirements for financial institutions, the majority of savings and loan services merged with their union, which transferred their financial activity and assets to the cooperative bank (renamed the Deželna banka Slovenije, Country bank of Slovenia), and transformed itself into a holding cooperative with slightly less than 50 percent share in the bank.

CONCLUSION

The development of cooperatives in the post-Yugoslav space after 1991 is marked by far-reaching economic and political changes resulting in the transition to a market economy based on private property and in the emergence of new, independent states. The transition to the new economic and political realities was heavily aggravated during the war destruction that took place in some regions of this space causing human and material losses, while the social capital as a necessary precondition for cooperative organization was seriously eroded. On the other hand, cooperatives have a potential to rebuild the trust within communities and the society. Therefore, a lot of foreign partners from the public and private sector (including cooperative movements from abroad) offered various kinds of support for the realization of cooperative initiatives.

Although the cooperative legislations after the break-up of the former common state seem to be framed each one independently from others, some common trends can be identified. First, taking account of the constitutionally guaranteed freedom of economic initiative in each one of the legal systems discussed, cooperatives are not allowed in all economic sectors. In all the legal systems discussed they are, for instance, excluded from directly carrying out banking services, although the credit cooperatives were the backbone of the former cooperative movement in this space before World War II. Before the transition, credit cooperatives were allowed in some countries (Croatia, North Macedonia, Serbia), or special financial institutions were foreseen within the cooperative system (like savings and loan services in Slovenia). Not only in this respect, the legal framework for cooperatives seems to be more restrictive than previously. On the other hand, there are some cases and initiatives that cooperatives provide banking services through jointly owned banks. In some countries, the banking legislation introduced new legal entities that are not cooperatives but operate substantially with a cooperative purpose and according to cooperative principles (credit unions, microfinance institutions). Some legal systems have adopted or plan to adopt legislation about social enterprises and similar entities with a purpose of general interest, that are not at all (for instance some microfinance organizations) or at least not formally cooperatives but are regulated by provisions that are to a great extent the same as cooperative principles. The tendency does not contribute to higher recognizability of cooperatives.

The distribution of cooperatives across economic sectors has not changed much from the previous system. The farmers' cooperatives still have the greatest economic weight, although they are not always the most numerous. Cooperatives emerge gradually and also grow in other sectors. In addition, recent legislation introduces new classes of cooperatives—the activities of which are not only of members' but also of general interest (for instance, social cooperatives).

The further development of cooperatives in the post-Yugoslav space will depend on internal factors and the socioeconomic environment.

Investment in the human factor, in members, especially in management and supervisory bodies, professional managers, and employees will be of critical importance. Improving business and management skills is crucial for taking advantage of market opportunities, for efficient governance, and attracting new members.

A stable development presupposes more intensive cooperation among cooperatives through setting up of informal and formal networks for supporting tasks, common business projects, and interest representation. In this respect, it is important that members consider cooperative principles and legal provisions as means for realizing the specific purposes of cooperatives.

The framers of the socioeconomic environment should be aware of the fact that cooperatives are in a minority in the corporate landscape in all countries discussed and, need treatment that would be at least equally favorable as for other economic actors.

REFERENCES

Agency for Intermediary, IT and Financial Services (APIF). *Pretraga Registra*, 2016. http://bizreg.esrpska.com/Home/PretragaPoslovnogSubjekta.

Agency of the Republic of Slovenia for Public Legal Records and Related Services (AJPES). *Informacija o poslovanju gospodarskih družb v republiki Sloveniji v letu*, 2015. http://www.ajpes.si/doc/LP/Informacije/Informacija_LP_GD_zadruge_2014.pdf.

Agency of the Republic of Slovenia for Public Legal Records and Related Services (AJPES). *Poslovni subjekti v poslovnem registru Slovenije po področjih dejavnosti SKD in po skupinah, stanje na dan 31. 12. 2015*, 2016. http://www.ajpes.si/doc/Registri/PRS/Porocila/posl_subj_skd_skup_31122015.pdf.

Agromedia. *Zemljoradnička zadruga Azanja- nekad i danas*, 2016. http://www.agromedia.rs/Zivot-na-selu/price-sa-sela/zemljoradnicka-zadruga-azanja-nekada-i-danas.

Central Bank of Bosnia and Herzegovina. *Izvještaj o finansijskoj stabilnosti 2014*, 2015. http://www.cbbh.ba/files/financial_stability_report/fsr_2014_bs.pdf.

Centralni Registar Privrednih Subjekata, 2016. http://www.pretraga.crps.me:8083/.

Četković, Đ. "Crna gora." In *Zadružni leksikon FNRJ I*, edited by M. Vučković. Zagreb: Zadružna štampa, 1956.

Državen zavod na statistika na Makedonija (State Statistical Office of Macedonia). *Struktura na zemjodelskite stopanstva, 2013: Prethodni podatoci* (Structure of Agricultural Holdings, 2013: Preliminary Data), 2013. http://www.stat.gov.mk/Publikacii/5.4.14.01_769.pdf.

Federalno ministarstvo poljoprivrede, vodoprivrede i šumarstva (Federal Ministry of Agriculture, Water Management and Forestry). *Srednjoročna strategija razvoja poljoprivrednog sektora u Federaciji Bosne i Hercegovine za period 2015–2019 godina*. http://fmpvs.gov.ba/upload_files/1440617190- 368_1286_1872_b.pdf.

Fulm Saving House, 2016. http://fulm.com.mk/default.asp?docID=263&lng=en.

Gnjatović, D. "Drugi zadatak privilegovane agrarne banke: kreditiranje poljoprivrednog zadrugarstva." *Bankarstvo* 40, nos. 5–6 (2011): 10–29.

Hrvatska narodna banka (Croatian National Bank). *Godišnje izvješće 2014,* 2014. http://www.hnb.hr/publikac/godisnje/2014/h-god-2014.pdf.

Hrvatska narodna banka (Croatian National Bank). *Popis kreditnih unija upisanih u sudski registar: Stanje na dan 31. Prosinca 2015,* 2016. http://www.hnb.hr/supervizija/kreditne%20unije/h-popis-kreditnih-unija.pdf.

Hrvatska udruga kreditnih unija (Croatian Association of Credit Unions). *Kreditne unije u republici Hrvatskoj*, 2012. http://www.hukreditneunije.hr/dokumenti/Kreditne_ Unije_u_RH.pdf.

Hrvatski centar za zadružno poduzetništvo (Croatian Center for Cooperative Entrepreneurship). *Analiza zadrugarstva u Hrvatskoj do 31. 12. 2014*, 2015. http://zadruge.coop/upload_data/site_files/analiza_2014_za_web.pdf.

Kovačević, R. "Hrvatska." In *Zadružni leksikon FNRJ I,* edited by M. Vučković. Zagreb: Zadružna štampa, 1956.

Kmetijski Inšttut Slovenije (Agricultural Institute of Slovenia). *Slovenian Agriculture in Numbers*. Ljubljana, Slovenia, 2014. http://kis.dev.splet1.si21.com/f/docs/Slovensko_kmetijstvo_v_stevilkah_OEK/Slovensko_kmetijstvo_v_stevilkah_2014_ANG.pdf.

Kraljevina Jugoslavija (Kingdom of Yugoslavia). *Statistički godišnjak 1929*. Beograd: Državna štamparija, 1932.

Kraljevina Jugoslavija (Kingdom of Yugoslavia). *Statistički godišnjak 1940*. Beograd: Državna štamparija, 1941.

Malešević, L. *Zadruge daleko od pravog zadrugarstva*, 2016. http://www.dnevnik.rs/ekonomija/zadruge-daleko-od-pravog-zadrugarstva.

Mataga, Ž. "Poljoprivredno zadrugarstvo u hrvatskoj: Razvoj i temeljni problemi." *Sociologija i Prostor* 43, no. 1 (2009): 17–42.

Ministarstvo poljoprivrede i zaštite životne sredine Republike Srbije (Ministry of Agriculture and Protection of Environment of the Republic of Serbia). *Strategija poljoprivrede i ruralnog razvoja Republike Srbije za period 2014–2024.* Godine. Službeni glasnik RS, br. 85, 2014.

Ministrstvo za gospodarski razvoj in tehnologijo (Ministry of Economic Development and Technology). *Evidenca socialnih podjetij*, 2016. http://www.mgrt.gov.si/si/delovna_podrocja/socialno_podjetnistvo/evidenca_so_p/.

Ministerstvo za zemjodelstvo, šumarstvo i vodostopanstvo (Ministry of Agriculture, Water Management and Forestry). *Nacionalna strategija za zemjodelstvoto i ruralniot razvoj za periodot 2014-2020 godina*, 2014. http://www.mzsv.gov.mk/NSZRR% 202014-2020.pdf.

Narodna Skupština Republike Srbije (National Assembly of the Republic of Serbia). *Predlog. Zakon o zadrugama*, 2015. http://www.parlament.gov.rs/upload/archive/files/lat/pdf/predlozi_zakona/3504-15%20-%20LAT.pdf.

Njegovan, Z. "Agrarno ili zadružno pitanje: Prilog za razumevanje zadrugarstva u Republici Srbiji." *Ekonomika preduzeća* 59, nos. 5–6 (2011): 297–307.

Pajkić, S. *Opljačkano, potcijenjeno, neiskorišteno zadrugarstvo Bosne i Hercegovine*. Fojnica: Štamparija Fojnica, 2014.

Pllashniku, Mehdi. "The Role of Development of Farmers' Cooperatives." *European Journal of Social Sciences, Education and Research* 4, no. 1 (2015): 87–94.

Registar poslovnih subjekata Federacije BiH, 2016. http://bizreg.pravosudje.ba/pls/apex/f?p=183:30:3346753356757936::NO:RP:P30_FIRSTTIME:TRUE.

Savezni zavod za statistiku (Federal Statistical Office). *Statistički godišnjak FNRJ/SFRJ*. Belgrade: Savezni zavod za statistiku, 1954–1991.

Schauer, D. *Prva doba našega zadružništva: (od nastanka do leta 1895)*. Ljubljana: Self-Published Work, 1945.

Ševarlić, M. "Analiza stanja i pravci razvoja zemljoradničkog zadrugarstva u Srbiji." In *Perspektive razvoja sela*, edited by D. Škorić, paper presented at the Serbian Academy of Sciences and Arts Sciences (April 17, 2013), 201–18. Beograd: SANU, 2014.

Stanojević, I. "Analiza zadružnog sustava u 2014, godini." *Agroeconomia Croatica* 5, no. 1 (2014): 51–57.

Stojanović, Ž., and D. Gnjatović. Zadrugarstvo u Srbiji. *120 godina Zadružnog saveza*. Beograd: Hesperia.edu, 2015.

Uradni list FNRJ. "Splošni zakon o zadrugah." *Official Journal of Fedarative Peoples's Republic of Yugoslavia* no. 59 (1946).

Uradni list FNRJ. "Temeljni zakon o kmetijskih zadrugah." *Official Journal of Fedarative Peoples's Republic of Yugoslavia*, no. 49 (1949).

Uradni list FNRJ. "Uredba o kmetijskih zadrugah." *Official Journal of Fedarative Peoples's Republic of Yugoslavia*, no. 5 (1954).

Uredba o kmetijskih zadrugah. *Uradni list FNRJ (Official Journal of Fedarative Peoples's Republic of Yugoslavia)*, no. 5 (1954).

Usepjanov, A. "Makedonija." In *Zadružni leksikon FNRJ II*, edited by M. Vučković. Zagreb: Zadružna štampa, 1956.

Ustavotvorna skupština Kraljevine Srba, Hrvata i Slovenaca (The Constituent Assembly of the Kingdom of Serbs, Croats and Slovenes). *Ustav Kraljevine Srba, Hrvata i Slovenaca*, 1921. http://www.arhivyu.gov.rs/active/sr-latin/home/glavna_navigacija/leksikon_jugoslavije/konstitutivni_akti_jugoslavije/vidovdanski_ustav.html.

Zakon o gospodarskih zadrugah. (Act on Economic Cooperatives). *Službeni list Kraljevske Bankse Uprave Dravske Banovine*, no. 81 (1937).

Zakon o kooperativama, 2015. http://www.sluzbenilist.me/PravniAktDetalji.aspx?tag=%7BC2F4C311-2B96-436A-B783-2717730EAF57%7D.
Zakon o kreditnim unijama, 2007. http://www.zakon.hr/z/488/Zakon-o-kreditnim-unijama.
Zakon o stambenim zadrugama, 2010. http://www.sluzbenilist.me/PravniAktDetalji.aspx?tag=%7BEA85BEC4-2506-48DC-A0AB-2DC84F84E344%7D.
Zakon o zadrugah. *Uradni list SFRJ (Official Journal of Socialist Federative Republic of Yugoslavia)*, no. 3 (1990).
Zakon o zadrugah. 1992. http://www.pisrs.si/Pis.web/pregledPredpisa?id=ZAKO217.
Zakon o zadrugama. 2011. http://www.zakon.hr/z/458/Zakon-o-zadrugama.
Zadružna zveza Slovenije. *Letno poročilo 2014*. Ljubljana: Zadružna zveza Slovenije, 2015.

Chapter 7

The Role of Cooperatives in Improving Financial Inclusion in the Philippines

Karen P. Quilloy and Jan Danica S. Asma

Ending poverty remains the greatest challenge at the global, national, and local levels. Although the incidence of poverty has been declining over the decades worldwide, alleviating the different dimensions of poverty, particularly its economic and human aspects, remains challenging. Lack of assets, limited economic opportunities, poor education and capabilities, and poor health conditions are the major causes of poverty in rural areas, where the majority of the poor reside. To move out of this trap, people's human and economic capabilities must be strengthened so that they can access available development opportunities and participate in the growth experienced by their economy. In particular, the poor must be provided with adequate access to credit and other financial products to enable them to become productive and generate cash flow sustainably, which will in turn contribute to broad-based development.

The critical role of financial services in increasing the earning potentials of the poor, empowering them, and improving the quality of their lives has led to a growing consensus among policymakers, development planners, academia, and development partners to promote financial inclusion as a tool for achieving inclusive growth and poverty reduction. Participating in the financial system improves the ability of people to start and expand businesses, invest in social services such as education and health, and protect themselves against financial shocks (World Bank 2016).

In the Philippines, financial inclusion has been identified as a priority target in the national agenda for inclusive growth and poverty reduction. Under the Philippine Development Plan 2011–2016, the government aimed for an inclusive and resilient financial system through a more efficient mobilization of financial resources and improved environment for the financial system. Accordingly, a framework and action plan called the National Strategy for

Financial Inclusion (NSFI) was launched in July 2015 to serve as a guidepost for the government and the private sector to systematically accelerate the level of financial inclusion in the country such that the financial system is accessible and responsive to the needs of the entire population. While the country's efforts have been achieving significant milestones, with the Philippines ranking first in Asia and third in the world in terms of having a conducive environment for financial inclusion based on the survey of Global Microscope, 2015 (The Economist Intelligence Unit 2015), there remains a wide range of challenges to deal with and opportunities to explore.

We know for a fact that basic financial services in rural areas are relatively less available and accessible compared to urban areas primarily because of the costs and risks associated with extending the service to the rural population. Given that the poor mostly reside in rural areas, they often have no, if not limited, to financial services, particularly to credit and savings, and are, therefore, constrained from tapping the economic and entrepreneurial opportunities available for them.

In 2015, only 26 percent of adult Filipinos had savings accounts, 20.6 percent were covered by microinsurance, and 10.5 percent had access to formal credit (Global Microscope 2015). In another survey done by Demirgüç-Kunt and Klapper (2013), 13 percent of the borrowing adult population were found to be relying on informal moneylenders as their main source of credit. A key factor that contributes to this low financial coverage is the absence of bank offices in many municipalities in the country due to the tendency of the formal institutions to concentrate in highly populous and urbanized regions, where there are more potential bankable clients. As of December 2014, 36 percent of the country's municipalities remain unserved by banks (BSP 2015). All these data signal that there is still much to do to achieve full financial inclusion in the Philippines, and it must continue to explore and innovate alternative ways to effectively increase access to a wide range of financial products and services.

One of the strategies for improving financial access is the development of the nonregulated financial service providers (FSPs) such as pawnshops, remittance agents, money changers/foreign exchange dealers, e-payment service providers, mobile banking agents, nonstock savings and loan associations (NSSLAs), and credit cooperatives. The presence of these FSPs has significantly reduced the proportion of unserved municipalities, thereby improving the access to finance of people in the unbanked areas.

This chapter focuses on the role and contribution of cooperatives as an effective access point for financial inclusion. It is divided into the following sections: (1) overview of financial inclusion in the context of the Philippines, (2) the state of financial inclusion in the Philippines, (3) the role of cooperatives in narrowing the gaps of financial inclusion, and (4) concluding remarks.

FINANCIAL INCLUSION IN THE CONTEXT OF THE PHILIPPINES

Financial inclusion is explained in this paper based on the framework used by the Philippine NSFI. In its broadest sense, financial inclusion is defined as the state where there is effective access to a wide range of financial products and services by all (BSP 2013). With effective access, we mean having physical and economic access of all market segments, including the unserved and underserved, to a full suite of good-quality financial products and services that are appropriately designed for the clients' needs and purposes and are relevant to lead to actual usage that can benefit them and improve their welfare. These financial products and services include savings, credit, insurance, remittances and payment services, and investments.

Prior to the development of NSFI, there was an established National Strategy for Microfinance in 1997. Since its formulation, financial inclusion has become a long-standing national policy objective and commitment to support it has increased. This strategy set the stage for financial inclusion initiatives in the country. It revolves around the following core principles:

1. greater participation of the private sector and/or microfinance institutions (MFIs);
2. an enabling policy environment to induce private-sector participation;
3. market-oriented financial and credit policies such as market-oriented interest rates; and
4. nonparticipation of government line agencies in the implementation of credit and guarantee programs.

The increased participation of the private sector, particularly the MFIs, has paved the way for the improved performance of the Philippine finance sector. As of 2011, there were already 14,938 MFIs, representing a range of institutions which include rural banks, thrift banks, cooperative banks, cooperatives, and nongovernment organizations (NGOs). Of these MFIs, about 98 percent are cooperatives, while the rest are banks and NGOs (Mercado-Bunker 2014).

The principles of the National Strategy for Microfinance have been implemented in the country's strategy for financial inclusion. In pursuit of a financial system that is accessible and responsive to the needs of all market segments, the Philippines commits to use alternative products and delivery channels to reach the underserved segments of the markets (e.g., the poor, women, and persons with a disability); implement a good regulatory policy that balances financial inclusion with financial stability; and adopt a holistic approach to financial literacy and education. The objective is to have a wide range of relevant, responsive, and quality financial products and services that effectively reach different market segments, especially the financially excluded sectors, through innovative delivery channels and in complementation with adequate financial education and consumer protection. These commitments are guided by the following set of principles of NSFI:

1. "Financial inclusion is not the end-goal. It is a means to achieve social cohesion and shared economic development."
2. "Financial inclusion is a worthy policy objective that can be pursued alongside the promotion of stability, integrity and efficiency in the financial system."
3. "Financial education and consumer protection are a fundamental complement to financial inclusion. Greater access alone can easily lead to a personal financial crisis if people do not clearly understand these financial products and services."
4. "Financial inclusion can be truly maximized to benefit the client if basic infrastructure and support systems are present. These include physical infrastructure like roads, communications (e.g., telephony, internet), power, and water, among others."

The strategy framework of the Philippines financial inclusion is focused mainly on clients, wherein the ultimate goal is for the various financial products and services to impact the well-being of the Filipinos. By looking at the elements of the Philippines financial inclusion, one can readily find where cooperatives can play a role in making the country's financial system more inclusive.

THE STATE OF FINANCIAL INCLUSION IN THE PHILIPPINES

Supply Trends in the Financial Inclusion of the Philippines

Several FSPs play an inclusive role in the financial environment of the Philippines. As mentioned earlier, these range from formal financial institutions such as banks and financial companies to semi-formal and informal sources such as NSSLAs, cooperatives, pawnshops, and money changers/ foreign exchange dealers among others (BSP-NSFI 2015). The Philippines banking system is comprised of universal and commercial banks, thrift banks, rural banks, and cooperative banks. As of the end of December 2015, there are about 10,124 banks, of which the universal and commercial banks dominate (60 percent) (table 7.1). In relation to this, 16,315 automated teller machines (ATMs) are situated in 63 percent of the cities and municipalities in the country, which translates to 14 banks and 23 ATMs per 1,000 adults (BSP 2015b).

Table 7.1 Number of Banking Offices by Type, Philippines, 2000–2015

	*Number of Banking Offices**			
Type of Bank	*2000*	*2005*	*2010*	*2015*
Universal and Commercial Banks	4,250	4,318	4,681	6,020 (59.5%)
Thrift Banks	1,391	1,293	1,418	2,018 (19.9%)
Rural and Cooperative Banks	1,913	2,059	2,778	2,086 (20.6%)
Total	7,554	7,670	8,877	10,124 (100.0%)

Source: BSP (2015b).
* Banking offices include head offices and branches.

On the other hand, it is noteworthy to also recognize the significant presence of rural and cooperative banks in the country, which increased from 1,913 to 2,086 between 2000 and 2015. These types of banks, which comprised 21 percent of all banks in 2015, are established in areas that universal and commercial banks do not reach, such as the rural areas and island provinces.

Bank offices are concentrated in urbanized regions with high population such as the National Capital Region, Region IV-A (CALABARZON), and Region III (Central Luzon) (NSFI 2015). The regions with low banking penetration are generally the low-income regions of the country, which include the Autonomous Region in Muslim Mindanao (ARMM), Cordillera Administrative Region (CAR), Eastern Visayas, Zamboanga Peninsula, and MIMAROPA. To facilitate financial service delivery in these areas, the Philippines government supported the development of microfinance, an alternative to banking, which is more inclusive and adaptable to the financial needs of communities.

Microfinance aims to help the poor improve their living conditions by providing them access to financial services like small credit, savings, and insurance (Mercado-Bunker 2014). As of 2011, there are 14,938 MFIs operating nationwide. These MFIs are comprised of banks, NGOs, and cooperatives. The Bangko Sentral ng Pilipinas (BSP) has been proactive in promoting microfinance to be part of the services of the banks. It requires the formal financial system to provide affordably priced products and services such as microfinance loans, micro-agricultural loans, microfinance housing loans, micro-deposits, and microinsurance. As of the second quarter of 2014, about 183 banks have microfinance operations that serve 1.16 million borrowers with outstanding loans amounting to PhP 9.3 billion (table 7.2).

Although their contribution is relatively small compared to banks and NGOs in terms of outstanding loans released and savings deposits accepted, cooperatives can be a key area for further developing microfinance in the country given the significant number of registered cooperatives in the country and their wide range of outreach in different sectors. The credit cooperatives and microfinance NGOs covered almost half of the LGUs in 2013 (table 7.3).

Table 7.2 Types of Microfinance Products, Philippines, Second Quarter 2014

Microfinance Product	*Number of Banks*	*Amount*
Microenterpise Loans	167	PhP 7.8 billion
Microfinance Plus	18	PhP 186 million
Micro-Agri Loans	32	PhP 278 million
Housing Microfinance Loans	17	PhP 328 million
Micro-deposit Accounts	69	PhP 3.3 billion
Microinsurance	40	19.9 million individuals with coverage

Source: BSP (2014).

Table 7.3 Types of Financial Service Providers, Philippines, 2013

Financial service offered	*Type of financial service provider*	*Number of FSPs*	*No. of LGUs reached*	*% share to the total no. of LGUs*
Full Service Savings and Credit	Banks	9,884	1,030	63.0
	Credit Cooperatives	2,822	814	49.8
	Nonstock Savings and Loans Association (NSSLAs)	198	66	4.0
	Microfinance NGOs	1,812	790	48.3
Credit and Other Services	Pawnshops	17,652	1,109	67.9
	Other Nonbank Financial Institutions (NBFIs)	145	53	3.2
Payments and Money Transfers	Remittance Agents and Money Changers/Foreign Exchange Dealers	10,834	903	55.3
	E-Money Agents	24,029	903	55.3
	Automated Teller Machines (ATMs)	14,528	627	38.4

Source: BSP (2013).

Another alternative to banks is micro-banking offices (MBOs), which make financial services available to unserved or underserved cities and municipalities where establishing a full bank office is not economically feasible. Since 2010, the BSP has allowed the establishment of an MBO, which is a simple branch that offers financial services ranging from credit, savings, remittances, foreign exchange, e-conversion, bills payment, and government pay-out benefits. As of 2014, there have been 501 MBOs established, serving 322 Local Government Units (LGUs), sixty-one of which do not have a regular bank branch (table 7.3).

Based on the data, the presence of nonbank FSPs gave customers an additional 50,000 access points or outlets aside from banks, which resulted in reduction of the percentage of unserved municipalities in the country from 36 percent to 12 percent (BSP-SFIP 2013). As of 2015, 87 percent of the cities and municipalities have at least one financial access point (BSP 2015a). Accessing financial services from nonbank FSPs is an effective ground for training and preparing individuals for future accessing of banks. While the number of deposit accounts in credit unions and financial cooperatives per 1,000 adults gradually decreased between 2004 and 2014, there is an increasing trend in the number of deposit accounts in commercial banks per 1,000 adults (figure 7.1). This pattern is a positive indication that more adults are able to shift to or access the formal financial institutions through the years.

A less formal type of FSP is pawnshops, which are present in 68 percent of LGUs in the country. Remittance agents and e-money agents are alsopresent, covering 55 percent of all LGUs (table 7.3). The latter, along with mobile banking, are technological innovations that have contributed significantly to expanding the reach of financial service delivery. E-money rules and regulations were issued in 2010 by BSP. From 2010 to 2013, the number of registered e-money issuers (EMIs) and active e-money agents had already reached 32 and 10,620, respectively, serving 965 LGUs (table 7.3). Around 220 LGUs (36 percent) of the 604 unbanked LGUs have access to e-money agents (BSP 2013).

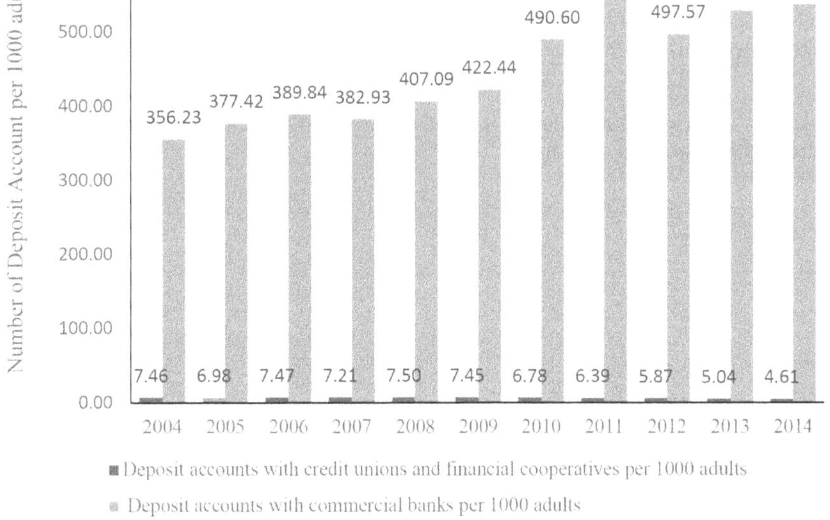

Figure 7.1 Number of Deposit Accounts per 1,000 Adults, Philippines 2004–2014
Source of basic data: IMF-Financial Access Survey 2014.

Demand Trends in the Philippine Financial Inclusion Relative to Its Asian Neighbors

On the demand side, the status of financial inclusion of the Philippines generally lags behind its neighboring countries in Asia. This is measured in terms of people's access to financial services like savings and loans. Most of the data presented here came from the Global Findex Report, 2014–2015.

Supply side-wise, impressive progress has been observed in improving financial inclusion in the Philippines. However, from the users' point of view, the state of financial inclusion of the country is still far from ideal, especially when compared to other Asian countries. Singapore can be considered to have the most financially inclusive system followed by Malaysia and Thailand (table 7.4). These three high-middle-income countries in the ASEAN region have a higher percentage of aged 15-plus accounts and savings compared to the world. Cambodia, Myanmar, Lao People's Democratic Republic (Lao PDR), Vietnam, Indonesia, and the Philippines have relatively lower access to financial services compared to East Asia and the Pacific and the world.

In terms of the savings landscape in the Philippines, the Consumer Expectations Survey of BSP[1] reveals that only 29 percent of Filipino households have savings as of the third-quarter of 2015 (table 7.5). The proportion is even lower for low-income households, where only 18 percent were able to save. As to where thcy save their money, the majority (70 percent) save in banking institutions but, a significant proportion of the households are also found to save at home (43 percent). The next most common saving institution is the cooperative (14 percent). These figures show that many households are

Table 7.4 Account at a Financial Institution, by Country and by Sociodemographic Characteristic, 2014 (% aged 15+)

	Sex		*Income*		*Age group*		*Education*	
	Male	*Female*	*Bottom 40%*	*Top 60%*	*Older adults*	*Young adults*	*Primary*	*Secondary*
Cambodia	14.94	10.68	8.83	15.29	12.54	12.59	10.54	28.31
Indonesia	34.62	37.24	21.94	45.33	36.18	35.17	15.78	53.49
Lao PDR*	27.44	26.16	20.72	31.22	28.48	22.97	21.95	34.67
Malaysia	83.01	78.09	75.57	84.08	81.95	76.2	58.6	84.36
Myanmar	28.6	17.08	16.07	26.98	25.08	13.12	20.61	26.21
Philippines	21.97	33.88	14.92	37.13	33.37	13.86	15.18	33.47
Singapore	96.64	96.07	96.2	96.47	97.03	92.94	...	...
Thailand	81.24	75.44	71.97	82.34	79.76	70.55	73.19	85.36
Vietnam	29.81	31.86	18.74	39.46	28.91	37.44	15.34	40.02
East Asia and Pacific (Developing only)	70.78	66.72	60.73	74.22	70.5	60.26	63.6	76.28
World	64.09	57.36	53.3	65.7	65.09	44.92	46.98	72.29

...= not available
Source: Global Findex 2014.
* 2011 data.

Table 7.5 Proportion of Households Who have Savings by Income Group and Type of Saving Institution, Philippines, 2015

	Income group[1]			
Type of saving institution	*Low-income group (<PhP10,000)*	*Middle-income group (PhP10,000–PhP29,999)*	*High-income group (≥PhP30,000)*	*All households*
Banks	44.8	71.8	89.9	70.1
Cooperatives	13.8	15.8	13.5	14.5
Paluwagan[2]	6.4	8.1	3.5	6.2
House (kept at home)	55.6	43.2	31.3	42.8
Credit/loans and other associations	11.7	8.0	10.0	9.6
Others	1.8	1.4	0.8	1.3
Average	18.1	36.9	69.6	28.9

[1] Average exchange rate of Philippine pesos (PhP) per U.S. dollar (US$) was PhP47.17 in December 2015.
2 "Paluwagan" is an informal group saving and lending system in the Philippines similar to Rotating Savings and Credit Association (ROSCA).
Source: BSP (2015a).

still excluded from the formal financial system. With the cooperative, which is a semi-formal financial institution being in between the banks and informal saving institutions, a great potential or role for cooperatives can be seen as a bridge for transitioning from informal to formal systems.

Consequently, data from Global Findex 2014 further show that a greater percentage of the top 60 percent income earners, older adults, and persons with secondary education have accounts and savings in a financial institution (table 7.6). It is alarming though to know that among the young adults and top 60 percent income earners of the Philippine population, only 14 percent and 37 percent, respectively, were able to save in financial institutions.

In terms of the percentage of savers who are fifteen years and older, the Philippines ranks at the bottom half of the Asian region, placed just above Vietnam, but lower than Lao PDR (figure 7.2). The proportion of the population with savings in the country is less than a third of that of Singapore, the top country with the highest percentage of saving population (table 7.6).

In the region, the Philippines has the lowest percentage of the bottom 40 percent of the population in terms of income that borrows from a financial institution. Compared to Cambodia where 26 percent of its bottom 40 percent were able to borrow from a financial institution, the Philippines reported only 8 percent of its bottom 40 percent (table 7.7). One of the reasons for this trend is the dependence on and preference for informal financial sources.

However, what is remarkable is that even the top 60 percent of income earners also depend on informal lenders. When we look at the trend of

Table 7.6 Savings at a Financial Institution by Country and by Sociodemographic Characteristic, 2014 (% aged 15+)

	Sex		Income		Age group		Education	
Country	*Male*	*Female*	*Bottom 40%*	*Top 60%*	*Older adults*	*Young adults*	*Primary*	*Secondary*
Cambodia	4.84	2.6	2.7	4.24	4.51	1.23	3.11	7.23
Indonesia	26.36	26.76	13.8	35.12	27.74	22.6	11.02	40.08
Lao PDR	19.77	18.98	13.25	23.85	16.94	18.73	16.18	24.57
Malaysia	35.12	32.28	25.56	39.24	34.41	32.05	22.34	35.79
Myanmar	15.38	10.4	6.75	16.8	14.14	8.85	9.24	19.13
Philippines	13.63	15.88	4.86	21.63	17.46	7.61	6.17	18.4
Singapore	45.71	46.68	42.92	48.73	47.68	38.82	...	...
Thailand	43.69	37.91	31.33	46.91	42.61	31.21	38.11	44.24
Vietnam	15.19	13.66	9.14	18.48	15.42	11.84	9.02	17.88
East Asia and Pacific	36.78	36.21	26.1	43.57	38.64	26.23	32.58	42.22
World	29.00	25.79	19.19	32.93	30.03	17.94	19.17	34.37

...= not available
Source: Global Findex 2014.
* 2011 data.

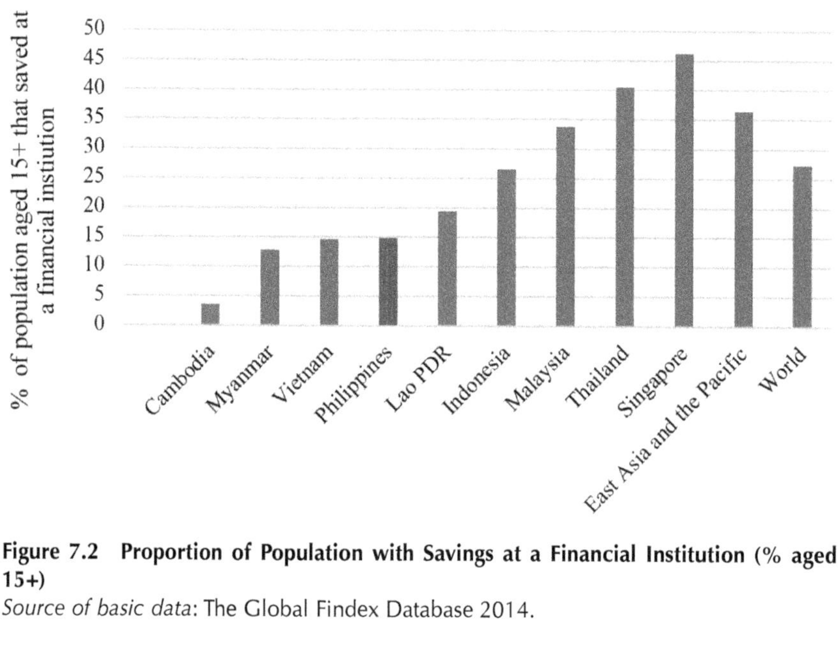

Figure 7.2 Proportion of Population with Savings at a Financial Institution (% aged 15+)
Source of basic data: The Global Findex Database 2014.

Table 7.7 Borrowed from a Financial Institution by Country and by Sociodemographic Characteristic, 2014 (% aged 15+)

	Sex		*Income*		*Age group*		*Education*	
Country	*Male*	*Female*	*Bottom 40%*	*Top 60%*	*Older adults*	*Young adults*	*Primary*	*Secondary*
Cambodia	25.48	29.36	25.77	29.03	29.69	22.47	29.27	15.00
Indonesia	15.15	11.17	11.33	14.35	15.37	5.60	9.52	16.30
Lao PDR	19.11	17.22	19.11	17.42	20.03	13.91	17.98	18.39
Malaysia	22.17	16.58	15.23	22.37	29.93	9.16	9.46	21.25
Myanmar	19.54	11.80	14.61	16.13	20.02	2.39	19.08	9.16
Philippines	9.89	13.60	8.20	14.26	15.10	2.91	7.72	13.49
Singapore	14.07	14.32	16.60	12.36	15.89	5.75	...	...
Thailand	17.39	13.67	16.22	14.83	16.21	11.58	14.69	16.42
Vietnam	15.43	21.33	19.88	17.43	23.02	3.08	24.77	14.69
East Asia and Pacific	11.78	10.18	7.95	13.05	12.05	5.89	8.55	14.52
World	11.83	9.57	8.69	12.04	12.26	5.11	7.29	13.54

...= not available
Source: Global Findex 2014.
* 2011 data.

borrowing from informal lenders, the percentage of those in the top 60 percent of Filipino income earners who borrow from informal sources is higher than the proportion reported in the bottom 40 percent of the income earners (table 7.8). The Philippines ranks second, next to Cambodia, among the countries with the highest proportion of the top 60 percent income earners depending on informal lenders. Similarly, it is surprising to note that the more educated population (with secondary education) borrow more from informal sources compared to the less educated Filipinos (with primary education). The same is true with Indonesia, Malaysia, Lao PDR, and Thailand. The Philippines is found to be the only country in the region where individuals with both higher income and education level have a higher proportion of the population borrowing from informal lenders compared to that of the population with lower income and education.

In the general perspective, the Philippines has the lowest percentage of those who are fifteen years old and above who borrowed from a financial institution (figure 7.3). All the other countries have a higher percentage of the said population group borrowing from a financial institution compared to the average in the East Asia and the Pacific, and the world. Despite having the lowest rate of borrowing, the Philippines is still among the top in the region next to Cambodia and Myanmar in terms of borrowing from an informal private lender (figure 7.4).

Based on the Global Microscope 2015 (EIU 2015), which assessed the regulatory environment for financial inclusion, the Philippines ranks third

Table 7.8 Borrowed from a Private Informal Lender by Country and by Sociodemographic Characteristic, 2014 (% aged 15+)

	Sex		*Income*		*Age group*		*Education*	
Country	*Male*	*Female*	*Bottom 40%*	*Top 60%*	*Older adults*	*Young adults*	*Primary*	*Secondary*
Cambodia	16.88	19.36	18.77	17.84	18.79	16.81	19.41	9.07
Indonesia	2.26	3.61	3.15	2.8	3.16	2.21	1.35	4.33
Lao PDR	4.72	5.04	5.12	4.71	4.91	4.83	6.01	3.04
Malaysia	1.54	0	1.81	0.15	1.1	0	2.08	0.61
Myanmar	15.22	17.02	18.08	15.05	18.48	9.77	21.55	6.79
Philippines	12.22	14.71	9.51	16.24	16.36	5.81	11.02	14.53
Singapore	1.06	1.04	1.21	0.92	1.07	0.92	...	...
Thailand	10.2	8.23	10.95	7.92	9.54	7.32	9.73	8.29
Vietnam	1.51	2.11	2.41	1.4	2.15	0.72	3.42	0.94
East Asia and Pacific	2.54	2.45	2.5	2.49	2.56	2.21	2.18	2.97
World	4.79	4.32	5.12	4.17	4.78	3.76	5.74	3.54

Source: Global Findex 2014.
* 2011 data.
...= not available

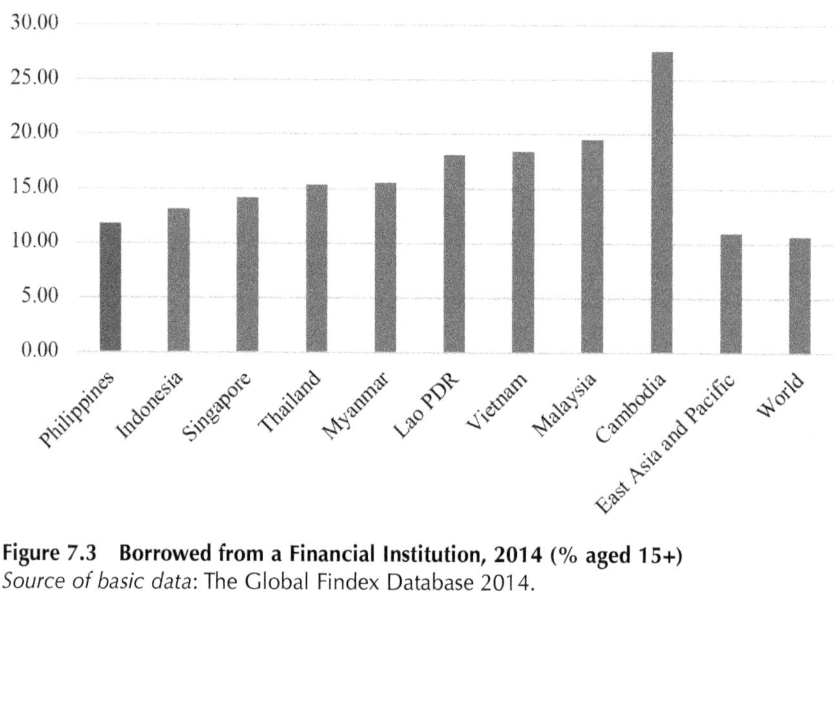

Figure 7.3 Borrowed from a Financial Institution, 2014 (% aged 15+)
Source of basic data: The Global Findex Database 2014.

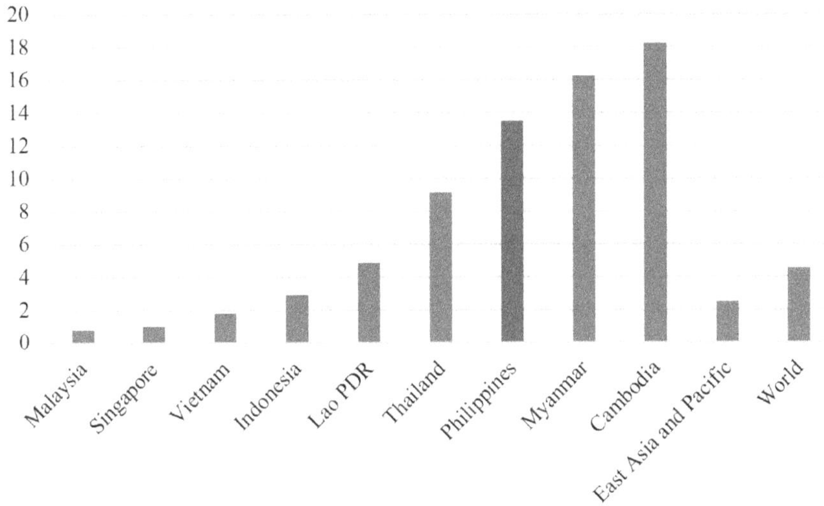

Figure 7.4 Borrowed from Private Informal Lenders, 2014 (% aged 15+)
Source of basic data: The Global Findex Database 2014.

out of fifty-five countries with a score of 81/100. It has been recognized as a leader in promoting and creating an enabling environment for financial inclusion. Several regulations were adopted, and circulars were issued to promote entry of new FSPs and widen the coverage while ensuring the provision of safe services to better serve the poor. However, despite successes in the provision of an enabling environment, it can be deduced from the information above that much improvement has yet to be done in the terms of enhancing access and use of financial services in the country. Only 26 percent of Filipino adults have savings accounts, and only 10.5 percent have access to credit. The challenge that the Philippines financial system faces is how to narrow the gaps in financial inclusion.

NARROWING FINANCIAL GAPS IN INCLUSION THROUGH COOPERATIVES

Cooperatives are one of the key access points in areas where financial inclusion is weak, such as in rural and far-flung areas. As an autonomous organization of, by, and for the people, a cooperative aims to meet the social, economic, and cultural needs and aspirations of its members and, ultimately, to improve their standards of living. This cooperative goal is consistent with the vision of financial inclusion to improve the well-being of people and achieve social cohesion and shared economic development.

It has been articulated in the study of Groeneveld (2011) that financial institutions are more motivated to reach people in the rural areas and provide them financial services if they have closer links with their capital suppliers and client base compared to FSPs, for which these key players are completely separate. Inherently, cooperatives are deeply linked with their member-owners as their needs and aspirations are the key basis for its organization. Anne Gaboury, president and chief executive officer of the Développement International Desjardins, the largest financial cooperative group in Canada and a leading contributor to microfinance in the world, also shared in an interview that the reach and impact of financial cooperatives are more meaningful because cooperatives are owned by the people who created and financed them using their pooled resources (Microfinance Gateway 2012). Because of its member- and community-based approach in the delivery of financial services, a cooperative is seen as a viable model for enhancing financial access and improving financial inclusion in areas that are difficult to reach and are often neglected by banks and other financial institutions.

Cooperative as an Access Point to Financial Products and Services

During the formative years of Philippine cooperatives (1898–1941), credit unions were the first and most prevalent type of cooperative in the country. Cooperatives provided credit to address the most pressing need of the disadvantaged and marginalized people, which was the lack or insufficiency of capital for agricultural activities. As lack of or limited finance continues to be a major constraint among many households, credit remains the most common type of service provided by local cooperatives to their members. Under the Republic Act 9520, otherwise known as the Philippine Cooperative Code of 2008, encouraging thrift and savings mobilization among the members, generating funds, and extending credit to the members for productive and provident purposes are among the major purposes for which a cooperative may be organized in the country. Among the common financial products and services of the cooperatives are loans, savings deposits, and insurance, which are provided to members along with financial education seminars.

One of the unique features of cooperatives, particularly the multipurpose cooperatives with financial services, is their integrated system of financing. Unlike other FSPs, cooperatives normally complement their financial services with nonfinancial support services to ensure and sustain their members' financial productivity as well as to minimize financial risks to the cooperatives. These support services may include marketing services, input provision, technical assistance, capacity building activities, technology and infrastructure, and financial literacy education, among others.

Credit Cooperatives

The cooperatives engaged in provision of credit and other financial services (e.g., savings) for productive and provident purposes are called credit cooperatives (Philippine Cooperative Code of 2008). They generate a common pool of financial resources or funds to provide financial assistance and other related services to their members. As of 2014, there are 3,194 credit cooperatives in the country, which comprise 13 percent of the total number of cooperatives registered with the Cooperative Development Authority (CDA), the lead government agency responsible for the country's cooperative development. However, these are not the only cooperatives that provide financial services.

Though no exact count can be provided due to lack of disaggregated data, cooperatives categorized under the multipurpose type often have a credit service in conjunction with other business activities. From the credit type, cooperatives are re-registered as multipurpose cooperatives once they operate with more than one type of business activity. Multipurpose cooperatives have the biggest share in the total number of cooperatives in the country. In 2014, the total number reached 14,912, comprising 47 percent of all CDA-registered cooperatives.

Credit cooperatives are not regulated by the central banking authority of the Philippines, BSP, but are regulated by CDA and, therefore, have relatively more flexibility when it comes to policies, terms and conditions, and loan and savings program design. They can effectively reach the low-income households and offer them financial products that fit their needs and capacity in terms of loan amount, loan maturity, savings balance, and interest rates. Among the common loan products offered by cooperatives to their members are salary loan, appliance loan, grocery loan, vehicle loan, educational loan, business enhancement loan, and housing loan.

Cooperative Banks

Aside from credit cooperatives, cooperative banks also exist in the Philippine financial system to provide a wide range of financial services in local communities and niche markets in support of the growth of the rural sector. In 2014, there were forty-seven cooperative banks registered with CDA (CDA 2015). This number is expected to gradually decline in the following years, as cooperative banks are being encouraged under the Strengthening Program for Cooperative Banks Plus (2013) to do mergers, consolidations, and bank acquisitions to further strengthen the whole cooperative banking sector of the rural banking system.

Cooperative banks are full-fledged licensed banks engaged in retail and commercial banking but with a cooperative ownership structure. They are organized by primary cooperatives or federation of cooperatives where their clients are their owners. Like a typical cooperative, a cooperative bank adheres to the cooperative practice of "one member, one vote." However, unlike credit cooperatives, which are usually exclusive to the members, financial services of cooperative banks such as savings and loans can be availed both by the members and nonmembers. Some cooperative banks also participate in the wholesale markets for bonds, money, and equities.

With their commitment to support rural communities, cooperative banks as well as other cooperatives with credit services also serve as financial intermediaries between the government financial institutions and the people from the rural sector, particularly farmers, fisherfolk and micro and small businesses and entrepreneurial households. For instance, in the Agro-Industry Modernization Credit and Financing Program, the Philippine government's umbrella credit program, cooperative banks and cooperatives are tapped as credit service conduits or fund retailers of its credit programs. The advantage of channeling credit through cooperatives is that cooperatives offer conditions on financial contracts that are appropriate and adaptable to the characteristics of the members.

Viability of Cooperative Business Model in the Financial System

With more than a century of existence and history of providing financial services, cooperatives have reached a significant portion of the unserved and underserved population in the Philippines, as evidenced by the financial inclusion data presented earlier. The "cooperative" way of doing business is one of the key factors that has sustained the effective delivery of financial services of cooperatives to their members and to the communities where they operate.

As a business model, a cooperative is guided by a set of agreed values and principles, which are responsive to the financial needs of its members. It is based on the values of democracy, self-help, and self-responsibility, equality and equity, and solidarity. It promotes a more equitable distribution of capital within a community and prevents the concentration of finances in a few centers of financial power. A cooperative fosters inclusiveness through its open and democratic nature and its commitment to serve the community.

Further, we can compare a cooperative with an investor-owned firm in terms of the key elements of a business model and identify the advantages of the cooperative model. First, the cooperative model formulates its value proposition in terms of maximizing benefits to its members rather than maximizing returns on investments. Second, it targets market segments where there is a need of members rather than targeting areas where there are more lucrative opportunities. Last, the value network of a cooperative is typically composed of suppliers and customers or clients who are its members or owners of the cooperative and, therefore, seeks to offer them the best value (Mazzarol 2009). In a cooperative, there is an opportunity to create complementary relationships between the suppliers and customers, unlike in profit-oriented financial institutions where the dynamics are more competitive, and cost reduction and maximization of shareholder returns are the key goals.

Financial Education and Consumer Protection

Two of the key elements for promoting financial inclusion in the Philippines are financial education and consumer protection. Overlooking the need for people to adequately understand the financial products and services and their use and value propositions might lead to a personal financial crisis.

For cooperatives engaged in financial service provision, continuing financial literacy is a component of any financial transaction. Educating the officers, employees, and members is critical in a cooperative because any crisis that may occur can have a negative effect on both the institution and the individual member clients. The members are the major source of capital assets of the cooperative, while the cooperative is the source of financial products of the members. Hence, both have to work together for the benefit of all.

As part of the strategy of cooperatives to increase financial awareness, minimize default risks, and optimize the intended impacts of the financial services, financial education seminars, particularly on credit or borrowing, are conducted before and during (and also after, if necessary) the application and/or release of loans. Inculcating the principles of self-support and financial independence among the members——that is, instilling the value of thrift and saving and teaching the efficient and productive use of credit through money management——is the key goal of cooperative financial education. The financial responsibilities of the members and the wise use of money are among the common foci of the seminars. Re-orientation programs and personal counseling are also conducted for members who happen to fail to be in good credit standing to provide them money advice and inspiration to work hard on improving their financial status.

With regard to consumer protection, cooperatives are by all means adhering to the principles of transparency, fair treatment, privacy of client information, effective redress, and prevention of over-indebtedness, as these are practices that support the cooperative values of democracy, equality, and equity as well as the cooperative principle of democratic member control and member economic participation. With consumer protection, consumers are informed ex-ante about financial matters, which allows them to make informed judgments and confident decisions on financial transactions.

Cooperatives that are members of the Microfinance Council of the Philippines, Inc. (MCPI) follow the MCPI code of ethics, which is comprised of the following points.

1. "Provide the poor with permanent and sustainable access to appropriate social and financial services";
2. "Charge market rates of interest on loans and savings, avoiding interest rate subsidies or excessive interest rates";
3. "Promote and maintain a client-friendly culture among our members of the Board, management and the entire staff of the organization";
4. "Provide access to all forms of information requested by members and clients regarding past, current, and future transactions";
5. "Adequately inform members and clients about policies, procedures and transaction costs in order to enable them to make informed choices and decisions";
6. "Treat members and clients with respect and dignity, empathizing with them most especially in times of crisis"; and
7. "Consistently assess the impact of our services with the objective of exerting extra efforts to lift members and clients out of poverty in the shortest time possible."

Indeed, cooperatives maintain a great framework to protect consumers from financial woes and serve them with fair treatment and to educate them to gain financial knowledge, skills, and confidence, which can all in turn result in financial stability and progress.

CONCLUDING REMARKS

This chapter tackles the state of financial inclusion in the Philippines, with particular focus on the contributions and potential role of cooperatives in the country's financial system. The significant role of nonbank financial institutions has been emphasized in the discussion where cooperatives emerge to be a potential driver of financial inclusion. While cooperatives are currently not the top alternative financial provider in the country in terms of monetary value and share, they are among the FSPs with the highest potential of bridging the people tied with the informal financial providers to the formal financial providers, and ultimately, in moving the financially excluded out of the informal financial sector. Their physical presence in the unserved and underserved areas and their wide range of sectors and population groups covered cannot be understated. As of 2013, there were 23,672 primary cooperatives in the Philippines, which serve at least 12.68 million Filipinos.

As a financial institution with the guiding principle of "people before profit," cooperatives also serve as effective financial intermediaries between the financially excluded and the formal banking sector. They can be a good starting point or vehicle for establishing the people's creditworthiness and training them to become financially responsible and wise citizens, which are essential to successfully mainstream them into the formal financial system.

However, all these potentials can only be realized if cooperatives operate in an environment where there are adequate infrastructure and technology, financial and human resources, enabling business conditions, and effective and conducive policies and institutions. For the Philippines, this is the continuing challenge that has to be faced and translated into opportunities and success.

NOTE

1. The Consumer Expectations Survey (CES) is a quarterly nationwide survey that is participated in by at least 5,000 sample households in the Philippines that are randomly drawn from the Philippine Statistics Authority Master Sample List of Households, which is considered a representative sample of households nationwide. The Third Quarter 2015 CES has a sample size of 5,894 households.

REFERENCES

ADBI. *Financial Inclusion in Asia Country Surveys*. Tokyo: Asian Development Bank Institute, 2014.

Ayyagari, Meghana, and Thorsten Beck. *Financial Inclusion in Asia: An Overview*. ADB Economics Working Paper Series no. 449, September 2015. https://dx.doi.org/10.2139/ssrn.270754.

BSP. *Strengthening Program for Cooperative Banks Plus Implementing Guidelines*. Manila, The Philippines: Bangko Sentral ng Pilipinas, 2013.

BSP. *State of the Financial Inclusion in the Philippines: 2013 Data Updates*. Manila, The Philippines: Bangko Sentral ng Pilipinas, 2013.

BSP. *Financial Inclusion Initiatives*. Manila, The Philippines: Bangko Sentral ng Pilipinas, 2014.

BSP. *National Strategy for Financial Inclusion*. Manila, The Philippines: Bangko Sentral ng Pilipinas, 2015.

BSP. *Consumer Expectations Survey: Third Quarter 2015*. Department of Economic Statistics Manila, The Philippines: Bangko Sentral ng Pilipinas, 2015a.

BSP. *Financial Inclusion Initiatives*. Manila, The Philippines: Bangko Sentral ng Pilipinas, 2015b.

BSP. *Online Interactive Statistics*. Manila, The Philippines: Bangko Sentral ng Pilipinas, 2016.

Cooperative Development Authority (CDA). *Annual Report 2015*. Manila, The Philippines: CDA, 2015.

Demirgüç-Kunt, Asli, and Leora Klapper. "Measuring Financial Inclusion: Explaining Variation in Use of Financial Services across and within Countries." *Brookings Papers on Economic Activity* 2013, no. 1 (2013): 279–340.

Global Findex (Global Financial Inclusion Database) 2014. http://databank.worldbank.org/data/reports.aspx?source=global-findex-(global-financial-inclusion-database)#.

Groeneveld, J. M. "Morality and Integrity in Cooperative Banking." *Ethical Perspectives* 18, no. 4 (2011): 127–35.

Hunter, Shawn. *Realizing Financial Inclusion in Asia: Achievements and Challenges*. Queensland: Foundation for Development Cooperation, 2014.

International Monetary Fund (IMF). Financial Access Survey, 2014. https://data.imf.org/?sk=E5DCAB7E-A5CA-4892-A6EA-598B5463A34C.

Llanto, Gilberto M. *Financial Inclusion, Education, and Regulation in the Philippines*. ADBI Working Paper 541. Tokyo: Asian Development Bank Institute, 2015. https://ssrn.com/abstract=2672722.

Mazzarol, Tim. *Co-operative Enterprise: A Discussion Paper & Literature Review*. Crawley: University of Western Australia, 2009.

Mercado-Bunker, M. "Financial Inclusion in the Philippines." Presentation at the 2014 Asia -Pacific Financial Inclusion Forum. Shanghai, 19 March 2014.

Microfinance Gateway. *Advancing Financial Inclusion through the Cooperative Model, Part 1*. An interview with Anne Gaboury of Quebec's Développement International Desjardins, Quebec, 2012.

Republic of the Philippines. *Philippine Cooperative Code of 2008. Republic Act 9520*. Manila, Philippines, 2009.

The Economist Intelligence Unit (EIU). *Global Microscope 2015: The Enabling Environment for Financial Inclusion*. Sponsored by MIF/IDB, CAF, Accion and the Metlife Foundation. New York: EIU, 2015.

World Bank. *Measuring Financial Inclusion around the World*. World Bank Research Digest 10, no. 2 (2016).

Chapter 8

Cooperatives and Rural Development: Historical Perspectives and Experiences from Tanzania

Emmanuel Maro Nyankweli and
Tafuteni Nicholaus Chusi

BACKGROUND

Tanzania is the second-largest country following the Democratic Republic of Congo, in East and Central Africa. It covers an area of 945,000 square kilometers. The 2012 estimates revealed a population of 44.9 million persons (National Bureau of Statistics [NBS] 2013). This population comprises more than 120 ethnic groups, 75 percent of which live in rural areas and depend on small-scale farming. The average annual growth rate of the gross domestic product (GDP), reported by the NBS, in Tanzania was 6.72 percent from 2002 to 2015, reaching an all-time high of 12.40 percent in the first quarter of 2007 and a record low of 2.60 percent in the third quarter of 2009. The GDP per capita in purchasing power parity is USD 2,472 (2015), with a growth rate of 6.3 percent per annum. Agriculture dominates the Tanzanian economy, accounting for 55 percent of the GDP and 80 percent of recorded total foreign exchange earnings, while providing employment for 70 percent of the labor force.

A cooperative is defined as a group of people having similar economic interests who undertake a planned economic activity by using their own resources for solving their own problems (Münkner 2002). The traditional Rochdale concept of a cooperative society roughly describes a cooperative as pseudo- or quasi-classical forms having formal features of a cooperative society. The International Cooperative Alliance-COOP defines cooperative as an autonomous association of persons united voluntarily to meet their common economic, social, and cultural needs and aspirations through a jointly owned and democratically controlled enterprise. This definition emphasizes that cooperatives are independent of the government and not owned by anyone other than the members. Thus, in this chapter, the understanding of cooperatives is guided by these definitions.

HISTORICAL CONTEXT OF COOPERATIVES IN TANZANIA

Cooperatives in Colonial Era

Cooperative development in Tanzania dates back to the early twentieth century, mainly in cash-cropping areas experiencing rivalry between the African peasants reacting against unfair marketing and processing practices and political discrimination (URT 2015). It can be reliably noted that cooperatives were founded by peasants in 1925 (Hyden 1975). The nodes of cooperative development were in the northern, southern Tanzania and Lake Victoria basin, notably in Kilimanjaro, Sukumaland, Bukoba, and Rungwe. The motive was to enable indigenous peasants to obtain at least part of trade profits from crops by reducing the role of middlemen, predominantly Asian traders, such as coffee and cotton traders (Maghimbi 2010). By 1933, eleven agro-marketing cooperative societies were established in Kilimanjaro; these societies were registered with the secondary society Kilimanjaro Native Cooperative Union, which is still functional (Maghimbi 2010; Hyden 1975). According to Hyden (1975), in colonial administration, cooperative societies are significant for their economic viability. These societies were subjected to close monitoring to maintain their economic viability and financial discipline. The registrar of the cooperatives had a mandate to deregister all unviable cooperative societies.

Cooperatives in the Independence Era

During the independence struggle, cooperatives added a role, namely political activism, to its original economic and financial roles because the Tanganyika African National Union (TANU) became a popular party in the country. In this era, cooperatives became a good recruiting ground, and TANU had facilitated the growth of farmers through the cooperative societies. The rural marketing societies were considered the agents of economic transformation in the post-independence era. According to Maghimbi (2010), the idea of cooperation appealed to ordinary peasants as much as it did to politicians and civil communities. Hence, the expansion of the cooperatives became one of the most prominent features of the new government after 1961. Before independence, the number of cooperatives had increased to 691 in urban and rural areas. In the rural areas, marketing cooperatives were established, whereas in the urban areas, consumer cooperatives were established. The consumer cooperatives culminated into the formation of the Cooperative Supply Association of Tanganyika (COSATA).

By 1962–1964, producer and marketing cooperatives were established throughout Tanzania, prompting the government to declare that all marketing activities of agricultural produces should proceed through the cooperatives (Hyden 1975). The COSATA, established in 1963, is the wholesale supplier to the cooperatives. It was considered the nucleus around which retail cooperative societies functioned in urban centers (Maghimbi 2010). Between 1961 and 1966, the cooperatives underwent quantitative expansion in the rural and urban areas. The number of registered societies increased from 857 in 1961 to 1,533 in 1966. In 1960, the cooperatives managed 145,000 metric tons of produce, whereas, in 1965, this number had increased to 496,000 metric tons (Maghimbi 2010; Hyden 1975).

The rapid expansion was attributed to the relaxation of the laws governing the registration of the cooperatives compared with the laws observed in the colonial times, which resulted in a high number of registrations. These registrations culminated into serious management problems, with inadequate supervision and lack of training for staff and committee members. Thus, despite their popularity, both rural and urban cooperatives did not yield favorable results because of inadequate managerial capacity, lack of democracy and training, and financial indiscipline that consequently led to declining loyalty among members. Therefore, a special commission was formed by the government to determine the problems encountered by the cooperatives to reboost the morale of and loyalty among members. The committee learned that most cooperatives had an exclusive top-down management and were established without genuine local demand and understanding and that members had accepted the idea because of the general enthusiasm generated by the independence. Furthermore, the cooperatives experienced a shortage of skilled manpower, and most were susceptible to political interferences. To overcome these circumstances, the government established the Unified Cooperative Commission; this commission governed the employment of all senior employees at the cooperative union level to eliminate nepotism and all forms of favoritism.

According to the United Republic of Tanzania (URT 1968), the government deliberately increased the formal powers of the Commissioner of Cooperative Development (in his capacity as a registrar) over the cooperatives and enacted the Cooperative Societies Act, 1968. This act empowered the registrar or his representative the ultimate powers to address numerous management concerns in the movement such that all expenditures, except for minor daily ones, must be approved by a senior officer in the Cooperative

Development Division, and the registrar or his representative can dissolve the management committees (URT 1968; 2014).

The URT (1968) indicated that the government aimed to strengthen the cooperative unions by creating one such union in each region. In concordance with the formation of larger unions, the government aimed to engage the unions in new activities (e.g., wholesale and transport businesses and petrol station management). It deliberately emphasized information sharing and education. The cooperative training institutions were motivated to more effectively cope with the increasing demand for more efficient management skills in the movement. Furthermore, a new avenue of a more extensive Nordic assistance was discovered in the field of cooperative development in Tanzania. The Swedish cooperative movement had been providing some specialists since 1964. However, from 1968, this aid was rendered on a bilateral basis between the Government of Tanzania and the governments of the Nordic countries to ensure effective management of and impart knowledge of cooperative functioning to cooperative leaders, staff, and members.

Cooperatives during the Arusha Declaration, 1967–1976

The Arusha Declaration was passed in January 1967, and socialism was established. However, the policy paper on socialism and rural development of 1969 was more relevant to the cooperatives. This document highlighted the limitations of the existing marketing societies and outlined novel avenues. It recognized cooperatives as basically a socialist institution. However, the marketing cooperatives, comprising of small-scale capitalists, and which themselves, have become a large employer of labor, had increasingly developed a capitalist character. The cooperative movement in Tanzania was considered to considerably strengthen the growth of socialism and self-reliance, representing a major advancement over a private, capitalist trading system. However, if the marketing cooperatives remained solely concerned with marketing, with the development of commercial farming among its members, they would become a capitalist institution.

Nyerere (1969) reported that cooperatives must play the central part in the development of rural socialism in Tanzania for fulfilling a progressive role, but they must be revolutionized. For achieving this goal, two changes were required. First, the society must become production-oriented through the development of cooperative farming units for its members at the primary level. Second, the democratic participation of the members of all cooperatives must be increased and emphasized. Therefore, reform cooperatives were established in the form of Ujamaa villages, where production is supposedly collective and not individualistic. By the end of 1971, approximately 4,000 Ujamaa villages were established, and most of them were in their initial development stage. Hence, only 120 villages had reached the registration stage as cooperative societies. The policy aimed to gradually absorb the remainder of these and other new villages into the cooperative movement in a similar fashion.

The integration of the Ujamaa villages into the cooperatives resulted in a parallel official government structure, where the Cooperative Development Division, established under the Ministry of Agriculture and Cooperatives, and the Ujamaa Village Division, established under the Ministry of Regional Administration and Rural Development, were merged into the Rural Development Division department headed by the Commissioner of Rural Development and managed by the Prime Minister's Office (Sizya 2001). Currently, the Rural Development Division is under the Ministry of Agriculture, Food Security, and Cooperative Development. The account of the socialist phase of cooperative development would be incomplete without some reference to the expansion of consumer cooperative shops in urban and rural areas. In the rural areas, such shops were established by the existing multipurpose society, whereas in the urban areas, such shops were started by specific consumer cooperative societies (Maghimbi 2010). This activity was a renewed attempt to reduce the share of retail markets held by middlemen and private traders (URT 2015; Hyden 1975). Despite their economic and political roles, the cooperatives played a significant role in the accessibility of social services, transportation, savings, and credits as well as in education in rural and urban centers (Banturaki 2012; Maghimbi 2010).

Cooperatives in the Post-Arusha Declaration Era, 1977–1982

Banturaki (2012) reported that the government abolished all primary cooperatives in 1976. Their crop-marketing functions were later taken over by communal (Ujamaa) villages. The abolished cooperative unions never bought crops directly from peasants but through primary cooperatives. The other services provided by the abolished cooperatives, such as wholesale and retail trade, were taken over by state-owned companies, such as the Regional Trading Companies and District Development Corporations.

Banturaki (2012) reported that in the beginning of the 1980s, the government realized that the crop authorities performed below expectations. Hence, in 1984, it reintroduced the cooperatives and remodeled the crop authorities into crop boards. These reforms were introduced when the government was addressing major economic crisis caused by both external and internal shocks, such as decreasing world market prices, increasing oil prices, Tanzania–Uganda war, unreliable weather conditions, inconsistent macroeconomic and sectoral policies, and inflation (Maghimbi 2010). In 1986, the government adopted and implemented the open-market policy through the structural adjustment program (Banturaki 2012). Few of the policy actions that had a significant influence on the cooperatives were the abolition of price controls; elimination of subsidies; liberalization of marketing of agricultural inputs and outputs, which facilitated the emergence of private sector participation in both commercial and production activities in the economy. Although farmers have not yet received the anticipated benefits of competitive marketing, it had some advantages, including the availability of more private buyers who avail alternative marketing opportunities for agricultural produces (e.g., coffee).

Reinstated Cooperatives, 1982–1990

This period between 1982 and 1990 was characterized by an explicit government contravention of basic cooperative principles and intervention in the management affairs of the reinstated cooperatives. The re-establishment of the cooperatives indicated the relinquishment of considerable centralized government control over produce marketing and over cooperative organizations themselves altogether. The public was demanding structural reforms in the local marketing organizations, to meet their needs. It also demanded democratic management and control by the members of the cooperatives. By contrast, the 1982 legislation for the reinstatement of the cooperatives was largely based on the recommendations of the ruling Chama Cha Mapinduzi (CCM) party, which directed all reinstated cooperatives to be multipurpose, a system that had been previously unsuccessful (URT 1982). Second, the cooperative unions were to exist at the regional level without considering other factors, which required successful cooperation. Third, and most importantly, the legislation brought the cooperatives under the CCM structure, as a political party mass organization. Under such a structure, the cooperative movement got direct commands, directives, and control from the CCM party and government (URT 1982). Therefore, the election of cooperative leaders at all levels and employment of cooperative unions' senior staff had to be screened and approved by the CCM. By forcing the cooperatives to recruit leaders not of their own choice, the political interference facilitated the involvement of incompetent noncommitted opportunists and other corrupt people into the cooperatives. Thus, the cooperatives obviously experienced serious mismanagement because of state and political party bureaucracy (Banturaki 2012).

Banturaki (2012) stated the confession of the government that its own policies and directives accounted for 87 percent of the total cooperative unions' debts, amounting to 40 billion Tanzanian Shilling by 1989. In addition, the cooperative members did not gain anything substantial from their own organization but experienced total frustration and despair at the cooperative prospects. The cooperative leaders directed their loyalty to the political party, where they were made accountable. The leaders were no longer accountable to the cooperative members, who were the "owners" of the cooperatives (Ewald 2011).

Banturaki (2012) further reported that following the 1985 political directives, by December 1987, all villages were registered as multipurpose village cooperatives following the party structure. The reinstated cooperatives were forced to undergo other structural changes. These necessitated the dissolution of their larger associations to form multipurpose village cooperatives following the legal method of "voluntary division" on political criteria rather than of "economic viability" on the "efficiency and effectiveness" criteria of a cooperative for serving its members (ibid). The members then rightly realized that the cooperatives were the property of the ruling party and government, and therefore, they could not cater to their own needs (Maghimbi 1992).

SUCCESS AND CHALLENGES OF COOPERATIVES IN TANZANIA

Success of Cooperatives in Tanzania

Since their inception in the 1930s, cooperatives have promoted the socioeconomic welfare of their members and the general cooperative stakeholders as well as ensured the socioeconomic development of local communities to which they belong. Precisely, the rural cooperatives with their multiple advantages of being grass-roots organizations, having high member participation and accessibility, showed rapid expansion, whereby the rural population acknowledged cooperative successes and achievements as the aces of cooperation. The cooperatives managed to show their potential of implementing production- and service-oriented activities, including agro-marketing functions, crop and milk processing, farm input distribution, wholesaling and retailing of basic commodities, transport, school education, farmer education, and democratization. More than 80 percent of agricultural production and marketing has been conducted through the cooperatives before the introduction of trade liberalization in the early 1980s and 1990s. With their inherent catalytic elements of being grassroot organizations and their modus operandi, cooperatives have established themselves as practical, dynamic, and potential instruments for providing the desired socioeconomic services to the people. Thus, the government acknowledged the potential of cooperatives and designated them as development promoters, potential agents of rural socioeconomic changes, vehicles for rural transformation, and hence, instruments for poverty reduction.

Contribution to Poverty Reduction

Cooperatives are highly ranked to rapidly reduce the poverty of most Tanzanians. Because small farmers joined the cooperatives, the cooperative members, were provided with subsidies in agricultural inputs. These subsidies made agricultural production very cheap while the cooperatives were struggling to obtain a high price for their products, hence ensuring stable income, both internally and externally, and reducing poverty.

Social Protection

Cooperative members provide social protection to each other through mutual support. Mutual support systems are mostly observed between the members. Nearly all cooperatives have established special borrowing schemes, and the members can borrow money and access to kind assistance in cases of emergencies. Some cooperatives have solidarity funds to which a member contributes regularly, and out of which, a member is helped with an agreed sum of money in events of death of a spouse, child, and or a family member.

Employment, Income, and Poverty Reduction

Cooperatives provide employment opportunities to their members, thus enabling them to earn and reduce their poverty. However, the standard of living of the members in villages (peasants) is low but more favorable than that of their nonmember counterparts. The standard of living of the members was determined by observing their housing and dressing; schooling of their children; freedom from debts; and ownership of assets such as bicycles, radios, and mobile phones. It was also measured by investigating the socioeconomic activities in which the members participated.

Cooperative Challenges

Lack of Adequate Capital

A major challenge encountered by cooperatives is inadequate internal capacity to maintain, finance, and sustain operations. Consequently, the cooperatives remain completely dependent on external support, particularly from government subvention. Capital is highly used for financing the activities of cooperatives; hence, the lack of adequate capital led to the dissolution of many cooperatives that had no strong capital base. Cooperatives have to perform numerous activities, such as employing competent personnel and adopting "best practices" under the provision of financial services to members, and without a strong capital base, these objectives cannot be achieved.

Poor Leadership and Incompetent Management

Poor leadership and incompetent management are among the factors contributing to the poor performance of cooperatives in Tanzania. This was a result of selfishness among leaders because they focused on fulfilling their personal interests instead of serving the interest of the members. Most cooperatives had inadequate leadership and skilled personnel, consequently experiencing a serious misuse of authorities and powers, improper allocation of scarce resource, and thus the embezzlement of funds. This can be reflected in the behaviors of nepotism and favoritism during recruitment, which is based on technical know who rather than technical know-how.

Lack of Cooperative Education and Awareness

Inadequate cooperative education, knowledge, and awareness among the cooperative staff, committee members, and leaders are serious challenges in the effective and efficient functioning of cooperatives. These factors can damage the morale of the members, increase mistrust among them, and discourage their participation in decision-making.

Trade Liberalization

Before trade liberalization, cooperatives enjoyed cheap crop financing by the government as well as the monopoly of agricultural crop marketing. Following the implementation of trade liberalization, cooperatives had no time to adjust to the world economic order. Thus, they could not manage to compete with the other commodities exported and imported from other countries and lost their monopoly advantage in the market economy. Furthermore, the withdrawal of subsidies was a serious threat to cooperatives.

Government Intervention in Cooperatives

Cooperative policy and legislation that provided the government with power to supervise the cooperatives led to government interferences in the governance and management of the cooperatives. Consequently, the cooperatives were politicized, corrupted, and mismanaged. The monopolistic position of the cooperatives in the economy never helped them to realize returns on their businesses, thereby weakening their financial base. Thus, the cooperatives could not provide services to their members; and the members lost morale to participate in the governance of their cooperatives.

Lack of Strategic Planning

This challenge has been encountered by Tanzanian cooperatives. The board members and cooperative staff have failed to develop strategic plans for their organizations, which would provide options for the progress and implementation of actions for conducting organizational operations.

Lack of Cooperative Training Institutions

Cooperative education training and awareness to staff and committee members offered by one institution were inadequate. The Cooperative College Moshi, established in 1963 (now known as Moshi Cooperative University), was and remains inadequate because all cooperatives in Tanzania depend on this institute. The expansion and establishment of new private and public training institutions are urgently required to determine the needs and serve most of the ever-increasing established urban and rural cooperatives.

CONCLUSION AND IMPLICATION

Cooperatives are indeed a tool for rapid development and poverty reduction in rural and urban areas because a free and strong cooperative movement empowers voiceless ordinary and subjugated people. Cooperatives and microfinance institutions when established and managed appropriately can significantly help in improving the lives of poor people. Most of these people live in slums in cities, and approximately 75 percent dwell in rural areas and depend on agriculture. They must be involved in the ownership, functioning, and management of their development process through their own local organizations. In addition, cooperatives are the foci of knowledge and information, technology testing and innovation, and learning and application and of the accumulation of saving and credit distributions. Cooperatives make the optimum use of local resources and thus, are the most effective models for cost reduction. The Arusha declaration cooperatives represented self-reliance and employment of the minority, youths, women, and disadvantaged people.

Cooperatives will remain a vital tool for rural and urban transformation if they are transformed into responsible organizations with true democracy, for the members and by the members themselves. However, efforts should be devoted to restore the lost faith among and reboot the morale of the members of cooperatives by adhering to the principles of inclusive governance, true democracy, and rule of law. Furthermore, participation of all members should be ensured, regardless of gender, ethnicity, and economic status. Strategic thinking and planning must be encouraged for establishing progressive cooperative societies. Cooperatives have been considered a masculine territory for decades; this stereotype must be changed with respect to the qualification of membership and leadership. Timothy and Nyankweli (2013) reported that women membership markedly improves the functions of Savings and Credit Cooperative Societies (SACCOS). It indicates that the saving rate of Tanzania can be significantly improved by encouraging women to join SACCOS. Thus, this study recommends encouraging and honoring the role of women in cooperatives.

REFERENCES

Banturaki, J. A. *Tanzania Cooperatives: Their Role in Socio-Economic Development*. Kampala: Perspectives for Cooperatives in East Africa, 2012.

Ewald, Jonas. *Challenges for the Democratisation Process in Tanzania. Moving Towards Consolidation 50 years after independence?* PhD dissertation. Gothenburg: University of Gothenburg, Faculty of Social Sciences, 2011.

Hyden, Goran. "Development of the Cooperative Movement in Tanzania." *Tanzania Notes and Records* 76 (1975): 51–56.

Maghimbi, Sam. "The Abolition of Peasant Cooperatives and the Crisis in the Rural Economy in Tanzania." In *The Tanzanian Peasantry: Economy in Crisis*, edited by Peter G. Forster and Sam Maghimbi. Aldershot: Avebury Publications, 1992.

Maghimbi, Sam. *Co-operatives in Tanzania Mainland: Revival and Growth. Series on the Status of Co-operative Development in Africa*. ILO Country Office for the United Republic of Tanzania, Kenya, Rwanda and Uganda. International Labour Office, Co-operative Programme (EMP/COOP). CoopAfrica Working Paper No.14, 2010.

Münkner, Hans. *The Supportive Environment for Cooperatives in the Context of the Current Political, Economic, Social, Demographic, and Ecological Environments* (paper presented at the Supportive Environment for Cooperatives: A Stakeholder Dialogue on Definitions, Prerequisites and Process of Creation). Ulaanbaatar, Mongolia, May 15–17, 2002.

National Bureau of Statistics. *2012 Population and Housing Census: Population Distribution by Administrative Units: Key Findings*. The United Republic of Tanzania, 2013. http://nbs.go.tz/nbs/sensa/PDF/2012 PHC POPULAR VERSION .pdf.

Nyerere, Julius K. "Socialism and Rural Development." In *Ujamaa Essays on Socialism*, 106–144. Oxford: Oxford University Press, 1969.

Sizya, Mwelukilwa J. *The Role Co-operatives Play in Poverty Reduction in Tanzania* (paper presented at United Nations in observance of the International Day for the Eradication of Poverty), October 17, 2001.

United Republic of Tanzania (URT). *Cooperative Societies Act*. Dar es Salaam: Government Publishers, 1968.

United Republic of Tanzania (URT). *Cooperative Societies Act*. Dar es Salaam: Government Publishers, 1982.

United Republic of Tanzania (URT). *The Cooperative Societies Act of 2013*. Dar es Salaam: Government Publishers, 2014.

United Republic of Tanzania (URT). *Co-operative Reform and Modernization Program (CRMP): 2005-2015*. Dar es Salaam: Government Publishers, 2005.

Vedastus, Timothy, and Nyankweli Emmanuel. "The Influence of Gender on the Performance." *The African Journal of Finance and Management* 21, no. 1 (2013): 1–8.

Chapter 9

Workers' Cooperative Movement in Argentina and other Latin American Countries: An Alternative to Unemployment and Precarious Work

Andrés Eduardo Ruggeri

Worker-recuperated enterprises (in Spanish, empresas recuperadas por los trabajadores; ERTs)[1] are closely related to the effects of the neoliberal economic policy on Argentina's production structure and working conditions. This indicates that among other factors, the emergence of ERTs is directly associated with the massive collapse of industries and consequent unemployment of millions of workers. Under these conditions, the first reaction of workers is to desperately try to retain their jobs that would facilitate escaping the impending social marginalization. The living conditions of unemployed workers are visible threats for their employed counterparts, driving them to develop survival strategies beyond old union tools that were no longer useful. The starting point of an ERT is highly complicated because of certain factors: shuttered business, unemployed workers who could not feed their families, rundown facilities, no capital, lack of involvement by the state, business frauds, and other elements warranting ERTs. Despite these factors, workers managed more than 150 enterprises in the worst crisis years and a similar number in the following years; presently, Argentina has 367 ERTs.[2] These ERTs undertake solidarity-based cultural and educational initiatives and provide work and dignity to their members. ERTs can practically show the potentials and limitations, in the current circumstances, of self-management as a social and economic practice. The practices of equality and collective management constantly clash with the needs of the market as well as with the values and ideas that workers have imbibed from the capitalist culture in which they were born and have lived all their lives.

WORKERS' COOPERATIVES IN THE NEOLIBERAL ERA

The present ERTs have distinguished themselves and drawn particular attention because of how they have addressed the failure of the neoliberal system. As a testament to their global influence, the concept and practices of empresas recuperadas have since been adopted in other Latin American countries, namely Brazil, Uruguay, and Venezuela (Ruggeri 2009, 2014; Atzeni and Vieta 2014). ERT-type conversions have also been conducted outside this region considering the international characteristics of the neoliberal crisis that has extended to the self-described "developed world." This has led to "Argentina-style" factories and workplaces in countries such as Turkey, Greece, Spain, Italy, France, Bosnia, Mexico, and the United States. However, the Argentine movement of ERTs and workers' cooperatives remains the largest and most widespread movement in the neoliberal era.

Neoliberal hegemony, which led to ERTs, was not independent of capitalist globalization, which introduced major changes in the production and consumption structures as well as in the organization of work and role of the state apparatus (Antunes 2005; Harispe 2009). Argentina, possibly the Latin American country where the postwar "welfare state" had been more successful in ensuring an operational network of social security, was seriously affected by this global neoliberal hegemony, which was highly manifested during the Carlos Menem government (1989–1999).

In the early 1990s, the Washington Consensus (Williamson 2004) established a wide range of neoliberal ideas typically adopted without verification by most governments in the region. In most Latin American countries, so-called adjustment programs, privatization, and downsizing of the state and financial appreciation processes were implemented, resulting in a desolated outlook by the mid-1990s (Basualdo et al. 2002). The old welfare states were abandoned, nullifying the achievements of worker movements and subjecting the society to the threat of massive unemployment. Neoliberalism soon generated a new society and a new model of state but has regressive characteristics; social and economic development is highly uneven. The new neoliberal state apparatus disintegrated the old model, privatizing public enterprises and dismantling most social security systems built over decades. The global forces radically changed the role of the state, which became almost exclusively devoted to ensuring the interests of large economic groups. Unemployment caused by the economy's rapid deindustrialization increased several times faster than did the resources and structures created for avoiding it. Thus, the marginal groups socially unified under the category of "unemployed" began organizing and emphasizing their demands, leading to numerous forms of organization and the proliferation of micro-experiences, cooperatives, and self-managed enterprises of all types.

This radical version of neoliberalism, existing in Argentina since 1989, was finally discontinued in December 2001,[3] a few years before the marked global collapse caused by the implementation of this policy on the international scale. Argentina was not only the sole country to experience this type of crisis but also was potentially the most extreme case. In other countries, resistance to what was being described as the global neoliberal system began to be manifested, particularly in anti-globalization protests, as in terms of popular governments beginning to win elections in Latin America, especially since Hugo Chavez's victory in Venezuela in late 1998. Because of this new context of resistance to global neoliberalism, many intellectuals and activists worldwide identified some of the popular forms of resistance and reactions to the crisis in Argentina as part of a global anti-globalization movement (Petras et al. 2002; Schoijet 2006; Bowman and Stone 2009). However, our experience, particularly in the case of ERTs, shows that despite being related to the global context, the Argentine process has its own characteristics.

By analyzing the characteristics of ERTs and their formation, particularly regarding political processes and changes in workers' subjectivities, we can assess the relationship between workers' movement and a possible global struggle against capitalism. Indisputably, Argentine and Latin American ERTs emerge more as a form of resistance against extreme situations caused by neoliberal crisis rather than as an anti-capitalist ideological choice. However, they simultaneously highlight critical concerns related to reformulating an economic and social project for achieving a worker-controlled economy.

GLOBAL CRISIS AND SELF-MANAGEMENT

For Latin Americans who have repeatedly experienced crisis in the past few decades, the situation in certain countries, such as Spain and Greece, seems like a déjà vu. A crisis caused by finance capital that is worsened—considering the argument that it is the only approach to confront it—by following the established and outdated ideas of "austerity" results in millions of workers being unemployed, reduced funding designated for social protections, forcing the state to discontinue public enterprises, and reducing expenses framing the "welfare state."

Contrastingly, they designate extensive funding for strengthening the tools of resistance to counter the inevitable social protest, facilitate the intense mobility of capital for investigating the optimal conditions for the exploitation and precarization of work and maximum capability for accumulating capital, designate high amounts from public funds for the "rescue" of the banking sector responsible for the crisis, they penalize those who try to respond differently. The differences between a crisis with these characteristics in the periphery of the capitalist system and that in the countries in the center of global capitalism are, precisely, the centrality of the affected economies, strength of the involved institutions and financial tools, strength of the hegemonic ideology and capitalist culture, and institutional and repressive forces of the states and their ability to respond as the guardians of capital's strongest interests.

Paradoxically, worker and grassroot movements in Argentina and other Latin American countries seem to have a weaker ability to resist because of the multiple mechanisms of social protection that they have been able to achieve in the past, thus weakening their antibodies for workers' struggle and organization and allowing a rapid and expensive reply by governing capitalists. The conformism and resignation to the possible changes, even in the most-moderated social democratic parties that comprise the largest part of Europe's left-wing government, hindered the adoption of the "human" version of global neoliberal capitalism. The two factors contribute to the defenselessness and disappointment of their base.

In the past five years, there have been many labor conflicts, and many enterprises and production establishments have collapsed in most European countries and the United States. The case of the Republic Windows and Doors factory (presently known as New Era Cooperative) in Chicago is one of the most established cases in North America. Nevertheless, Southern Europe's process of recuperation, in countries more markedly affected by the crisis, is more important. Cases, such as Vio.Me in Thessaloniki, Greece, played similar roles in Argentine ERTs in December 2001 (Azzellini 2014). The other lesser-known examples include, within the militancy of the radical Left-wing governments of these countries, various cooperatives that we could categorize as ERTs in Spain, particularly in Catalonia, and in certain places in France, some of them already functioning for several years.

In Italy, laws allow the formation of cooperatives from the moment of industry collapse. However, in this country, as is the norm when collapses are sudden and fraud rates are high, the actual difficulties that workers experience in taking over enterprises are large and torturous. There are distinct perspectives about the process' dimensions and identity. Some researchers claimed the existence of many ERTs; however, to date, the cases in which these businesses have identified themselves as ERTs have been very low such as the Rome-based Officine Zero and Milan-based Rimaflow (ibid). Both cases were factories that collapsed with very few possibilities of restarting production in their previous line of work. These factories were occupied by a group of their former workers that in collaboration with a group of social and political activists tended to recreate the Argentine model of "open factory" as the location of various activities and solidarity, cultural, and labor projects, without much chances of achieving recuperation as an industrial unit.

By refining the relevant data, some particularities were observed in these still unknown cases of European enterprises recuperated by their workers. First, in contrast to Latin Americans, Europeans seem to experience more difficulty developing the solidarity networks to sustain and support these businesses (although the aforementioned cases owe a large part of their survival to these same networks). The existing social security institutions create a situation where the closure of factories is not permanent for workers, which typically occurs in Argentina and Latin America. Unemployment insurance allows workers to continue receiving a regular income for a certain time, delaying their confrontation with the situation of having no income at all and thus discouraging the development of radical struggle methods to avert unemployment (Gómez Solórzano 2014).

WORKER-RECUPERATED ENTERPRISES IN ARGENTINA: AN APPROXIMATION

Argentina had 367 ERTs at the end of the last survey of the Programa Facultad Abierta (Open Faculty Program) team in 2016 at the University of Buenos Aires,[4] directed by the author (Programa Facultad Abierta 2016). This number was only 161 in 2004, 257 in 2010, and 311 in 2013 (Programa Facultad Abierta 2003; Ruggeri, Martinez and Trinchero 2005; Ruggeri et al. 2011; Centro de Documentación de Empresas Recuperadas 2014). This increase contradicts the widespread view that ERTs are exclusively the result of the 2001 crisis and therefore, represent a stagnant and declining process in subsequent years.

Presently, more than 360 self-managed enterprises in Argentina provide jobs for approximately 16,000 workers. In contrast to the perception of the dissolution or mere survival of ERTs, in the past two years, more than 2,400 new self-managed jobs have been added, including those in recently developed ERTs. According to our survey, 42 percent of ERTs belong to metallurgical or other manufacturing industries, 19 percent to the food industry, and 22 percent to nonproduction-related services such as health care, education, and tourism. Most ERTs are categorized as small and medium enterprises[5] according to the number of employees, with an average of a little more than thirty members. Average workers have quite specialized skills, but their placement is difficult in industries apart from those in which they have spent most of their careers.

The revival of production involves long processes of struggle and occupation of factories and other workplaces, typically involving several months (more than nine for cases that began in 2001, five for subsequent cases until 2011, and more than nine later). These long-term conflicts complicate retaining the highest-qualified workers or those whose skills have greater demand in the market (such as administrative and executive personnel). Thus, workers who remain in ERTs are typically those who have no other chance of re-employment.

A workforce comprises workers with a certain level of expertise and many years of service in the same company, with 5 percent of workers being young adults, 75 percent being older than thirty-five years, and 20 percent being older than fifty-five years. Most of the survey respondents were men. The small number of women is explained by the characteristics of the Argentine labor market as a whole, with certain industries and jobs occupied almost entirely by men (as in metallurgical or printing industries, where the few women employed work in administration or cleaning). Other industries, such as education, health care, and textile, employed a large number of women, although these cases are far fewer in our study sample.

Moreover, ERTs are widespread in Argentina, with a distribution that is closely related to the country's economic structure and industries that were the most affected by the neoliberal offensive of the 1990s. This is reflected in the fact that 50 percent of ERTs are located in the Buenos Aires metropolitan area, and most of those located outside the capital are in the industrial area of Santa Fe province. The remaining ERTs are distributed in twenty-one of the country's twenty-four provinces.

Another important feature of ERTs is their legal conformation as worker cooperatives. According to our data, 95 percent of cases were formed under this legal form. The remaining 5 percent were formed as other types of cooperatives, undefined cases that are involved in conflicts, and cases of co-management between workers and former owners or other business people. A cooperative form is favored for several reasons, such as lower taxes and the possibility of being recognized by a bankruptcy judge as "continued production" of a factory or business that has been declared bankrupt. Cooperative members can legally operate in the market and enjoy protection over the ownership of facilities, machinery, or other assets of the former company. Moreover, in forming a cooperative, workers can control the company without being held responsible for the typically large, sometimes multimillion-dollar, debts of former owners.

With respect to health and social security benefits, however, ERTs have serious problems in ensuring workers' rights, mainly because of the lack of specific regulations that apply to these cases of cooperativized former wage workers. The absence of a specific law for workers' cooperatives subjects ERTs and other similar cooperatives to legal ambiguity. Recently, this situation has increasingly become a subject of internal debate, considering the "aging" of recuperated enterprises, with most workers having been veterans when the self-management process began (Ruggeri 2014).

Regarding productivity, despite the efforts of their members, most recuperated enterprises have not achieved the maximum production output of their installed capacity. Significant improvements were made between the start of the operations and the first two years of work. However, subsequent expansion has been problematic and slow, and ERTs sometimes reach a point of stagnation. The associated reasons are diverse, including the disastrous state of the plant and machinery in most cases, forcing workers to invest heavily to make the enterprise operational. These continuous or long-term investments are almost impossible under conditions of the lack of capital, leading to situations demanding sacrifices in which workers contribute their labor power without receiving an income that exceeds the survival threshold. Simultaneously, this collective behavior—against the odds of market logics—shows an important level of maturity because it is a pledge of commitment to ensure future development and progress of the self-managed enterprise.

ERTs have mentioned difficulty in entering the market as the main reason for their economic problems. Even after several years of work, ERTs have not been able to achieve a sales level that would allow them to make the optimal use of their production capacities. Most administrative and executive personnel who oversee sales abandon the enterprise amid conflicts, and production workers collectively assume their tasks. In some cases, ERTs resort to a form of subcontracting (trabajar a façon), in which a capitalist external to the company contributes prime materials and supplies and pays a fixed price for the final product. As product marketing is undertaken by this capitalist, the cooperative's profit levels are very low. However, in some very difficult cases, this is an option for allowing operations to begin.

A decisive factor in this situation is the role of the state, which potentially can help prevent these problems from becoming obstacles that can result in the failure of the strategy. However, in addition to a legal system and a legislature that is highly vulnerable to changes in "public opinion," which is not favorable for ERTs, the executive power at its different levels is yet to develop instruments more than those for partial assistance. Some subsidies do reach ERTs, representing support that is important, but not sufficient.

There is still no defined public policy consistent with the goal of consolidating workers' self-management. However, the lack of a legal framework yields two negative outcomes. On the one hand, it leaves too many aspects up to the judges' interpretation and makes decisions subjectively. On the other hand, it places ERTs in illegal or precarious situations. Moreover, no development or training program exists that would provide workers with tools for collective management based on actual situations.

Presently, many workers encounter the same challenges faced by millions of other workers during critical periods in Argentina. Either workers defend their jobs under self-managed forms or they become part of a structurally unemployed sector; most workers are unsuitable for reabsorption in the labor market because of their age, gender, or trades.

COLLECTIVE MANAGEMENT MECHANISMS

What distinguishes enterprises self-managed by their workers from other types of enterprises is their main political and symbolic capital: the collective form of management. This self-management process is dynamic and must be voluntarily maintained by workers. The new collective enterprise emphasizes workers' decision and joint management practices.

Self-management is the most frequently cited characteristic of recuperated enterprises; however, the specific strategies it uses are not reported statistically or presented adequately in case-by-case reports. We observed that in each case the dynamic nature of self-management and how it is practiced depend on the conditions of the original group of workers during the conflict that led to the ERT development, its ability to achieve legal recognition despite many difficulties, the specific strategy it uses to restart production, and the characteristics of the collective of formerly wage workers who now lead it. In particular, studies have reported the effects of the intensity and nature of the initial conflict on the dynamics of self-management (Fajn 2003; Rebón 2004; Ruggeri, Martinez and Trinchero 2005). They have shown a complex relationship among the intensity of the conflict, direct democracy that workers need to collectively establish, and egalitarian mechanisms subsequently used in addressing queries related to decision making and equality in the workday and income levels. The studies have also established a relationship between ERTs that have undergone occupation processes and possible political pressure, such as obtaining expropriation laws or other measures in their favor.

Almost all ERTs have adopted the cooperative form; therefore, they must consider formal legal mechanisms that regulate the cooperatives' operation, basically in terms of decision making, which is essential for any self-management process. Cooperatives recognize two basic management bodies: administrative council and general assembly of members. In traditional cooperatives, the administration council has the management power and calls assemblies only while preparing annual reports and in leadership elections. All other decisions are made by the council, and only an annual assembly is required by the law. However, in recuperated enterprises, the relationship between the bodies completely differs. Our research revealed a situation quite different in the ERTs than in traditional cooperatives in Argentina. In only 8 percent of the surveyed ERTs, decisions were made by the administrative councils. Most ERTs gave their councils various operational functions that, because of their immediacy, form of implementation, or routine nature, were impractical for assemblies to address. Furthermore, 30 percent of ERTs explicitly mentioned that the assemblies are more important than the administrative council; 62 percent responded that their administrative councils are responsible for administrative, commercial, legal, and customer relationship concerns. According to these findings, administrative councils functioned more as the representatives and daily administrators of cooperatives' routine affairs, rather than as an authority equivalent to a board of directors, as sometimes happens in many traditional cooperatives.

The 8 percent where everything is decided by the administrative council coincides with the 8 percent that hold assemblies once a year. National legislation on cooperatives requires these annual assemblies, which should be minuted and are subject to external oversight. However, the reality for most ERTs is closer to the image perception that has become popular and to the management model of conducting more frequent assemblies. An overwhelming 88 percent of respondents mentioned holding periodic assemblies, and surprisingly, among them, 44 percent and 35 percent hold assemblies weekly and monthly, respectively.

Evidently, the assemblies are crucial for ERT workers. Some analysts have attributed the importance of the assembly body to the expansion of direct democracy during the mass mobilizations of 2001 and 2002 (Fajn 2003; Rebón 2004), but highlighting other factors is important. We contend that the following findings facilitate understanding the current development of ERTs. First, the depth of the conflict cumulates to the dissolution of the previous forms of the organization, both in hierarchical management and trade unions. Marked changes occurred in the structures of workers' relations. The leveling of the social status of the members makes an assembly a more logical form for debate and decision making. Second, assemblies are a constant element in working-class organizations. Even bureaucratic union leaderships must use assemblies as a validation mechanism during labor conflicts. An assembly is a working-class tradition, not the product of crisis-related mobilizations or emergence of new social movements. Notably, most ERTs were formed at the same time as those mobilizations, which may have promoted this practice in those years. Last, an assembly is the most effective way of ensuring that members of recuperated enterprises participate in making decisions regarding self-management. It is difficult to consider self-management without assemblies, as confirmed by the present findings.

According to these data, the relationship between the administrative council and general assembly acquires particular ways in ERTs that are more in concordance with their origin in workers' struggle for jobs than with traditional cooperativism. The imprint of these origins and their class background clearly appear in the inverted traditional roles of the council and assembly. While this may be true in different contexts and to different degrees, it tends to impose the influence of the collective of direct democracy over that of representative democracy.

However, reducing self-management to decision-making methods or workers' rights of equal participation does not consider the repercussions of a production process that is different, although in various degrees, from the process of capitalist enterprises. Changes in the organization of work and production process itself in the ERTs must be examined considering the abundant difficulties and challenges involved in the transformation of the logic of economic production. These may be the aspects extensively revealing the depth of changes in workers' self-management.

In ERTs, where attempts are made to democratize the production process itself, it is possible to excel more than recovering jobs and to envision a different conception of work and, therefore, a different logic of production as well as worker–worker and worker–society relationships.[6] Simultaneously, this is the area where changes are the most difficult and which involves more factors.

As discussed, production conditions tend to vary among enterprises, and the needs and shortages that emerge when production is restarted immediately pose the question of how to organize labor. The collective ability to restart the entire production process is a real test of workers' knowledge about the company's operation (both mechanical and nonmechanical dimensions) and their ability to overcome any potential obstacles.

We analyzed the internal workings of ERTs and observed complex and heterogeneous situations. An analysis of these data enables determining certain commonalities and mark a starting point for a more complete analysis of management forms, work organization, and distribution of income among workers. Because the self-management dynamic is very complex, we have not limited our discussions to a single aspect (such as decision making or equal income among workers) or a single aspect of the entire organizational and laboring process.

Simultaneously, the heterogeneous solutions that ERT workers apply to similar problems show that, at least for the time being, there is no single or right course of self-management. Evidently, based on cooperatives' rules and traditional practices, no standard solution can be provided for a problem. Workers' creativity and problem-solving efforts are at times demanding.

SELF-MANAGEMENT AND WORKERS COOPERATIVISM IN THE CAPITALIST CONTEXT

Although the self-management concept is often used in a broad sense (Peixoto de Albuquerque 2003), for all types of social and political relations, we limited it to cases of workers' economic management.

By self-management, we refer to "workers' management of an enterprise unit without capitalists or bosses, conducting their own organization of work under nonhierarchical forms" (Ruggeri 2014). In brief, self-management indicates that workers collectively decide the organization of the labor process, production norms, use of surplus, and company's relationship with the rest of the economy and society. Notably, we are discussing strategies for building new economic and social organizations and supporting grass-root movements intersecting with working-class struggles to improve the living conditions of many workers, while still living in a larger capitalist society.

As mentioned previously, the biggest difficulty with self-management cases, such as ERTs, is the economic aspect: maintaining horizontality and solidarity while also being economically effective. New definitions are required for "effectiveness," "profitability," "growth," and "viability," that are not defined in market terms—to be able to achieve a decent life for workers. ERTs can subsequently practically demonstrate the potentials and limitations, in the current circumstances, of self-management as a social and economic practice. We are specifically referring to the economic conditions of self-management, analyzing concrete processes, not abstractions and idealizations. What are the conditions for and problems in achieving self-management in ERTs? What solutions have been found, if any, and what progress has been made?

The theory and the concept of self-management and its practical implementation can be reconstructed and expanded considering concrete experiences. According to our review of relevant literature, this study is the first to analyze cases of self-managed enterprises, such as ERTs, in Argentina and other Latin American countries (including new cases in European countries such as Greece, Italy, and Spain) and report their dynamics beyond spotty existence at historical junctures.

The following sections provide some key problems and solutions that workers have been reporting in daily practice, that are mostly novel and not yet well formulated in the academic circle.

Political and Socioeconomic Context

Without considering the relationship among production, social and cultural logic, and political context of self-management cases, any analysis of the problems of ERTs would be an abstract, ahistorical intellectual process. In any circumstance of social transformation, understanding its context is critical for understanding its determinations and starting point. We have noted the neoliberal context in which ERTs emerged in Argentina as well as in their defensive and reactive (rather than proactive) characteristics. Workers' objectives were initially limited to responding to reality; however, they have evolved and become more profound because of their conflicts with the capitalist society and market. In the political and socioeconomic contexts, it is possible to understand the enormous difficulties encountered by ERTs and to assess their achievements.

We note that the self-management process cannot be completely avoided from the influence of the capitalist market, in which the companies operate. The challenge is to preserve and develop a particular logic of economic rationality for self-management, even accommodating the market's rules of competition. Thus, although workers feel like being the "owners" of their labor process, they cannot escape from the ultimate aspect of alienated labor: the production of commodities for exchange on a market whose logic and purpose is beyond their control. They alone cannot compensate for the lack of a social order, in which self-managed labor can exist without the hegemonic social relations created by capital. However, the creation of a protective market niche through the "institutional purchase" of universities or churches may alleviate the marketing pressures and increase the exchange price of goods.

A different scenario would be in the context of production relationships where the market is not the main mechanism for the appropriation and distribution of production. The introduction of self-management enterprises in a mixed economy run by a socialist state would place the starting point of this process in a qualitatively different place, which cannot be addressed in this study. A study of the Yugoslavian experience, with all its historical limitations, may provide some basic clues (Jakopovich 2009).

Lack of Capital

ERTs typically begin operating solely with their workforce, and, in some cases, with whatever raw materials remained in stock. Without access to credit, it is very difficult for ERTs to operate, except at the cost of considerable sacrifice, often made by the members and their families. Some government subsidies aim to ease this situation, as briefly highlighted in the document, but the results are unsatisfactory (Ruggeri 2014).

How workers achieved the level of capital or financial resources to begin and maintain production is one of the most decisive and interesting aspects of these case studies. Devising approaches for achieving this level without exploiting workers (as in the gap-filling survival tactics by taking orders for bosses in sub-contraction) and still meeting people's needs in an environmentally sustainable way is, in fact, the main challenge of this form of management.

If self-managed enterprises are not based on capitalist accumulation, they must follow an organizational way of life that controls, or even eliminates, the adoption of any type of capitalist logic justifying the exploitation of workers in the workplace and in the society. Democratic and solidarity-based management strategies, with all of the complexity of its mechanisms for participation, are the foundation for generating a noncapitalist logic for guiding ERTs. In the Argentine context, the absence of that type of a noncapitalist logic at the national economy level complicates the task even more. The practices of equality and collective management in ERTs constantly clash with the needs of the market as well as with the values and ideas that workers have imbibed from the capitalist culture in which they were born and have lived all their lives. Therefore, who deserves to have more? Is equalization of all fair and just? How do worker-inherited beliefs, cultural values, and (transformed) subjectivities influence the daily functioning of ERTs?

Problem of Self-Exploitation and "External Boss"

ERTs' lack of working capital, often combined with difficulties in developing a marketing structure (clearly related to the previous factor) and their small-scale operations, forced a significant number of recuperated enterprises to resort to production for third parties, namely a façon work (Fajn and Rebón 2005; Ruggeri 2009, 2014). In this case, a business or business owner, referred as "the client" by workers, provides the raw materials and guidelines for production and rents, ERTs' workforce, and the use of machinery and facilities. This "external boss" subsequently pays a significantly lower price to the ERTs for their finished product than the price the ERTs would earn if production were their own. In these cases, self-management is reduced to certain parts of the outsourced production process, and, what is worse, the surpluses almost entirely are earned by the indirect boss. We conclude that exploitation, in the form of extraction of the surplus value, is more masked in these cases than in market relations. The boss possesses the working capital and draws the lion share of the value earned from the production, whereas the self-managed collective is reduced to controlling only parts of the means of production and a small share of the labor value.

In a certain sense, this activity leads to "self-exploitation," a concept in academic discourse that is frequently associated with recuperated enterprises (Fajn and Rebón 2005; Heller 2004). In cases of a façon work, it is clear that exploitation is being practiced by a boss disguised as a "client" and that it is accepted by ERT workers considering the lack of a more suitable alternative in the market. In other cases, self-exploitation is associated with long workdays, maintaining features of the work process inherited from the former capitalist enterprise, low income, and other circumstances that are negative for workers, even compared with their private business counterparts. However, these analyses of self-exploitation in ERTs typically equate self-managed workers with wage workers, ignoring all features characterizing ERTs: the factors leading to their creation, state of the business, and collective decision making typical of these enterprises. They also fail to consider other circumstances involving the humanization of the workplace, such as comradeship, solidarity, and collective action. Even more significantly, these analyses do not address the basic question of whether ERTs have the essential element required for exploitation: capitalist accumulation. Here, we report our counter-arguments and different perspectives. The acute challenge is whether ERTs are, or can be, economically viable, which can relatively well satisfy workers' needs.

Relationship to the Market

Self-managed enterprises can collectively address the problems of production, typically by using democratic forms of management, and are guided by the logic of solidarity among workers and with the society. This solidarity-based and egalitarian logic contradicts the logic of maximizing profits and market competition under the rules of capitalism. However, the rhythms or more time-consuming process of internal democracy under workers' management, their ways of addressing problems, and the solidarity exercised among workers and between workers and the society cannot be protected from the encroachment of market competition, thus forcing self-managed enterprises to adapt market rules in at least part of their operations.

The strategy using which these opposing logics are reconciled or adapted to each other is another powerful characteristic of ERTs and one of ERTs' main problems. Despite having to comply with the rhythm and pace of production imposed on them by the operation of the markets into which they are incorporated, recuperated enterprises try not to be subjected to other forms of exploitation that are widespread worldwide.

For example, these enterprises maintain a humane workspace, which is one of the major changes in their working conditions. Moreover, the inclusion of nonproductive and solidarity-based activities in their facilities, particularly when these activities are related to the community—using collective work time, space, and organization for actions not a part of the capitalist rationality—is an unusual form of altering the social functions of the enterprises and increasing workers' awareness about their role in the society.

The purpose of production is often debated among ERT leaders and members. Capitalist businesses seek capital accumulation by using different forms of organizing production to maximize self-interest by exploiting workers. Contrastingly, self-management enterprises must devise a strategy to grow and operate under a rationale that does not seek this accumulation. They must strive to build a business allowing workers to enjoy basic living standards that can provide jobs to others and will be socially integrated.

Labor Process

Self-management implies a different dynamic in relationships among the involved workers, not just in management decisions but also in the production process. This indicates that workers appropriate the labor process, with the possibility and obligation of changing the rules governing the work process.

However, almost none of the ERTs have introduced significant changes in the organization, pace, or characteristics of the labor process (Novaes 2007; Vieta 2009; Ruggeri 2009, 2014). Those types or changes would require not only an injection of capital but also the ability to deconstruct the previously existing process and recreate it under new conditions; the changes may only be a few but significant. These changes are related to workers' personal freedoms and the dignity arising from knowing that they, the workers, really do control the company's activities. These changes are particularly manifested in the characteristics, length, and pace of the working day, which are more humane than those on a typical workday of wage workers.

Notably, these changes in the quality of working life do not make self-managed workers less productive but yield opposite results. In most cases, when such changes are made compatible with a good administration of the pace and organization of work, they lead to increased production efficiency. In brief, labor productivity in ERTs, as in our research, can also be competitive.

Production and Technology Problems

Some of the richest and most complex aspects and dynamics of self-managed enterprises include the following: the relationship among the available technological tools, their role in organizing production, and their importance when determining possibilities for changes in the labor process and the possibility of making socio-technological adaptations (Novaes 2007) and what we, more broadly, refer to as social innovations (Trinchero 2009; Ruggeri

2009). One of the major limitations of ERTs is performing self-managed production within a technological framework designed for capitalist accumulation. Technology is not neutral; its design, use, and even its dismissal are part of how production relationships are structured (Novaes 2007; Dagnino 2009). How a machinery is arranged in a plant and how the chain of production is organized can, and in most cases do, imply the need for an authoritarian management structure to perform the work and devise a new structure to reproduce the previous strategy of organizing production, thus restricting self-management conditions.

Therefore, self-managed production is conditioned by an appropriation of production technologies designed for building social relationships in a people-centered way. Socio-technological adaptation and social innovation allow workers to develop new social relationships aimed to build their enterprises. This approach is highly difficult when not articulated by a state or research institution that has science and technology policies for including self-managed enterprises in a production strategy with noncapitalist objectives.

Effects on Local and Community Development

The effects of Argentine ERTs on local communities are not only economical in maintaining and generating jobs but also have cultural and social dimensions. ERTs have facilitated rebuilding and creating social associations between workplaces and local communities.

Most ERTs acknowledge the enormous social solidarity they sparked in broad segments of the population, a factor critical for their recovery. They have engaged in solidarity-based activities with their local communities to reciprocate the solidarity and support received during the conflicts that led them to become ERTs. These activities, which may appear antieconomic or irrational, include lending space and facilities for cultural activities, schools for lowest-income groups in the community, and donations from and collaboration with social organizations and movements.

These are not strategies for acquiring political legitimation; they are workers' heartfelt gesture of returning the received solidarity. These community actions, which differ from "corporate responsibility," play a fundamental role in creating a caring community.

CONCLUSION

As enterprises that are neither state nor private and are different from traditional cooperatives, ERTs have been driving genuine self-management in practice, despite many challenges and limitations. The Argentine ERT experience may be useful for contemplating the reality and potentials of self-managed labor beyond the abstract proposals of ideologues or jurists and considering the common circumstances of Latin American workers.

This adoption of a diverse form of workers' sharing tasks and lines of work, which were previously performed under the contradiction between labor and capital, does not occur without resistance. Sometimes, we observed the lack of commitment and responsibility of some groups and individuals. Major obstacles, both internal and external, cannot be resolved without conflict, which affects the viability of recuperated enterprises.

The Argentine case reveals that the management of production units by workers is difficult. However, this task has been possible in the past decade and is ongoing. The lessons from these processes, involving not only hardships and sufferings but also joys and celebrations over workers' achievements, should nurture critical thinking that builds practices from square one. The alternative of the political economy is, and should be, guided by the logic of solidarity, thus eliminating the subjugation of the self-destructive nature of capital flight, factory collapse, and endless capital accumulation in global capitalism.

NOTES

1. We have used ERT in this chapter, instead of the English acronym worker-recovered enterprises (WREs).
2. 2016 Report: Workers' recovered enterprises in the beginning of Macri's administration (Programa Facultad Abierta, 2016).
3. Macri's government, elected in November 2015, is reimplementing this policy.
4. Programa Facultad Abierta (Open Faculty Program) is a research and extension program directed by the author since 2002. It is affiliated to the Faculty of Philosophy and Letters of the University of Buenos Aires, Argentina. It specializes in ERT support, assessment, and research. Since 2004, the program has been managing the Documentation Centre of Recovered Enterprises, located in the facilities of the Cooperative Chilavert Graphic Arts, a recovered printing company in Buenos Aires.
5. PYMES (pequeñas y medianas empresas in Spanish).
6. Several researchers have addressed this point (Fajn and Rebón 2005; Ruggeri 2009, 2014; Novaes 2007).

REFERENCES

Antunes, Ricardo. *Los Sentidos del trabajo: Ensayo Sobre la Afirmación y la Negación del Trabajo* [The Senses of Work: Essay on the Affirmation and Denial of Job]. Buenos Aires: Taller de Estudios Laborales/Herramienta, 2005.

Atzeni, Maurizio, and Marcelo Vieta. "Between Class and the Market: Self-Management in Theory and in the Practice of Worker-Recuperated Enterprises in

Argentina." In *The Routledge Companion to Alternative Organization*, edited by Parker Martin, George Edward Cheney, Valérie Fournier and Chris Land, 47–63. London: Routledge, 2014.

Azzellini, Dario. "¡Sí podemos! Empresas recuperadas por sus trabajadores en el hemisferio norte durante la crisis actual." *En Org & Demo*15, no. 1 (Jan/Jun 2014): 9–36. https://DOI:10.36311/1519-0110.2014.v15n1.3980.

Basualdo, Eduardo, M., Azpiazu, D. y otros. *El Proceso de Privatización en Argentina*. Buenos Aires, Página/12, Universidad Nacional de Quilmes, abril 2002.

Bowman, Betsy, and Bob Stone. "La Cooperativizaciòn como Alternativa al Capitalismo Globalizador [Cooperativization as Alternative to Capitalism Globalizing]." In *La Economía de los Trabajadores: Autogestión y Distribución de la Riqueza: Selección de Trabajos Presentados al Primer Encuentro Internacional [The Economics of Workers: Self-Management and Distribution of Wealth. Choosing Jobs Presented by First International]*, edited by Programa Facultad Abierta, 49–95. Buenos Aires: Ediciones de la Cooperativa Chilavert, 2009.

Centro de Documentación de Empresas Recuperadas. *Nuevas Empresas Recuperadas 2020-2013*. Buenos Aires: Ediciones Continente, 2014.

Dagnino, Renato. *Tecnologia Social: Ferramenta para Construir Outra Sociedade [Social Technology: Another Tool for Building Society]*. Campinas: IG/UNICAMP, 2009.

Fajn, Gabriel. *Fábricas y Empresas Recuperadas: Protesta Social, Autogestión y Rupturas de la Subjetividad* [Recovered Factories and Businesses: Social Protest, Self and Subjectivity breaks]. Buenos Aires: Centro Cultural de la Cooperación, 2003.

Fajn, Gabriel, and Julián Rebón. "El Taller ¿Sin Cronómetro? Apuntes Acerca De Las Empresas Recuperadas [El Taller without Timer? Notes about the Recovered Companies]." *Revista Herramienta* 28, 2005. http://www.herramienta.com.ar/revista-herramienta-n-28/el-taller-sin-cronometro-apuntes-acerca-de-las-empresas-recuperadas.

Gómez Solórzano, Marco. Trabajo precario global. En Gómez Solórzano y Pacheco Reyes (comp.) *Trabajo informal, economía solidaria y autogestión. Precariedad laboral y resistencia en la globalización.* Buenos Aires: Ediciones Peña Lillo/ Continente, 2014.

Harispe, Hernán. "Trabajo y Sindicalismo [Work and Unionism]." In *La Economía de los Trabajadores: Autogestión y Distribución de la Riqueza: Selección de Trabajos Presentados al Primer Encuentro Internacional [The Economics of Workers: Self-Management and Distribution of Wealth: Selected Works Presented by First International]*, edited by Programa Facultad Abierta. Buenos Aires: Ediciones de la Cooperativa Chilavert, 2009.

Heller, Pablo. *Fábricas Ocupadas: Argentina 2000-2004 [Occupied Factories: Argentina 2000-2004]*. Buenos Aires: Ediciones Rumbos, 2004.

Jakopovich, Dan. *Sources of the Democratic Deficit in the Yugoslav System of 'Self-Government.* Z Net, 2009. http://www.zcommunications.org/sources-of-the-democratic-deficit-in-the-yugoslav-system-of-self-government-by-dan-jakopovich.

Novaes, Henrique Taham. *O Fetiche da Tecnologia: A Experiência das Fábricas Recuperadas*. São Paulo: Expressão Popular- Fapesp, 2007.

Peixoto de Albuquerque, Paulo. Autogestão [Self-management]. In *A Outra Economía [The Other Economy]*, edited by Antonio David Cattani. 39–46. Porto Alegre: Veraz Editores, 2003.

Petras, James, H. Veltmeyer, J. C. Volnovich, P. V. Hazaki, and R. Castel. *Produciendo Realidad: Las Empresas Comunitarias: Grissinopoli, Río Turbio, Zanón, Brukman y Gral. Mosconi* [Producing Reality: Community Enterprise: Grissinopoli, Río Turbio, Zanon, Brukman and Gral Mosconi]. Topia Editorial. Buenos Aires: Colección Fichas, 2002.

Programa Facultad Abierta, Facultad de Filosofía y Letras. *Informe del Relevamiento de Empresas Recuperadas por sus Trabajadores*. Buenos Aires: Universidad de Buenos Aires, 2003. http://www.recuperadasdoc.com.ar/Informes%20relevamientos/Informe%20Primer%20relevamiento%202003.pdf.

Rebón, Julián. *Desobedeciendo al Desempleo: La Experiencia de las Empresas Recuperadas* [Unemployment Disobeying: The Experience of Recovered Companies]. Buenos Aires: Ediciones Picaso/La Rosa Blindada, 2004.

Ruggeri, Andrés. *Las Empresas Recuperadas: Autogestión Obrera en Argentina y América Latina* [Recuperated Enterprises: Worker Self-Management in Argentina and Latin America]. Buenos Aires: Facultad de Filosofia y Letras, Universidad de Buenos Aires, 2009.

Ruggeri, Andrés. *Las Empresas Recuperadas en la Argentina. 2010. Informe del Tercer Relevamiento de ERT* [The Recovered Companies in Argentina, 2010: Third Report of the Survey of ERT]. Buenos Aires: Ediciones de la Cooperativa Chilavert, 2011.

Ruggeri, Andrés. *Qué son las empresas recuperadas?* Buenos Aires: Continente/Peña Lillo, 2014.

Ruggeri, Andrés, Carlos Martínez, and Héctor Hugo Trinchero. "Las Empresas Recuperadas en la Argentina: Informe del Segundo Relevamiento del Programa Facultad Abierta [The Recovered Companies in Argentina: Report from the Second Survey, Open Faculty Program]." Buenos Aires: Facultad de Filosofía y Letras, Universidad de Buenos Aires, 2005.

Schoijet, Mauricio. *La Crisis Argentina: Los Movimientos Sociales y la Democracia Representative* [Argentina's Crisis: Social Movements and Representative Democracy]. México: SITUAM-Plaza and Valdés Editores, 2006.

Trinchero, Héctor Hugo. "De la Exclusión a la Autogestión: Innovación Social Desde la Experiencia de las Empresas Recuperadas por sus Trabajadores (ERT) [From Exclusion to Self-management: Social Innovation from the Experience of the Companies Managed by their Workers (ERT)]." In *La Economía de los Trabajadores: Autogestión y Distribución de la Riqueza: Selección de Trabajos Presentados al Primer Encuentro Internacional [The Economy of Workers: Self-management and Distribution of Wealth: Selected Papers presented at the First International]*. Buenos Aires: Programa Facultad Abierta. Ediciones de la Cooperativa Chilavert, 2009.

Vieta, Marcelo. "Desafíos e Innovaciones Sociales en las Empresas Recuperadas por sus Trabajadores [Challenges and Social Innovations in Companies Managed by their Workers].” In *Las Empresas Recuperadas: Autogestión Obrera en Argentina y América Latina [Recuperated enterprises: Worker self-management in Argentina and Latin America]*, edited by Andrés Ruggeri. Buenos Aires: Editorial de la Facultad de Filosofía y Letras, 2009.

Williamson, John. “A Short History of the Washington Consensus.” Paper commissioned by Fundación CIDOB for a conference “From the Washington Consensus towards a New Global Governance,” Barcelona, September 24–25, 2004. http://www.iie.com/publications/papers/williamson0904-2.pdf.

Chapter 10

Managing Cooperatives in South Africa: An Economic Perspective

Ravinder Rena

Since the twenty-first century, many significant improvements have been made in science and technology globally. Despite these improvements, more than 350 million persons worldwide are still poor and vulnerable to seen and unforeseen negative socioeconomic factors. Most of these people cannot protect themselves from most of these factors because of having limited or no resources for sustenance. The pooling and collective use of these limited resources utilized may result in noticeable welfare changes. Thus, cooperatives represent a strong, viable, and vibrant economic alternative which have led to the belief that more can be achieved that would benefit poor and vulnerable people who, by operating by themselves, would not achieve any of the outcomes achieved by the cooperatives.

Cooperatives can achieve many economic targets despite operating in a competitive global market. According to Rural Business and Cooperative Development Service (RBCDS 1995), cooperatives can increase their bargaining power when dealing with other competitive organizations. Furthermore, they have economies of scale, can broaden their scope of obtaining products or services otherwise unavailable, provide market opportunities, can obtain goods that are unavailable, and can secure operating loans from financial institutions for the operation and improvement of the organization.

Cooperatives have effectively controlled the economic conditions of many people. In such an increasingly competitive economic world, cooperatives have provided a certain set of exclusive tools enabling the members to achieve more economic goals. With the withdrawal of most governments from regulating the economic activities, cooperatives are being considered as valuable instruments to manage most of these activities. Such activities may include increasing savings among the working population, providing risk management for agricultural or similar cooperatives and community (and even nationally) interactions, and creating more work opportunities.

In South Africa, cooperatives have not yet gained much popularity. They have only been considered for small-scale farmers and small and developing merchants in addition to low-income earners in the country. This is the possible explanation for the many cooperatives for farmers in South Africa.

In South Africa, it is certainly recognized that cooperatives offer an opportunity for impoverished communities to more actively participate in the economy. Cooperatives are believed to be a mechanism through which these communities can organize themselves and draw strength from the group. The dominant hindrance is the unpopularity of the mechanism of cooperatives among many South Africans, how they work, and how they can contribute to economic development. Furthermore, cooperatives are considered a third force in the world, and some large businesses and governments have collapsed because of competing among themselves and not formulating cooperatives.

This chapter examines how cooperative societies can contribute to economic development. Emphasis is placed on the nature and design of such cooperatives, how the economy can benefit from such societies, and how to appropriately formulate and manage these cooperative societies in South Africa. Although cooperative societies have been widely analyzed in the international community, extensive and comprehensive research on this topic has not been conducted in South Africa. Hence, this study aims to fill this gap in the literature.

This chapter is based on a descriptive analysis. The structure of the chapter is as follows: the second section provides a background on cooperative societies (which is considered the theoretical framework); the third section analyzes the national and institutional perspectives of cooperatives; the fourth section highlights and discusses the challenges encountered by cooperatives in the country; and the fifth section provides the summary and conclusions of the chapter.

HISTORICAL BACKGROUND OF COOPERATIVES

The International Cooperative Alliance (ICA 1995) defines a cooperative as an independent association where people gather voluntarily for meeting their conjoint economic, social, and cultural needs and ambitions by a jointly owned and democratically controlled enterprise. The Universal Wireless Communication Consortium (UWCC 2002) explains a cooperative as a business that is voluntarily controlled and owned by its member patrons. These patrons also manage the operations of the cooperative society to their benefit on a nonprofit or cost basis. Laidlaw (1974) defines a cooperative as a business enterprise aimed at providing complete identity of the component factors of ownership, control, and service use, which distinguishes it from other businesses.

The first cooperative was recorded in 1750. This cooperative was established in France, by the Franche–Comté community, among local cheese producers in this community. Apart from this cooperative, there appears to be no consistency regarding the exact origin of cooperative societies, although some arguments state it to be in Europe (Shaffer 1999; Holyoake 1908).

Cooperatives were gradually established in other countries, namely Greece, the United Kingdom, and the United States. Cooperative principles emerged with the development of more cooperatives. The Equitable Pioneers of Rochdale Society (EPRS) was established in 1844. This cooperative constituted twenty-eight members of the community who were unemployed and considered combining their limited resources for the welfare of the group. The EPRS was the first cooperative formed under the cooperative principles, and as such, it was considered the first modern cooperative (Gibson 2005; Abell 2004).

Between 1850 and 1855, the successful EPRS cooperative business established small businesses, such as a flour mill, textile plant, and shoe factory. These businesses rapidly expanded throughout the country and were highly successful. More than 400 British cooperative societies were formulated by 1863 and were modeled after the Rochdale Society. The cooperatives became popular worldwide as they steadily grew into a model for similar cooperatives worldwide. Abell (2004) reported a similar movement in some countries, namely France, Belgium, Germany, Austria, Denmark, Italy, Finland, Sweden, and Norway.

In 1895, the ICA was established as a nongovernmental umbrella organization for facilitating all friendly and economic transactions and interactions among cooperative societies, nationally and internationally. Its main objective is to promote and fortify autonomous cooperative societies worldwide. Moreover, the ICA aims to enhance information exchange among cooperative societies. Such an exchange can be promoted through international conferences, directories, research and reports, and two quarterly publications (ICA News and the Review of International Cooperation). To meet the main objective, the ICA organizes sectorial, regional, and international meetings.

Since its inception, the ICA has provided underlying cooperative principles that have been typically accepted by cooperators worldwide. These cooperators advocated for more cooperative societies, and more people decided to establish them. In 1895, the founding congress had 194 members, and this number has increased exponentially to more than 800 million members from different organizations such as agriculture, energy, fisheries, and tourism (Levin 2002).

The following subsection describes the development of cooperatives in South Africa during both pre-apartheid and post-apartheid periods because it pertains to the agricultural sector. These periods are distinct in terms of the support provided to cooperatives and largely explain why cooperatives were so successful during the apartheid periods and why they are struggling to survive in the post-apartheid period in South Africa.

South African Historical Perspective on Cooperatives: The Apartheid Era

The apartheid regime actively supported cooperatives in the agricultural sector to develop an economically successful class of white commercial farmers who worked at the expense of black farmers. According to Piesse et al. (2005), the Land Acts of 1913 and 1936 was implemented (in addition to other laws and regulations) by the South African government to benefit white commercial farmers and not their black counterparts. The implemented laws drove all the black people to marginalized homelands, away from designated white areas.

In addition to the implementation of the legislative laws, other measures were issued to ensure that cooperative white farmers develop successfully and thrive. For instance, these cooperatives received subsidized loans from the Land and Agricultural Bank (Land Bank) that was established in 1912 as well as received input supplies and markets for the output from the Cooperative Societies Acts of 1922 and 1939 and the Marketing Act of 1937. Under these conditions, agriculture thrived in the cooperatives of white farmers. Traditionally, cooperatives have three main areas of operations: (1) buying and selling agricultural input and equipment, (2) buying and selling agricultural commodities, and (3) providing transport services (Piesse et al. 2005).

The cooperatives of white farmers received loans at subsidized interest rates from the Land Bank. The government used cooperatives to provide assistance, typically as debt consolidation, to farmers who might have encountered any disasters. These agricultural cooperatives subsequently acted as financial intermediaries. Furthermore, the Marketing Act of 1937 (later amended to Act 59 of 1968) enabled using various policy instruments to market agricultural products, such as export monopolies, pool schemes, and single-channel schemes. These instruments (implemented under twenty-three marketing boards) were established under the act. Thus, cooperatives had regional monopoly power because they represented white farmers in the marketing boards (Piesse et al. 2005).

However, the high costs of the price supports, subsidies, and misallocation of resources to support commercial farmers were not sustainable in the long term. Therefore, a series of reforms began to be implemented in the 1980s. These reforms were also a result of political changes. According to Ortmann and King (2007), in the 1990s, subsidies and tax concessions were abolished in addition to the deregulation of agricultural financing and marketing. The role of agricultural cooperatives was reduced; thus, those cooperatives became less dependent on government support.

According to the Department of Trade and Industry (DTI 2012, 31), transformation occurred toward the support of black-owned agricultural cooperatives by the government during the 1970s and 1980s. The registration of cooperatives (even the black-owned cooperatives) was also introduced, and this initiative was promoted by the Cooperative Act of 1981. This support for black-owned agricultural cooperatives was launched as part of the apartheid economic grand plans for the "homelands." However, these plans seemed unreasonable and unfair toward their cooperatives. Therefore, these cooperatives remained weak and underdeveloped, leading to the collapse of other cooperatives.

These major policy reforms had material effects on the role of cooperatives in South Africa. Cooperatives no longer have the privilege of being appointed as agents of various marketing boards, thus losing their regional monopoly powers, and are no longer involved in distributing government subsidies. They still provide short- and medium-term credit to farmers but have to perform this function on a commercial basis because the Land Bank now also has to compete with commercial banks for this business (Ortmann and King 2007).

Cooperatives during the Post-Apartheid Era

In South Africa, the Cooperative Act of 2005 underlined that all cooperative societies must be self-sustaining and self-reliant. These notions were promoted by the political change as well the historical development of cooperatives in South Africa. Furthermore, this act stipulated how cooperatives can contribute to socioeconomic development by creating employment and generating income, particularly for the black population. This can provide a tool to alleviate poverty among the black people of South Africa.

The Cooperative Act of 2005 was the first initiative toward the development and creation of a legal environment supporting black cooperatives. According to Ortmann and King (2007), the DTI devised a policy to develop cooperatives after a participatory process (DTI 2004). This policy focused on emerging cooperatives although it considered and supported cooperatives formulated under the previous (apartheid) government. Furthermore, to enhance the development of cooperatives, the DTI established a Cooperatives Development Unit, which was in charge of reviewing policies and strategies, promoting the cooperative concept, and coordinating donor activities and government institutions.

The government of South Africa is committed to supporting the growth of cooperatives in South Africa, particularly among previously disadvantaged communities. The government has formed the Cooperatives Advisory Board, which acts as a representative of all cooperatives and advises the Ministry of Trade and Industry on all matters related to cooperatives in South Africa (RSA 2005). However, it was clearly stipulated that only genuine cooperatives registered under the ICA principles will receive any support measures, and such assurance has to be provided by any cooperative organization seeking assistance.

It is revealed that cooperatives in the agricultural sector are considerably less intellectually and administratively capable of performing optimally the movement of the Registrar of Cooperatives to the DTI. This movement resulted in a centralized approach for addressing all concerns, even those pertaining to cooperatives. Therefore, such an approach (in addition to the new Cooperative Act) enables an easier process to formulate and run a cooperative.

A high number of large cooperatives have converted to investor-owned firms (IOFs) in South Africa. However, there still exist controversies regarding the agricultural community, whether such a community operates optimally under cooperatives or IOFs (AgriTV 2003). A main concern remains regarding the interests of farmers: whether such interests are best recognized by cooperatives with its own members or IOFs managed and owned by shareholders. Some advantages of IOFs include the ability to attract better quality and improved management, having easier accessibility to various sources of capital, having an entrepreneurial flair, and having the orientation of shareholders' interests and those of customers. On the other hand, cooperatives do not receive a competitive return on their capital; thus, they do not provide higher-quality services than do IOFs. Furthermore, cooperative members always have the risk of conflicts between the members and shareholders. Good service might be provided, but returns on investment are always low and capital growth is poor compared with the returns from IOFs (AgriTV 2003).

Numerous statistics will be examined in future, suggesting that the cooperative regime for emerging cooperatives was a failure under the post-apartheid regime in South Africa. Satgar (2007, 17) reported that two phases characterize the post-apartheid cooperative movement in South Africa. In 1995, the groundwork was conducted. This marked the beginning of the first phase, where the South African National Association was assembled, comprising thirty cooperatives and some cooperative associations. A provisional committee was formed, and all provinces were encouraged to establish cooperative forums. By 1997, more sectorial bodies, such as the Agricultural Cooperative Business Chamber, South African Cooperative Network, National Community Cooperative Union, and Savings and Credit Cooperative League (SACCOL) assembled and formed the National Cooperative of Association of South Africa (NCASA).

The ICA, in collaboration with the new government, supported the formation of cooperative associations. In addition to the support from Canadian International Development Agency, these cooperative associations received significant financial support from the Canadian Cooperative Association. However, the changes in organizations in a top-down manner resulted in the failure to appropriately establish provincial and sectorial structures. With such concerns and poor provincial and sectorial structures, except for SACCOL, many original sectorial cooperatives withdrew. Furthermore, with such concerns, the Canadian Cooperative Association withdrew its funding for cooperatives. Other concerns related to the funding from the Canadian Cooperative Association include a stipulation, in a top-down manner, and some operations of the formed organizations.

The second phase was mainly concerned with the restructuring of all cooperative organizations, including provincial and sectorial organizations, with the assistance of the South African government. National, provincial, and sectorial leaderships were combined and restructured, and the board of cooperatives was expanded. The newly formed organizations retained the strong emphasis on building provincial cooperative associations, and most of them were divided and under-resourced.

By the end of the last phase, the national-restructured organizations attempted and failed to define the roles of cooperatives at the national level in the policy environment. Severe mistakes were made, which led to the collapse of the National Cooperative Association. The failure of the NCASA is not a collapse of the entire cooperative system as a whole, although the organization will be rebuilt and restructured gradually (Satgar 2007, 17). Against this political framework, we examined the management of cooperatives in South Africa. The following section provides a review of some pertinent literature.

NATIONAL AND INSTITUTIONAL PERSPECTIVES

In South Africa, three main assumptions govern the formation of cooperatives. The first assumption concerns the role of the state. This assumption states that the state may contribute to the establishment of cooperatives, and such assistance must always ensure that the cooperatives are autonomous and self-sustaining. Although the state may contribute to such establishment, the

Cooperative Development Policy and Cooperative Act clearly stipulate that the state should not intrude the ownership and control of these institutions. Moreover, the policy framework and legislation create the cooperative sector with the support of many institutions that may assist (either by mandates, resources, or policy) and address the structural imbalances in cooperatives. Briefly, legal reforms and policies for cooperatives are cautious of systemic hindrances that may potentially hinder the development of cooperatives in post-apartheid South Africa. As mentioned previously, although cooperatives might receive support from the state, they should always remain autonomous and self-sustained (Ortmann and King 2007).

The second assumption concerns the maintenance of the authenticity of people-centered cooperatives in South Africa. The new Cooperative Act, in addition to the Cooperative Development Policy implemented by the South African government, retains such authenticity in accordance with the international cooperative movement. Thus, cooperatives cannot be "ideologized" and limited only to the formation of capitalism in South Africa. Cooperatives should first focus on meeting human needs and not be considered as means to foster capital accumulation. This assumption has already been violated in most instances, with many government officials viewing cooperatives as organizations that should confine profit maximization and discipline of competition (Satgar 2007, 8).

The third assumption of cooperatives states the fact that cooperatives may be supported by the state in establishing themselves does not guarantee the development of genuine, independent, and self-sustaining cooperatives. The new South African government system aims to create a dynamic cooperative movement; the set legislation and policies strive to ensure that the different cooperatives can develop and organize themselves from a primary level until becoming a national apex body. It is necessary to have a cooperative movement that can completely represent the voices of its members in any development process for the state or market to not distort the identity of such cooperatives. Fundamental aspects to achieve such cooperatives are the symbolic and material capacities of the national cooperative movement. Hence, the post-apartheid South Africa government aims to empower these cooperatives. Building a cooperative movement is quite challenging, despite assistance from a vibrant civil society. Such challenges are elaborated in the Challenges for Cooperatives section (Satgar 2007, 8).

To comprehensively understand cooperatives and formulate a strong cooperative movement, it is imperative to understand the critical factors influencing the success of cooperatives and those that may weaken them. This section reports observations of previously established cooperatives.

The members of a functioning cooperative should have mutual trust because all cooperatives are based on trust and social cohesion. Moreover, the lack of shared vision, strong social associations, and financial trust weakens the relationships among the members. In environments where management is difficult and choices are tough (for primary productive and service cooperatives), trust among the members is fundamental.

Tension may arise within cooperatives because of the complexity of decision-making in democratic systems. The management of cooperatives in a democratic system, such as in South Africa, typically lacks clarity or consensus concerning the scope of decision-making authority. Cooperative Boards sometimes overstep their mandate and fail to provide information to all members. Moreover, the leading boards may lack corporate governance skills and find it complex to manage even the simplest democratic process.

A complex range of skills is required to appropriately manage an enterprise. Managing joint resources appears complex because more transparency is required by the different members of the cooperatives who would have pooled their resources. The management process becomes more challenging when the organization is working with people with no work or managerial experience. Such skills, particularly financial management, are required because all members must participate in the decision-making process, and failure to recognize such needs may cause tension in a cooperative.

In addition to managerial skills, technical skills are required for cooperatives. With initially having many members who are unemployed, have no prior business experience, and have low skills levels, cooperatives may require hiring (or buying) short-term technical skills to avoid the chances of collapse. Such cooperatives may include agricultural, productive, and housing cooperatives, which require specialized technical knowledge. Such technical skills may not be available within cooperatives themselves, and cooperatives should train their members or employ people with the necessary skills.

Cooperatives should always focus on the interests of their members than on any other individual interests. Some cooperatives focused on greed, self-interests, free riders, and opportunism, which have only led to their collapse. Thus, clear systems and precise policies are required to protect the collective interests more than individual interests. Moreover, champions are not required in any cooperative, and thus the vision and mission of cooperatives should be cautiously practiced. The leaders (board of directors) should always maintain high ethical standards and not be self-ambitious or corrupt in any operations. Failure to maintain these standards may lead to the collapse of the cooperative.

Self-sufficiency should be a culture in all cooperatives. Although different cooperatives may require a certain level of assistance from the government during certain stages of their development, these cooperatives should consider long-term self-sufficiency. For instance, although a social housing cooperative may require high levels of subsidy during the construction stages, post construction should be self-sufficient.

Cooperatives should never be considered a source of money; they lack actual commitment to self-sufficiency. Such perverse incentives should be avoided. Start-up funding should be carefully managed, and the screening process should be carefully reviewed to avoid any abuse from opportunists. The Cooperative Incentive Grant is an example that should be carefully monitored to avoid such an abuse.

All cooperatives must be well diversified with the members having diverse skills, income, and backgrounds to enhance the sharing of greater knowledge and resources. Cooperatives should also have a broad network of support, including legal, managerial, technical, financial, and administrative networks because it is more likely to enhance the success of cooperatives.

A cooperative society must clearly state the number of members it requires. Some cooperatives have had concerns of excessive labor when they only had a few opportunities for the relative markets being targeted; such cases have occurred in primary cooperatives (work or agricultural cooperatives). This mismatch may have emerged from social goals or conditions laid by donors and external agencies. Regarding the same concern of clarity, social and economic rationales of cooperatives must be clear. However, it is quite complex and challenging to viably run a cooperative; all members on board should have a shared understanding. Nonetheless, economic and social rationales must be clear. A clear business plan for cooperatives should be presented and evaluated for economic viability. The plan should distinctly indicate the required inputs, goods, or services provided for the production process and target market. A plan that fails to clearly present these aspects may not be approved.

Some cooperatives fail to access appropriate support to smoothen their functioning. Some cooperatives barely survive with limited or no access to skills, services, supplies, finance, information, credits, and markets. Most of these cooperatives require multidimensional assistance to develop gradually. Such incentives can be based on compliance with cooperative principles or turnover and profit terms (Boulle and Harrison 2007, 12).

Cooperatives in South Africa

South Africa is estimated to have 43,062 cooperatives. The geographical distribution of these cooperatives (as of March 31, 2009) shows that KwaZulu-Natal (KZN), Gauteng, Eastern Cape, and Limpopo provinces have more registered cooperatives (26 percent, 20 percent, 16 percent, and 12 percent, respectively) than do other provinces. Other provinces (Mpumalanga, North West, Western Cape, Free State, and Northern Cape) have registered few cooperatives, with Mpumalanga having the most of cooperatives (8 percent) and Northern Cape having the least (2 percent) cooperatives in 2009. Such a distribution is possibly because of different support measures available in each province as well as the availability of opportunities to establish cooperatives in the different provinces, among other reasons. Cooperatives in KZN appear to be outstanding in terms of best practice and new cooperative establishments within the country. Possible lessons for achieving such success can be acquired and adopted in other provinces in the country (DTI 2012, 35).

Though the rate of cooperative registration has been high; however, the rate of survival is very low. High rates of collapse are estimated among cooperatives. Interventions within sectors of the cooperatives are highly imperative. Empirical evidence indicates high collapse rates within sectors, which appear to be mostly associated with the lack of strong support networks among cooperatives. Furthermore, these support systems could not adequately cover the entire value chain of some cooperatives. Disorganized and poor cooperative movements have caused the collapse of many cooperatives. It was revealed that trading (98.2 percent), multipurpose and transport (94 percent), and service (91.5 percent) sectors have the highest collapse rates (DTI 2012, 40–41).

CHALLENGES FOR COOPERATIVES

Challenges for Cooperative Societies in South Africa

Presently, the state of cooperatives appears to be in flux worldwide. According to Taimni (1997), "cooperatives encounter one or more of the following crises: ideology, capital, credibility, and management in almost all parts of the world."

Cooperatives in South Africa have continued to emerge despite the collapse of the National Cooperative Association. These new cooperatives (in addition to the existing ones) encounter the setback of having to establish and build themselves. Self-establishment is a crucial part of primary, secondary, or sectorial cooperatives; such cooperatives require appreciation as they have an ethical basis rooted in the idea of self and collective empowerment. Such a tradition of learning from experiences deserves to be passed on to other generations.

The seven international principles of cooperatives capture the core of ethical practices that define the identity of a cooperative. These principles must always be emphasized concretely in all activities and struggles of the cooperative. For instance, democratic member control (the second principle of ICA) indicates leadership. All members of cooperatives (both women and men) should account for the decisions they take as the members.

Therefore, accountability should be entrenched within the leadership of the cooperative movement. Some cooperatives have failed to comply with this principle.

The successful establishment of any cooperative is anchored on financial stability, and such finance should also come from within the cooperative. The failure of cooperative members to pay their membership fee markedly weakens the cooperative and leads to it inevitable collapse. A strong financial foundation ensures the survival and independence of the cooperative.

Intragovernmental coordination is a factor influencing the development of cooperatives in South Africa. Although various government-linked institutions support cooperative development, their roles and contribution should be institutionalized. The national Cooperative Advisory Board is established by the new Cooperative Act (2005) to state policy recommendations and other strategic and important concerns related to the development of cooperatives. Therefore, this structure should have representatives from all government-linked institutions that promote the development of cooperatives to increase their awareness of the principles of cooperatives and align them with their own objectives.

Another challenge for cooperatives is to avoid the duality of "black cooperatives" and "white cooperatives." "Broad-Based Black Economic Empowerment (BBBEE) reportedly fosters a racial divide among cooperatives." The government must focus on eliminating the notion of any racial divisions and different support systems to different racial cooperatives. Most supporting organizations should overcome such barriers and foster cooperation between black and white cooperatives (Satgar 2007).

The historically white cooperatives and developing black cooperatives are weakly associated. BBBEE has failed in its approach to foster cooperation and solidarity between these cooperatives. Some of its approaches actually reintroduce racial divisions. However, efforts are being made to eliminate these divisions by ensuring that all decisions are based on the cooperative principles; such principles must be encouraged. Briefly, all approaches by BBBEE should not undermine cooperatives developed in post-apartheid South Africa (Satgar 2007).

Another challenge for cooperatives is the concern of tax reforms among cooperatives. Formally (before 1970), agricultural, trading, and farming cooperatives had important tax benefits and exemptions to promote their growth. Such benefits incentivized capital formation and promoted improved financial benefits for the members. However, these benefits were withdrawn after 1977. Cooperatives were taxed at the company rate, whereas only a few agricultural cooperatives obtained a concession through the Income Tax Act. New tax dispensation for tax exemptions, prohibition, and limits for cooperatives has been implemented in South Africa to protect both developing and established cooperatives. Such dispensations facilitate dealing with pressures encountered by cooperatives in an open economy.

The measurement of the social and economic influences of cooperatives is another challenge. Statistics for cooperatives in South Africa do not measure the influence of the societies; therefore, the Registrar of Cooperatives presents a biannual "State of the Cooperative Sector Report," which explains the performance of cooperatives. This report contains information on surpluses, turnovers, assets, growth trends, membership densities, and the contribution of cooperatives to employment creation. Because "concern for the community" is an ICA principle, it is fundamental for the report to state the extent to which cooperatives actively contribute to community development.

Developing new markets is challenging for cooperative development in post-apartheid South Africa. Community demand markets have acted as a major market for cooperative development in South Africa. However, such markets could not sustain all products of the developing cooperatives. Hence, other channels of operations are required to promote these products (Satgar 2007).

Cheney (1995) identified other major challenges for cooperative development, including wage solidarity, competition and expansion, cultural transformation, programs to increase productivity and participation, and centralization and reorganization. Thus, a cooperative should be a business organization capable of social movement to maintain its special characteristics. These attributes make cooperatives difficult to manage as they are a business enterprise with a human dimension. Imitating other business to increase efficiency and pursuing a social purpose make cooperatives different (Laidlaw 1974).

The provision of educating and training all cooperative members (officers and the general members too) is challenging for many developing cooperatives. Some members require training from start to finish, whereas some others only require retraining. A cooperative having members with a low education level has the risk of losing its crucial human and personal characteristics that distinguishes it as a cooperative. Education is crucial for any cooperative. Furthermore, the officers, directors, members of staff, all members (if educated) are easier to lead although difficult to drive; they might also be impossible to enslave, but they are easy to govern.

Cooperatives encounter challenges in deciding the business that is most suitable for enterprise development. These cooperatives always have difficulty deciding the type of business activity that is suitable for the public, private, or cooperative sector.

Adaption is a challenge for cooperatives. Total independence and self-sufficiency are not easily achieved by a developing cooperative. Cooperatives are highly dependent and interdependent on other support units, mainly the state-provided support systems. Correspondingly, public enterprises and the state also largely depend on private enterprises or cooperatives. Thus, cooperatives cannot be considered an exclusive economic system. They are rather considered a part of any economy. They operate cooperatively with other businesses. Cooperatives should subsequently adapt to the complex environment.

Some sectors of cooperatives could not work in close collaboration, leading to their collapse. Some cooperatives lack strict discipline within the society because of their voluntary and democratic nature. The management team of cooperatives is often reluctant to act according to any action against even the societies' bylaws. Such consequences have many other consequences, particularly in emerging economies such as South Africa. This internal hindrance that it creates itself when they prefer acting by common consent and persuasion has weakened the cooperative society.

Considering the different needs of the members, owners, customers, and patrons, the cooperative board of directors encounters a tough decision-making process. They should make decisions after considering all these groups of people. The managers, board of directors, and members of cooperatives must understand the business and cooperative structure. Business earnings of cooperatives must be adequately high to pay patronage, systematically rotate the investment of members, and consider customers by offering them goods and services at reasonable prices or fair market values.

When rebuilding the cooperative movement in South Africa, the sectorial bodies in all provinces should be the backbone. Taimni (1997) suggested that cooperatives should completely use all resources and maximize productivity at all times; place more emphasis on internal capital formation and accumulation; ensure highest efficiency while providing services to members; more favorably design the structures by enhancing the management capabilities and competencies; improve and sustain integrated vertical structures; perform value-added operations to improve the socioeconomic conditions of the members; and emphasize honesty, care, openness, and concern for communities and environments.

To enhance the success of cooperatives in South Africa, a balance should be maintained between national and international levels and between social and economic purposes, and a favorable public image should be maintained. On ensuring these factors, the efficiency of cooperatives may increase and their development may improve in a developing community.

SUMMARY AND CONCLUSIONS

A cooperative society provides mutual benefits to its members. This unique form of business, although beneficial to all members, requires considerable commitment, energy, time, and technical resources for its appropriate establishment. For the successful operation of cooperatives, mutual needs of the members must be fundamentally recognized. The business must be developed by potential members by suggesting new ideas and business plans. These members must also nominate knowledgeable directors who will employ a competent manager. Furthermore, such members must fund the cooperative business.

To increase their efficiency and maximize effectiveness, cooperatives must be a distinct sector within the national economy of any country. They are the intermediate body between the public and private sectors, partly private and public enterprises. Thus, they are an economic sector in their own right and should not be limited by either laws or regulations of the public or private sector.

Cooperatives must contribute to reducing poverty and unemployment in South Africa by acting as the third force. They will be a countervailing and alternative power supporting big business development in South Africa and contribute to social protection in the country. Therefore, cooperatives are considered an economic enterprise and a social organization. Accordingly, cooperatives must thus significantly contribute to addressing some serious human problems.

An established cooperative with legislative support, delivery institutions, and support programs rapidly develops in these environments and facilitates significant and positive contributions to employment creation, economic and human resource development, and economic ownership by local communities. Such cooperatives have been successful in countries such as Italy, Kenya, Canada, India, Spain, and Bangladesh (Abell 2004).

The instruments of support, such as legislative support, may be the factors contributing to the success of these cooperatives based on the Western model. These models date to 1904, when cooperatives were established in India. The Cooperative Societies Act of 1904 enabled socioeconomic revolutions mostly in underdeveloped rural areas. These reforms mainly benefited subsistence farmers during crises. In 1912, legislative support was provided to assist the development of these cooperatives, and they were considered an integral part of the development that would aid poverty alleviation and economic growth of the country. The Multi-State Cooperative Societies Act of 2002 is the new act governing the movement of cooperatives (DTI 2012, 25).

The South African government should implement a legislative support, policy support, and institutional framework to provide assistance for cooperative development. These measures should assist disadvantaged people, either through financial support or the creation of employment opportunities, and promote the formalization of the informal economy. The government can mainly contribute to cooperatives, in addition to providing financial support for primary establishment, by facilitating access to support services, predominantly support to cooperative human resource development.

REFERENCES

Abell, Peter. *Cooperative Movement.* Encyclopaedia Encarta 2004 Edition, 2004.

AgriTV. *Are Large Agricultural Co-operatives a Dying Species,* 2003? Accessed on January 15, 2014. http://www.agritv.co.za/co_vs_corp.html.

Boulle, J., and K. Harrison. *Western Cape Cooperative Strategy.* Centurion, South Africa: Development Bank of South Africa, 2007.

Cheney, George. "Democracy in the Workplace: Theory and Practice from the Perspective of Communication." *Journal of Applied Communication Research* 23, no.3 (1995): 167–200.

Cropp, Robert, and Gene Ingalsbe. "Structure and Scope of Agricultural Cooperatives." In *Cooperatives in Agriculture*, edited by Cobia David, 35–67. New Jersey, USA: Prentice-Hall Inc., 1989.

Department of Trade and Industry. *A Co-operative Development Policy for South Africa.* Pretoria, South Africa: Department of Trade and Industry, 2004.

Department of Trade and Industry. *Co-operative Enterprise Development Strategy of South Africa.* Pretoria, South Africa: Department of Trade and Industry, 2006.

Department of Trade and Industry. *The DTI Integrated Strategy on the Development and Promotion of Cooperatives: Promoting an Integrated Co-operative Sector in South Africa (2012-2022) Pretoria.* Accessed on January 29, 2014. DTI available at http://www.dti.gov.za/economic_empowerment/docs/coops/legis_policy/coop-strategy.pdf.

Gertler, Michael. *Rural Co-operatives and Sustainable Development.* Saskatoon: Centre for the Study of Cooperatives, University of Saskatchewan, 2001.

Gibson, Ryan. *The Role of Cooperatives in Community Economic Development.* RDI Working Paper No. 2005-3, 2005.

Grove, Frank. *What Is Cooperation? The Philosophy of Cooperation and It's Relationship to Cooperative Structure and Operations.* Madison: UWCC Occasional Paper No. 6, 1985.

Holyoake, George, J. *The History of Co-operation.* London: T. F. Unwin, 1908.

Hoyt, Ann. *And Then There Were Seven: Cooperative Principles.* Madison: University of Wisconsin Center for Cooperatives, 1996. Accessed on January 28, 2014. www.uwcc.com.

International Co-operative Alliance. *Welcome to the International Cooperative Alliance*, 2003. Accessed on January 28, 2014. www.coop.org.

Laidlaw, Alex. *The Cooperative Sector.* Columbia: University of Missouri, 1974.

Circom, Yair, L. *How Non-profit and Economy can Co-exist: A Cooperative Perspective.* Ireland: International Cooperative Research Institute, 2005.

Levin, Michael. *The Promotion of Cooperatives.* ILO Cooperative Branch, 2002. www.ica.coop/europe/ra2002/speech.

Ortmann, Gerald, and Robert King. "Agricultural Cooperatives II: Can They Facilitate Access of Small-scale Farmers in South Africa to Input and Product Markets?" *Agrekon* 46, no. 2 (2007): 219–244.

Philip, Kate. *Co-operatives in South Africa: Their Role in Job Creation and Poverty Reduction.* South Africa Foundation (SAF), 2003. Accessed on January 29, 2014. http://www.sarpn.org.za/documents/d0000786/index.php.

Piesse, Jenifer, Tobias Doyer, Colin Thirtle, and Nick Vink. "The Changing Role of Grain Cooperatives in the Transition to Competitive Markets in South Africa." *Journal of Comparative Economics* 33, no. 1 (2005): 197–218. https://doi.org/10.1016/j.jce.2004.10.002.

RBCDS. *What Are Cooperatives?* Washington: Cooperative Information Report, 1995.

RSA (Republic of South Africa). *Co-operatives Act 14 of 2005.* Government Gazette, August 18, 2005. Cape Town, South Africa: Government Gazette, 2005.

Satgar, Vishwas. *The State of the South African Cooperative Sector.* Cooperative and Policy Alternative Centre (COPAC), 2007. Accessed on January 30, 2014. http://www.copac.org.za/files/State%20of%20Coop%20Sector.pdf.

Schaars, Marvin. *Cooperatives: Principles and Practice.* Madison: University of Wisconsin Centre for Cooperative, 1978.

Shaffer, Jack. *Historical Dictionary of the Cooperative Movement.* London UK: The Scarecrow Press, 1999.

Taimni, Krishnan. *Cooperatives in the New Environments: A study of the Role of the Registrar of Cooperative Societies in Selected Countries in Asia.* Rome: FAOUN, 1997.

USDA (United States Department of Agriculture). *Agricultural Statistics 2004.* Washington, DC: National Agricultural Statistics Service, USDA, 2004.

UWCC. *Cooperatives.* Madison: University of Wisconsin Centre for Cooperative, 2002. Accessed on January 12, 2014. www.uwcc.com.

Chapter 11

Strengthening the Role and Further Development of Cooperatives in the Republic of Armenia

Suren Movsisyan

The modern cooperative era is reported to have emerged in 1844 in Rochdale, England (International Cooperative Alliance). "A cooperative is an autonomous association of persons united voluntarily to meet their common economic, social, and cultural needs and aspirations through a jointly owned and democratically controlled enterprise" (ICA Statement on Cooperative Identity 1996).

The agricultural sector constitutes nearly 20 percent of Armenia's gross domestic product (GDP; National Statistical Service of Armenia 2015) and is one of the main pillars of the country's economy. During the Soviet period in Armenia, the production norms and volumes were established by government planning agencies and implemented by collective enterprises, namely sovkhozes and kolkhozes. Following the collapse of the Soviet Union in 1991 and the privatization of land and main means of production, all farmers were given land of an average of 1.4 hectares. However, the lack of necessary bargaining power resulted in weak relationships with the processors and other actors in the value chain (Vardanyan 2011).

After the cooperative movement started emerging in Armenia from 1993, the United Methodist Committee on Relief (UMCOR) under its community association project began providing assistance to seven rural communities for the establishment of cooperatives in Ararat and Vayots Dzor Marzes (UMCOR 1994–2007).

Before 1999, 297 consumer cooperatives were already registered in Armenia (Urutyan 2012) and in the same year, the marketing assistance program of the United States Department of Agriculture formed the "Lejan Milk Producers Association" consumer cooperative in the village of Lejan, Lori Marz. Following these developments, several individual farmers began establishing their own cooperative enterprises. As of January 1, 2013, this number reached 307, including 127 in the agricultural sector.

PROBLEM STATEMENT

Previously in Armenia, no feasibility study has been conducted for establishing a cooperative and determining the stated relative skepticism regarding the production efficiency of the agricultural cooperative model. Therefore, this chapter examines the most common research concerns and initiates an academic approach to address the food security problem and unsustainable farming practices in the country.

Research Question

The primary research question of the study is as follows: Is building trust among farmers a key for strengthening the role and further development of cooperatives in the Republic of Armenia?

Purpose of the Study

The study analyzes the various factors resulting in the farmers' resistance to establishing cooperatives. In addition, it provides a more favorable solution for improving the welfare of rural households and facilitating the development of the agricultural sector in the Republic of Armenia.

Significance of the Study

The essence of this study is to look through the psychological, economic, legal, and behavioral aspects of the problems in establishing agricultural cooperatives in the Republic of Armenia.

First, this enhances the awareness of cooperatives in the country and can be a valuable source of information for the Ministry of Agriculture in Armenia and the rural communities as well. Second, the study facilitates educating people living in villages near the nation's borders, which does not have access to much information. Finally, this is beneficial for students and researchers who are interested in the agricultural sector for study and/or work purposes.

Assumptions

The following assumptions have been proposed considering the background information and views on the expansion of cooperatives for the development of agriculture in the Republic of Armenia.

- The rural population lacks awareness about cooperatives.
- Trainings on cooperatives have low demand in Armenia because potential clients are unaware about the socioeconomic benefits of establishing cooperatives.
- There is considerable and unexplored market potential, and cooperative development is still in its inception stages.

Limitations

The research identified numerous limitations and shortcomings. The fundamental limitation of the study is its exploratory methodology. However, because the characteristics of and problems in introducing agricultural cooperatives are similar all across Armenia, the research efficiently represents the general situation in the entire country. Another bias during the interviewing process is the possibility of influencing the respondents when they do not understand the question.

Delimitations

Because of time and financial constraints, the scope of the interviews conducted during the research was only limited to the Yervandashat agricultural consumer cooperative. A wider sampling would have had positive effects on the general analysis of the situation. The focus group included only one of the ten regions and villages in that region that were randomly selected. This form of sampling is biased and might not be representative of the rest of Armenia.

The main disadvantage of qualitative research methods is that the findings cannot be generalized to wider populations with the same degree of certainty suggested by quantitative analyses. However, this is only a disadvantage if the research question also requires statistical data. Adopting a mixed-method approach can enable overcoming this problem. Thus, the qualitative interviews conducted in the study framework aimed to comprehend people's understanding and behavior regarding the agricultural cooperatives and not provide a quantitative statistical review. However, it is very difficult to conduct a nationwide research. The empirical characteristic of this study in addition to the qualitative data required is a favorable combination and justifies the applied research method.

VARIABLES AND QUESTIONNAIRE ITEMS

The dependent variable is the members' views of the agricultural cooperative form in Armenia. The following question covers this attitudinal variable: "I think that joint farming in an agricultural cooperative is an efficient way for implementing agricultural production in Armenia." Answers to this question were measured on a 6-point Likert scale, with 1 representing "agree" and 6 representing "disagree."

The independent variables are based on the marital status (dummy variable = 1 if the respondent is married and 0 otherwise [base category]), the socio-economic factors of age and household size, and four social capital factors: involvement, trust, satisfaction, and loyalty. One or more questions in the questionnaire covered each of these capital factors. The study is based on the following social capital dimensions, questions, and variables:

Involvement

The members' involvement is represented by explicit actions concerning the agricultural cooperatives' operations and welfare. The members have high willingness to be informed about the financial status, participate in discussions, and be prepared to govern the firm. The following questions assess the social capital factor of involvement in cooperatives:

- "To which extent do you read the balance sheet and profit and loss account of the annual report?" A 6-point Likert scale was used: very carefully (1) to not at all (6); variable: "dreadbal."
- "Do you always participate in the general assembly meetings?" A 6-point Likert scale was used: running from every time (1) to never (6); variable: "dpart."
- "Would you be willing to become a member of the leadership?" The alternatives were yes (1) or no (2); variable: "dlead."

Trust

Trust is based on both individual members' relationship with other members and their views of the leadership. The following questions assess the social capital factor of trust in cooperatives:

- "To which extent is it important for you to have friends and relatives close to you within the cooperative (as colleagues)?" A 6-point Likert scale was used: very important (1) to not important at all (6); variable: "clfriend."
- "To which extent does the leadership care about the opinions of the members?" A 6-point Likert scale was used: very much (1) to not at all (6); variable: "dleadcare."

Satisfaction

Because the members' degree of satisfaction with the cooperative is a relative concept, it has been compared with the conditions before the establishment of the cooperative as well as the attractiveness of private farming.

- "Compared with the situation of collective/state farms, namely during the Soviet Union period, do you think that you—as an ordinary member—have more influence in decision making now?" The answer alternatives were yes (1) or no (2); variable: "dmeminfl."
- "Have you, after you became a member of the production cooperative, considered the option of becoming a family farmer?" The answer alternatives were yes (1) or no (2); variable: "farmlater."

Loyalty

Loyalty is considered an expression of both individual's propensity to act and the individual's actual behavior. Because the possibility of the members complaining about disloyalty is less, loyalty is measured in terms of opinions.

"To which extent do the members have positive opinions about the way the cooperative is run?" A 6-point Likert scale was used: very often (1) to never (6); variable: "dopinion."

Socioeconomic Structure of the Sample

The average age (forty-seven years) was relatively high. Younger people seemed to change their professions or move to other regions or countries

Table 11.1 Socioeconomic Structure of the Sample (N = 36)*

Attribute	*Mean*	*SD*
Age (years; respage)	46.47	8.77
Gender (binary; 1 = male, 2 = female) (gender)	1	0
Household head (binary; 1 = yes, 2= no) (hhead)	1	0
Household size (number of persons) (hhpsize)	3.22	0.64
Education (1 = primary education; 2 = secondary education; 3 = university) (education)	1.08	0.65
Agricultural education (1 = on the job only; 2 = Armenian National Agrarian University) (agriceduc)	1.08	0.28
Years of work experience (workexpy)	18.47	6.02

Note: SD = Standard Deviation
Source: STATA analysis based on the interview with Yervandashat cooperative, April 2014.

as only less than 6 percent of the respondents were younger than thirty-five years. The sample only comprised men and they were all household heads of households comprising three or four persons.

The educational level was relatively low. The rate of primary education was high, whereas that of formal agricultural education was rather low because most respondents received on-the-job agricultural education. Only 8 percent of the respondents had an agricultural university degree.

RESULTS

Descriptive Findings

Table 11.2 Mean Value of the Social Capital Variables (N = 36)

Social Capital Dimension/ Social Capital Variable	*Mean*	*SD*
Involvement		
- reading annual reports (very often = 1, never = 6)	4.36	0.90
- attending meetings (very often = 1, never = 6)	1.72	0.85
- willingness to become leader (yes = 1, no = 2)	2	0
Trust		
- close friends in cooperatives (very important = 1, not at all = 6)	3.89	1.65
- caring leadership (very much = 1,; not at all = 6)	1.83	0.70
Satisfaction		
- more influence in decision making than in the Soviet period (yes = 1, no = 2)	1.83	0.38
- considered private farming after transformation (yes = 1, no = 2)	2	0
Loyalty		
- positive opinion about cooperatives (very often = 1, never = 6)	1.83	0.81

Note: SD = Standard Deviation.
Source: STATA analysis based on the interview with Yervandashat cooperative, April 2014.

Involvement

The members' involvement in the cooperative was quite low. Relatively few members read the cooperative's annual reports; conversely, the attendance to annual meetings was considerably high. No respondent was willing and prepared to stand for board elections and accept leadership responsibilities.

Trust

It is important for the respondents to work in collaboration with relatives and friends at the cooperative. A strong positive feeling existed about the cooperative leadership is being concerned about the opinions of the members.

Satisfaction

Most members were not satisfied with the influence of their decisions in the cooperative. Compared with the work at the predecessor farm during the Soviet period, the ordinary members stated that they did not have more influence in decision making presently; therefore, not much has changed. Meanwhile, none of them considered the option of becoming private farmers after the transformation into an agricultural cooperative in the recent years.

Loyalty

Most members had positive opinions about their cooperatives.

RESEARCH METHODOLOGY

This study was based on both primary and secondary data. The primary research was conducted in Yervandashat, Armavir region.[1] Reliable and valid questionnaires[2] were developed to facilitate the collection of qualitative and quantitative data, enabling the clear examination of the current situation of the agricultural sector in the Armavir region of the Republic of Armenia. The primary data were collected using the following methods: focus group (including seven cooperative members) and personal interviews (with the chairperson of the cooperative and members), whereas the secondary data were data that were already collected and analyzed by other researchers from reliable internet sources and reports.

ECONOMETRIC ANALYSIS

The dependent variable of the econometric analysis is obtained from responses to the survey question "I think that joint farming in an agricultural cooperative is an efficient way for implementing agricultural production in Armenia." Answers to this question were measured on a 6-point

Likert scale, with 1 representing "agree" 6 representing "disagree." The dependent variable measures the stated relative skepticism regarding the production efficiency of the cooperative model among the respondents. The underlying, yet unobservable, continuous distribution of this relative skepticism is based on the 6-point Likert scale. Therefore, the analysis method had to account for the value of the dependent variable remaining unobserved but was approximated through the observed categorical responses on the scale.

The ordered logit model was used; the explanatory variables were based on previously discussed measures of social capital. The logit model in addition to the ordered probit models is an established estimation approach if the dependent variable y is discrete, while the order of discrete categories has a meaningful interpretation, such as "increasing order of answers," or in the present case, Likert scores 1–6 implying subsequently higher levels of skepticism regarding the degree up to which the cooperative may efficiently implement agricultural production in Armenia.

STATA Ordered Logit Regression Output

.* Ordered Logit Regression

.ologit agriced respage hhpsize married dreadbal dlead clfriend dleadcare dmeminfl farmlater

note: married dropped because of collinearity
note: dlead dropped because of collinearity
note: farmlater dropped because of collinearity
Iteration 0: log likelihood = −52.452448
Iteration 1: log likelihood = −46.43288
Iteration 2: log likelihood = −45.952334
Iteration 3: log likelihood = −45.950222
Iteration 4: log likelihood = −45.950221

Ordered logistic regression Number of obs = 36
LR chi2(6) = 13.00

Prob> chi2 = 0.0430
Log likelihood = −45.950221 Pseudo R2 = 0.1240

TEXT BOX 11.1

agriced		Coef.	Std. Err.	z	P>|z|	[95% Conf. Interval]	
respage		0.0317559	0.0512182	0.62	0.535	−0.06863	0.1321418
hhpsize		0.5163523	0.5212019	0.99	0.322	−0.5051848	1.537889
dreadbal		0.5656853	0.4241157	1.33	0.182	−0.2655663	1.396937
clfriend		0.2765275	0.268191	1.03	0.303	−0.2491171	0.8021722
dleadcare		−0.6711435	0.5214689	−1.29	0.198	−1.693204	0.3509168
dmeminfl		−2.246228	0.9358999	−2.40	0.016	−4.080558	−0.4118977
_cut1		−2.097579	4.525838	−10.96806	6.7729		
_cut2		−.3359566	4.552235	−9.258174	8.58626		
_cut3		1.647881	4.552723	−7.275292	10.57105		
_cut4		3.382652	4.562758	−5.560189	12.32549		

. listcoef, help

ologit (N=36): Factor Change in Odds

Odds of: >m vs <=m

TEXT BOX 11.2

agriced		b	z	P>|z|	e^b	e^bStdX	SDofX
respage		0.03176	0.620	0.535	1.0323	1.3209	8.7651
hhpsize		0.51635	0.991	0.322	1.6759	1.3898	0.6375
dreadbal		0.56569	1.334	0.182	1.7607	1.6632	0.8993
clfriend		0.27653	1.031	0.303	1.3185	1.5792	1.6523
dleadcare|	−0.67114	−1.287	0.198	0.5111	0.6264	0.6969
dmeminfl		−2.24623	−2.400	0.016	0.1058	0.4278	0.3780

b = raw coefficient
z = z-score for test of b=0
P>|z| = p-value for z-test
e^b = exp(b) = factor change in odds for unit increase in X
e^bStdX = exp(b*SD of X) = change in odds for SD increase in X

SDofX = standard deviation of X

. listcoef, percent help

ologit (N=36): Percentage Change in Odds

Odds of: >m vs <=m

TEXT BOX 11.3

agriced |	b	z	P>|z|	%	%StdX	SDofX
respage |	0.03176	0.620	0.535	3.2	32.1	8.7651
hhpsize |	0.51635	0.991	0.322	67.6	39.0	0.6375
dreadbal |	0.56569	1.334	0.182	76.1	66.3	0.8993
clfriend |	0.27653	1.031	0.303	31.9	57.9	1.6523
dleadcare |	−0.67114	−1.287	0.198	−48.9	−37.4	0.6969
dmeminfl |	−2.24623	−2.400	0.016	−89.4	−57.2	0.3780

b = raw coefficient
z = z-score for test of b=0
P>|z| = p-value for z-test
% = percent change in odds for unit increase in X
%StdX = percent change in odds for SD increase in X
SDofX = standard deviation of X

Logit Coefficients

. * Ordered Logit Regression

. ologit agriced respage hhpsize married dreadbal dlead clfriend dleadcare dmeminfl farmlater

note: married dropped because of collinearity
note: dlead dropped because of collinearity
note: farmlater dropped because of collinearity
Iteration 0: log likelihood = −52.452448
Iteration 1: log likelihood = −46.43288
Iteration 2: log likelihood = −45.952334
Iteration 3: log likelihood = −45.950222
Iteration 4: log likelihood = −45.950221

Ordered logistic regression Number of obs = 36
LR chi2(6) = 13.00

Prob> chi2 = 0.0430
Log likelihood = −45.950221 Pseudo R2 = 0.1240

TEXT BOX 11.4

agriced	Coef.	Std. Err.	z	P>|z|	[95% Conf. Interval]	
respage	0.0317559	0.0512182	0.62	0.535	−0.06863	0.1321418
hhpsize	0.5163523	0.5212019	0.99	0.322	−0.5051848	1.537889
dreadbal	0.5656853	0.4241157	1.33	0.182	−0.2655663	1.396937
clfriend	0.2765275	0.268191	1.03	0.303	−0.2491171	0.8021722
dleadcare	−0.6711435	.5214689	−1.29	0.198	−1.693204	0.3509168
dmeminfl	−2.246228	.9358999	−2.40	0.016	−4.080558	−0.4118977
_cut1	−2.097579	4.525838			−10.96806	6.7729
_cut2	−.3359566	4.552235			−9.258174	8.58626
_cut3	1.647881	4.552723			−7.275292	10.57105
_cut4	3.382652	4.562758			−5.560189	12.32549

1. The coefficient of the respage variable is 0.032; for every one-year increase in age, other components being constant, the predicted log odds of joint farming in an agricultural cooperative is an efficient factor for increasing agricultural production in Armenia by 0.032. Because the p-value associated with respage (0.535) is higher than the $\alpha = 0.05$ level of significance, the test fails to reject the null hypothesis (i.e., $H0{:}\beta_1 = 0$). This indicates that the parameter estimate associated with respage is statistically nonsignificant, with 5 percent significance level.
2. The coefficient of the hhpsize variable is 0.52; for every additional member of a household, other components being constant, the predicted log odds of joint farming in an agricultural cooperative is an efficient factor for increasing agricultural production in Armenia by 0.52. Because the p-value associated with hhpsize (0.322) is higher than the $\alpha = 0.05$ level of significance, the test fails to reject the null hypothesis (i.e., $H0{:}\beta_2 = 0$). This indicates that the parameter estimate associated with hhpsize is statistically nonsignificant, with 5 percent significance level.
3. The coefficient of the dreadbal variable is 0.57; for every one-unit increase in the variable, other components being constant, the predicted

log odds of joint farming in an agricultural cooperative is an efficient factor for increasing agricultural production in Armenia by 0.57. Because the p-value associated with dreadbal (0.182) is higher than the $\alpha = 0.05$ level of significance, the test fails to reject the null hypothesis (i.e., $H0{:}\beta_3 = 0$). This indicates that the parameter estimate associated with dreadbal is statistically nonsignificant, with 5 percent significance level.

4. The coefficient of the clfriend variable is 0.28; for every one-unit increase in clfriend, other components being constant, the predicted log odds of joint farming in an agricultural cooperative is an efficient factor for increasing agricultural production in Armenia by 0.28. Because the p-value associated with clfriend (0.303) is higher than the $\alpha = 0.05$ level of significance, the test fails to reject the null hypothesis (i.e., $H0{:}\beta_4 = 0$). This indicates that the parameter estimate associated with clfriend is statistically nonsignificant, with 5 percent significance level.
5. The coefficient of the dleadcare variable is −0.67; for every one-unit increase in dleadcare, other components being constant, the predicted log odds of joint farming in an agricultural cooperative is an efficient factor for reducing agricultural production in Armenia by 0.67. Because the p-value associated with dleadcare (0.198) is higher than the $\alpha = 0.05$ level of significance, the test fails to reject the null hypothesis (i.e., $H0{:}\beta_5 = 0$). This result indicates that the parameter estimate associated with dleadcare is statistically nonsignificant, with 5 percent significance level.
6. The coefficient of the dmeminfl variable is −2.25; for every one-unit increase in dmeminfl, other components being constant, the predicted log odds of joint farming in an agricultural cooperative is an efficient factor for reducing agricultural production in Armenia by 2.25. Because the p-value associated with dmeminfl (0.016) is less than the $\alpha = 0.05$ level of significance, the test rejects the null hypothesis (i.e., $H0{:}\beta_6 = 0$). This result indicates that the parameter estimate associated with dmeminfl is statistically significant, with 5 percent significance level.

Odds Ratios

. * Odds Ratios

. listcoef, help

ologit (N=36): Factor Change in Odds

Odds of: >m vs <=m

TEXT BOX 11.5

agriced |	b	z	P>|z|	e^b	e^bStdX	SDofX
respage |	0.03176	0.620	0.535	1.0323	1.3209	8.7651
hhpsize |	0.51635	0.991	0.322	1.6759	1.3898	0.6375
dreadbal |	0.56569	1.334	0.182	1.7607	1.6632	0.8993
clfriend |	0.27653	1.031	0.303	1.3185	1.5792	1.6523
dleadcare |	−0.67114	−1.287	0.198	0.5111	0.6264	0.6969
dmeminfl |	−2.24623	-2.400	0.016	0.1058	0.4278	0.3780

b = raw coefficient
z = z-score for test of b=0
P>|z| = p-value for z-test
e^b = exp(b) = factor change in odds for unit increase in X
e^bStdX = exp(b*SD of X) = change in odds for SD increase in X
SDofX = standard deviation of X

The odds ratio (Ω) was calculated directly by considering the antilog (i.e., e to the power) of the logit coefficient.

The logit coefficient of the respage variable is 0.032; its odds ratio (Ω) is $e^{.032}$ or 1.032. Thus, for every one-year increase in age, other components being constant, the odds of joint farming in an agricultural cooperative is an efficient factor for increasing agricultural production in Armenia by 1.032. This result implies higher levels of skepticism.

The logit coefficient of the hhpsize variable is 0.516; its odds ratio (Ω) is $e^{.516}$ or 1.676. This indicates that for every additional member of a household, other components being constant, the odds of joint farming in an agricultural cooperative is an efficient factor for increasing agricultural production in Armenia by 1.676. This result implies higher levels of skepticism.

The logit coefficient of the dreadbal variable is 0.566; its odds ratio (Ω) is $e^{.566}$ or 1.761. This indicates that for every one-unit increase in dreadbal, other components being constant, the odds of joint farming in an agricultural cooperative is an efficient factor for increasing agricultural production in Armenia by 1.761. The result implies higher levels of skepticism.

The logit coefficient of the clfriend variable is 0.277; its odds ratio (Ω) is $e^{.277}$ or 1.319. This indicates that for every one-unit increase in clfriend, other components being constant, the odds of joint farming in an agricultural cooperative is an efficient factor for increasing agricultural production in Armenia by 1.319. The result implies higher levels of skepticism.

The logit coefficient of the dleadcare variable is −0.671; its odds ratio (Ω) is $e^{-.671}$ or 0.511. This indicates that for every one-unit increase in dleadcare, other components being constant, the odds of joint farming in an agricultural cooperative is an efficient factor for increasing agricultural production in Armenia by 0.511. This result implies higher levels of skepticism.

The logit coefficient of the dmeminfl variable is −2.245; its odds ratio (Ω) is $e^{-2.245}$ or 0.106. This indicates that for every one-unit increase in dmeminfl, other components being constant, the odds of joint farming in an agricultural cooperative is an efficient factor for increasing agricultural production in Armenia by 0.106. This result implies higher levels of skepticism.

. * Percentage change in Odds Ratios

. listcoef, percent help

ologit (N=36): Percentage Change in Odds

Odds of: >m vs <=m

TEXT BOX 11.6

agriced |	b	z	P>|z|	%	%StdX	SDofX
respage |	0.03176	0.620	0.535	3.2	32.1	8.7651
hhpsize |	0.51635	0.991	0.322	67.6	39.0	0.6375
dreadbal |	0.56569	1.334	0.182	76.1	66.3	0.8993
clfriend |	0.27653	1.031	0.303	31.9	57.9	1.6523
dleadcare|	−0.67114	−1.287	0.198	-48.9	−37.4	0.6969
dmeminfl |	-2.24623	-2.400	0.016	-89.4	-57.2	0.3780

b = raw coefficient
z = z-score for test of b=0
P>|z| = p-value for z-test
% = percent change in odds for unit increase in X
%StdX = percent change in odds for SD increase in X
SDofX = standard deviation of X

Percent changes in the odds ratios were interpreted by subtracting 1 from the odds ratio and then multiplying the difference by 100: Percent change in the odds = (Ω −1) × 100.

For every one-year increase in age, with other components being constant, the odds of joint farming in an agricultural cooperative is an efficient factor for increasing agricultural production in Armenia by 3.2 percent ($[1.032 - 1] \times 100 = 3.2$ percent); all other components were constant.

For every one-unit increase in hhpsize, with other components being constant, the odds of joint farming in an agricultural cooperative is an efficient factor for increasing agricultural production in Armenia by 67.6 percent or ($[1.676 - 1] \times 100 = 67.6$ percent); all other components were constant.

For every one-unit increase in dreadbal, with other components being constant, the odds of joint farming in an agricultural cooperative is an efficient factor for increasing agricultural production in Armenia by 76.1 percent or ($[1.761 - 1] \times 100 = 76.1$ percent); all other components were constant.

For every one-unit increase in clfriend, with other components being constant, the odds of joint farming in an agricultural cooperative is an efficient factor for increasing agricultural production in Armenia by 31.9 percent or ($[1.319 - 1] \times 100 = 31.9$ percent).

For every one-unit increase in dleadcare, with other components being constant, the odds of joint farming in an agricultural cooperative is an efficient factor for reducing agricultural production in Armenia by 48.9 percent or ($[0.511 - 1] \times 100 = -48.9$ percent).

For every one-unit increase in dmeminfl, with other components being constant, the odds of joint farming in an agricultural cooperative is an efficient factor for reducing agricultural production in Armenia by 89.4 percent or ($[0.106 - 1) \times 100 = -89.4$ percent).

The likelihood ratio (LR) chi-squared statistic was used to test the null hypothesis and revealed no relationship between the independent variables.

$$\mathrm{LR}\chi^2 = -2 * \begin{pmatrix} \text{log likelihood at the first iteration} \\ -\text{log likelihood at the final iteration} \end{pmatrix}$$

$$= -2 * \left(-52.452448 - \left[-45.950221\right]\right) = 13$$

χ^2 (chi-square) tests for relationships among the variables. The null hypothesis (Ho) is that no relationship exists. Because the p-value of the observed chi-squared value (0.0430) is less than the $\alpha = 0.05$ level of significance, the test rejects the null hypothesis. This indicates a relationship among respage, hhpsize, dreadbal, clfriend, dleadcare, and dmeminfl, with 95 percent confidence level.

The interpretation of pseudo R^2 is not as straightforward as that of the "explained variance" that R^2 has in ordinary least squares.

$$R^2_L = -2 \times \begin{pmatrix} \text{log likelihood at the first iteration} \\ -\text{log likelihood at the final iteration} \end{pmatrix}$$

$$/\left(-2 \times \left[\text{log likelihood at the first iteration}\right]\right)$$

$$= -2 \times \frac{\left(-52.452448 - \left[-45.950221\right]\right)}{\left(-2 \times -52.452448\right)}$$

$$= 0.124$$

Specification Error

. ologit agriced respage hhpsize married dreadbal dlead clfriend dleadcare dmeminfl farmlater, nolog
note: married dropped because of collinearity
note: dlead dropped because of collinearity
note: farmlater dropped because of collinearity

Ordered logistic regression Number of obs = 36
LR chi2(6) = 13.00
Prob> chi2 = 0.0430
Log likelihood = −45.950221 Pseudo R2 = 0.1240

TEXT BOX 11.7

agriced |	Coef.	Std. Err.	z	P>|z|	[95% Conf.	Interval]
respage |	.0317559	.0512182	0.62	0.535	−.06863	.1321418
hhpsize |	.5163523	.5212019	0.99	0.322	−.5051848	1.537889
dreadbal |	.5656853	.4241157	1.33	0.182	−.2655663	1.396937
clfriend |	.2765275	.268191	1.03	0.303	−.2491171	.8021722
dleadcare |	−.6711435	.5214689	1.29	0.198	−1.693204	.3509168
dmeminfl |	−2.246228	.9358999	−2.40	0.016	−4.080558	−.4118977
_cut1 |	−2.097579	4.525838			−10.96806	6.7729
_cut2 |	−.3359566	4.552235			−9.258174	8.58626
_cut3 |	1.647881	4.552723			−7.275292	10.57105
_cut4 |	3.382652	4.562758			−5.560189	12.32549

. linktest, nolog

Ordered logistic regression Number of obs = 36
LR chi2(2) = 13.78

Prob> chi2 = 0.0010
Log likelihood = -45.563383 Pseudo R2 = 0.1313

TEXT BOX 11.8

agriced		Coef.	Std. Err.	z	P>|z|	[95% Conf. Interval]	
hat		1.391814	.5408229	2.57	0.010	.3318209	2.451808
_hatsq		−.1421026	.1623686	−0.88	0.381	-.4603393	.1761341
_cut1		−2.30597	.8954589			-4.061037	−.5509025
_cut2		−.2848622	.5368351			−1.33704	.7673153
_cut3		1.745503	.5731285			.6221917	2.868814
_cut4		3.399531	.7293632			1.970005	4.829056

The output from the logit command showed that one of the six variables, namely dmeminfl, is a statistically significant predictor. In the following link test, the variable_hatsq was not significant (p = 0.381, less than the α = 0.05 significance level). This confirms that we selected strong predictors. However, it also indicated that we do not have a specification error (because the link test is not significant); thus, the model is correctly specified.

Multicollinearity

Multicollinearity (or, briefly, collinearity) occurs when two or more independent variables in the model are approximately determined using a linear combination of other independent variables in the model. In case of perfect collinearity, that is, when an independent variable is a perfect linear combination of the others, it is impossible to obtain a unique estimate of regression coefficients with all independent variables in the model. The analysis cannot assume that the variable that Stata eliminates from the model is the "correct" variable to omit from the model; thus, the study relied on a theory to determine which variables should be omitted.

```
*Multicollinearity
.collin agriced respage hhpsize married dreadbal dlead clfriend dleadcare
  dmeminfl farmlater
(obs=36)
corr(): matrix has zero or negative values on diagonal
r(504);
```

Because the number of observations is small (i.e., n = 36), the model could not assess multicollinearity.

FEASIBILITY STUDY OF YERVANDASHAT COOPERATIVE[3]

This section describes the feasibility analysis of the Yervandashat Consumer Cooperative. The final results analyzed the distribution of each key output variable, including profit, yields, and net present value (NPV). The feasibility analysis of future business decisions under risks is based on this distribution. The financial statement simulation model is programmed in Excel by using the add-in SIMETAR©, a simulation and risk analysis software (Richardson, Schumann, and Feldman 2008). The NPV is the most determinative output variable from the model for evaluating the feasibility of expanding the capacity of the dried fruit production factory. The model calculates the NPV as follows:

$$NPV = -(\text{Beginning Net Worth}) + \sum_{j=1}^{n} \frac{\text{Family Living Dividends} + \text{Family Living Bonus}}{(1+i)^j} + \frac{\text{Ending Net Worth}}{(1+i)^n}$$

The equation calculates the NPV (assuming a discount rate of i = 31.75 percent) of family living dividends and bonuses paid to households and the net worth throughout the investment (five years) and further compares that value to the net worth at the beginning of the investment. If the NPV is higher than zero, the business is considered an economic success (Richardson and Mapp 1976).

The major income-generating products are dried apricot, black plum, red plum, and peach. Income is calculated as follows:

$$(1)\ \text{Income} = P_{\text{Dried Apricot}} \times Q_{\text{Dried Apricot}} + P_{\text{Dried Black Plum}} \times Q_{\text{Dried Black Plum}} + P_{\text{Dried Red Plum}} \times Q_{\text{Dried Red Plum}} + P_{\text{Dried Peach}} \times Q_{\text{Dried Peach}}$$

Income is stochastic because it is based on prices, which are randomly drawn from probability distributions estimated from historical series. Other random variables include inputs.

In 2014, the farm obtained a five-year loan of 5,000,000 AMD from Acba–Credit Agricole Bank Armenia CJSC, at a 24 percent interest rate. The loan amortization table was used to amortize the loan accordingly.

The cooperative is taxed as a corporation and has a depreciation deduction of 250,000 AMD annually, is subject to income and value-added taxes, and has no other tax deductions. The model assumes that the base crop mix is fixed for five years. Because all costs are for 2013, all costs, excluding the manager's and electrician's salaries, were inflated by the Prices Paid Index. However, the consumer price index (CPI) was used to inflate the manager's salary. The model assumed that the manager did not receive any bonuses. For estimating the CPI, payment protection insurance, and GDP deflators, the historical data from 2000 to 2013 were used, which were provided by the National Statistical Service of the Republic of Armenia. Based on these data, the simulation was conducted, and the corresponding values of the deflators for 2014–2018 were estimated (tables 11.3–11.6). The operating loan was estimated as 5 percent of the total annual cash costs. The interest for the operating loan was computed as the product of the loan amount and local interest rate. Furthermore, the estimations of the local interest rate amounted to the national interest rate plus the local interest rate basis of 0.085. The local interest rate basis was computed as the difference in the average rate of Armenia's ProCredit Bank's "AgroProgress" USD loan, which varied from 14 to 18 percent, and Central Bank's refinancing loan rate of 7.5 percent. If the farm incurs a cash flow deficit, the deficit is financed for one year, and the interest of this short-term cash flow deficit loan is estimated based on the local interest rate for the operating loan. The land value is inflated on the basis of the GDP deflator.

The Yervandashat Cooperative did not lease any machinery; thus, it did not pay any rent. Meanwhile, the total depreciation expense was 250,000 AMD annually, as determined using the straight-line depreciation method. The risk-adjusted discount rate for calculating the NPV and present value of the ending net worth is 0.3175. The farm had 1,000,000 cash reserves at the beginning, which it spent for acquiring fuel for 2013. In addition, any cash on hand by January 1, 2014, was assumed to receive interest calculated at 11.5 percent annually (annual interest rate of Armenia's ProCredit Bank's "ProApaga" savings account).

Table 11.3 Operating Loan Rate and Interest for Cash Reserves

First year to simulate	*2014*
Hectares Owned	40.0
Hectares Cash Rented	4
Land Value Dec 31	5,796,000
Machinery	
Baling Machinery	6,000,000
4 Solar Dryers (each costs 1,000,000 AMD)	4,000,000
Belarusian Tractor	7,200,000
Electric Dryer	2,697,500
Spray machine	1,500,000
Other machinery and tools (i.e., plow, chisel, cultivator)	1,000,000
Total Machinery Cost	22,397,500
% Change Land Value	4%
Beginning Cash Reserves	1,000,000
Manager's and Electrician's Base Salary	100,000
Manager's and Electrician's Bonus % NCFI	0%
Discount Rate for NVP	0.3175
Depreciation Tax Deduction	250,000
Other Tax Deductions	-
Local Interest Rate Basis	0.085
Operating Loan % Year	5%
Interest for Cash Reserves	0.115

Source: Simetar Simulations based on the interview with Yervandashat cooperative, April 2014.

Financial Statements

Table 11.4 shows the income statement projections for 2014–2018. The projections revealed substantial fluctuations in the net cash farm income (NCFI), from 61,337,748 AMD in 2014 to 94,694,278 AMD in 2018.

Table 11.5 shows the cash flow statement projections for 2014–2018. As shown in table 11.5, the ending cash steadily increased from 35,523,220 AMD in 2014 to reach its peak of 221,673,320 AMD in 2018.

Table 11.6 shows the balance sheet projections for 2014–2018. As shown in this table 11.6, the difference between total assets and liabilities gradually increased from 36,551,060 AMD in 2014 to 227,256,299 AMD in 2018.

Financial Model

The five-year financial model encompasses the following components:

1. NPV
2. PV of the ending net worth
3. The annual net cash income (NCI)
4. Annual ending cash reserves
5. The simulation part of stochastic variables

Table 11.4 Income Statement Projections for 2014–2018

	Financial Statements				
Income Statement	*2014*	*2015*	*2016*	*2017*	*2018*
Receipts					
Dried Apricot	95,101,497.17	103,051,828.14	111,320,608.46	119,907,838.13	128,813,517.16
Dried Black Plum	16,599,678.49	18,030,684.78	19,520,835.16	21,070,129.63	22,678,568.18
Dried Red Plum	4,022,441.86	4,366,218.08	4,724,000.47	5,095,789.05	5,481,583.80
Dried Peach	820,201.30	926,141.79	1,038,040.80	1,155,898.32	1,279,714.37
Revenue	116,543,818.82	126,374,872.78	136,603,484.89	147,229,655.13	153,253,383.51
Expenses					
Apricot Planting Cost	22,185,080.24	22,272,611.25	22,360,142.26	22,447,673.27	22,535,204.28
Black Plum Planting Cost	3,011,316.06	3,023,197.18	3,035,078.29	3,046,959.41	3,058,840.53
Red Plum Planting Cost	2,710,184.45	2,720,877.46	2,731,570.47	2,742,263.47	2,752,956.48
Peach Planting Cost	2,252,402.21	2,261,289.04	2,270,175.87	2,279,062.70	2,287,949.53
Apricot Harvesting Cost	10,289,900.54	10,733,976.01	11,181,222.79	11,631,640.88	12,085,230.29
Black Plum Harvesting Cost	678,681.32	709,675.05	740,891.34	772,330.20	803,991.62
Red Plum Harvesting Cost	128,723.00	134,204.30	139,724.69	145,284.17	150,882.74
Peach Harvesting Cost	14,987.55	16,254.83	17,531.60	18,817.87	20,113.63
Interest on Operating Loan	464,301.85	481,528.98	509,716.05	549,321.41	568,037.20
Land Debt Interest	1,200,000.00	1,050,902.74	866,022.14	636,770.20	352,497.79
Carry over debt interest	-	-	-	-	-
Total Expenses	42,935,577.22	43,404,516.83	43,852,075.50	44,270,123.58	44,615,704.08
Earnings before Taxes (EBT)	73,608,241.59	82,970,355.95	92,751,409.39	102,959,531.56	113,637,679.43
Value-Added Taxes	12,270,493.87	13,831,158.34	15,461,659.95	17,163,353.91	18,943,401.16
Net Cash Farm Income (NCFI)	61,337,747.72	69,139,197.62	77,289,749.45	85,796,177.65	94,694,278.27

Source: Simetar Projections based on the interview with Yervandashat cooperative, April 2014.

Table 11.5 Cash Flow Statement Projections for 2014–2018

Cash Flow Statements	*2014*	*2015*	*2016*	*2017*	*2018*
Beginning Cash Reserves Jan 1	1,000,000	35523219.94	78298242.47	121432227.5	169168105.7
NCFI	61,337,748	69,139,198	77,289,749	85,796,178	94,694,278
Interest Earned	115,000	4,085,170	-	-	-
Total Cash Inflows	62,452,748	108,747,588	155,587,992	207,228,405	263,862,384
Principal Payment	621,238.57	770,335.83	955,216.43	1,184,468.38	1,468,740.79
Repay the Deficit Loan	-	-	-	-	-
Income Taxes	26,207,046.97	29,577,408.14	33,098,587.38	36,773,511.36	40,617,644.59
Family Living Dividends	101,242.24	101,601.40	101,960.57	102,319.74	102,678.91
Family Living Bonuses	-	-	-	-	-
Total Cash Outflows	26,929,527.78	30,449,345.38	34,155,764.39	38,060,299.48	42,189,064.29
Ending Cash	35,523,219.94	78,298,242.47	121,432,227.53	169,168,105.70	221,673,319.68

Source: Simetar Projections based on the interview with Yervandashat cooperative, April 2014.

Table 11.6 Balance Sheet Projections for 2014–2018

Balance Sheet	*2014*	*2015*	*2016*	*2017*	*2018*
Cash Reserves Dec 31st	35,523,219.94	78,298,242.47	121,432,227.53	169,168,105.70	221,673,319.68
Land and Building	6,027,840.00	6,268,953.60	6,519,711.74	6,780,500.21	7,051,720.22
Total Assets	41,551,059.94	84,567,196.07	127,951,939.27	175,948,605.91	228,725,039.90
Loan Outstanding	5,000,000.00	4,378,761.43	3,608,425.59	2,653,209.16	1,468,740.79
Deficit Loan	-	-	-	-	-
Total Liabilities	5,000,000.00	4,378,761.43	3,608,425.59	2,653,209.16	1,468,740.79
Net Worth	36,551,059.94	80,188,434.64	124,343,513.68	173,295,396.75	227,256,299.11

Source: Simetar Projections based on the interview with Yervandashat cooperative, April 2014.

6. The validation of stochastic variables for 2014
7. The probability of positive annual NCI
8. The probability of positive annual cash reserves
9. Stochastic efficiency (SERF), indicates the most preferred crop mix for risk-neutral, moderately risk-averse, and extremely risk-averse people
10. The stoplight chart is presented and interpreted for probabilities of the NPV being less than 0 AMD and exceeding 100,000,000 AMD
11. Roy's ranking on the basis of the NCFI

12. The probability distribution function (PDF) for dried apricot, black plum, red plum, and dried peach for 2014
13. Cumulative distribution function (CDF) and PDF for four scenarios of the NPV.

DISCUSSIONS

To assess the risk components associated with each scenario, the study states the mean NPVs and their distributions. The data on the CDF depicts a 0 percent probability of obtaining a negative NPV under each of the four scenarios. Because the graphs of the NPV intersect under all scenarios, no first-degree stochastic dominance existed. Therefore, the CDF graph cannot show under which scenarios the NPV is the most preferred, and other tools have to be used to rank the NPV.

The PDF graph shows a 95 percent probability that under all scenarios, our NPV will be between 23,000,000 and 48,000,000 AMD, a 2.5 percent probability of the NPV being less than 23,000,000 AMD, and a 2.5 percent probability of the NPV exceeding 48,000,000 AMD.

Figures 11.3 and 11.4 show that because the financial model is a multiyear project, the power utility function was chosen; the lower risk aversion coefficient (RAC) is equal to 0, and the upper RAC corresponds to 4.000001. Four NPVs are preferred by all decision-makers because the certainty equivalence is maximum for every relative RAC ranging from 0 to 4.000001.

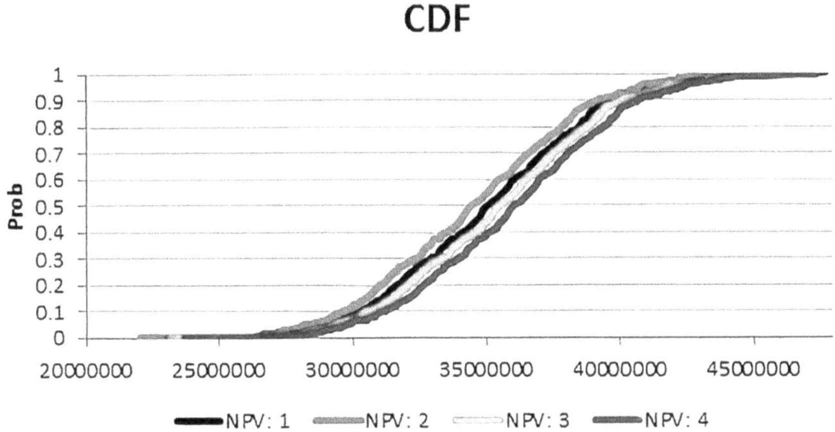

Figure 11.1 CDF of NPVs of Yervandashat Cooperative under Four Scenarios
Source: Simetar Simulations based on the interview with Yervandashat cooperative, April 2014.

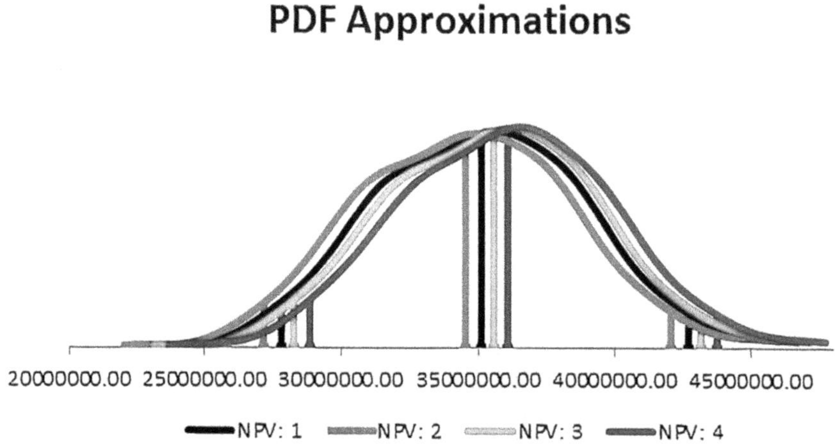

Figure 11.2 PDF of NPVs of Yervandashat Cooperative under Four Scenarios
Source: Simetar Simulations based on the interview with Yervandashat cooperative, April 2014.

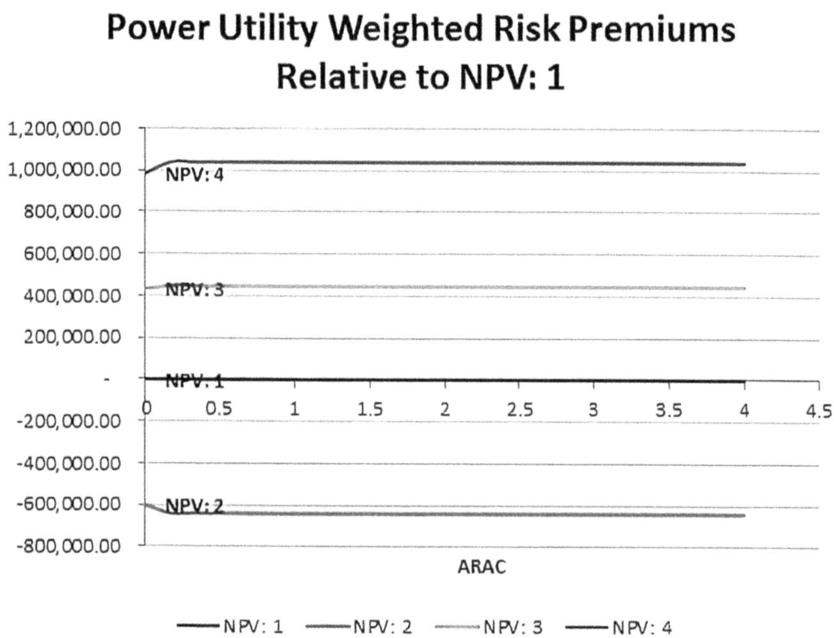

Figure 11.3 Power Utility-Weighted Risk Premiums of Yervandashat Cooperative
Source: Simetar Simulations based on the interview with Yervandashat cooperative, April 2014.

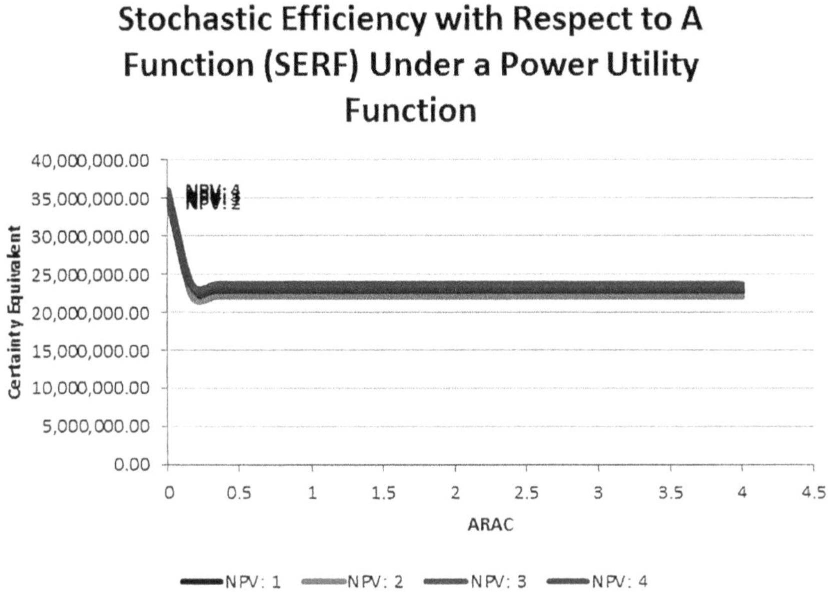

Figure 11.4 SERF under a Power Utility Function
Source: Simetar Simulations based on the interview with Yervandashat cooperative, April 2014.

Figure 11.5 illustrates the stoplight chart, showing that the probability of NPV_1, NPV_2, NPV_3, and NPV_4 exceeding the upper target (green) of 50,000,000 AMD is 0 or 0 percent. The probability of the values being between 0 AMD and 50,000,000 AMD is 1 or 100 percent (yellow) and that of the values being negative (red) under each of the four scenarios is 0 or 0 percent.

Table 11.7 shows that during 2014–2018, there is a 100 percent probability of obtaining positive NPVs for both annual NCI and annual cash reserves.

Table 11.8 presents that under all scenarios, there is a 0 percent probability of obtaining negative NCFI in two consecutive years; thus, all scenarios are equally preferred.

Table 11.9 shows the results of various multivariate tests. The first test is the two-sample Hotelling T2 test, which yielded a test value of 10.42, critical value of 15.87, and p-value of 0.153, indicating a 100 percent probability of the mean vectors being reproduced. Therefore, this test fails to reject the null hypothesis that the mean vectors are equal, indicating their equivalence, with 95 percent confidence level. The next test is the Box's M test. This test investigates whether the covariance matrix associated with simulated data is statistically equal to the covariance matrix for the original input data. The test fails to reject the null hypothesis that the covariance matrices are equivalent, thus

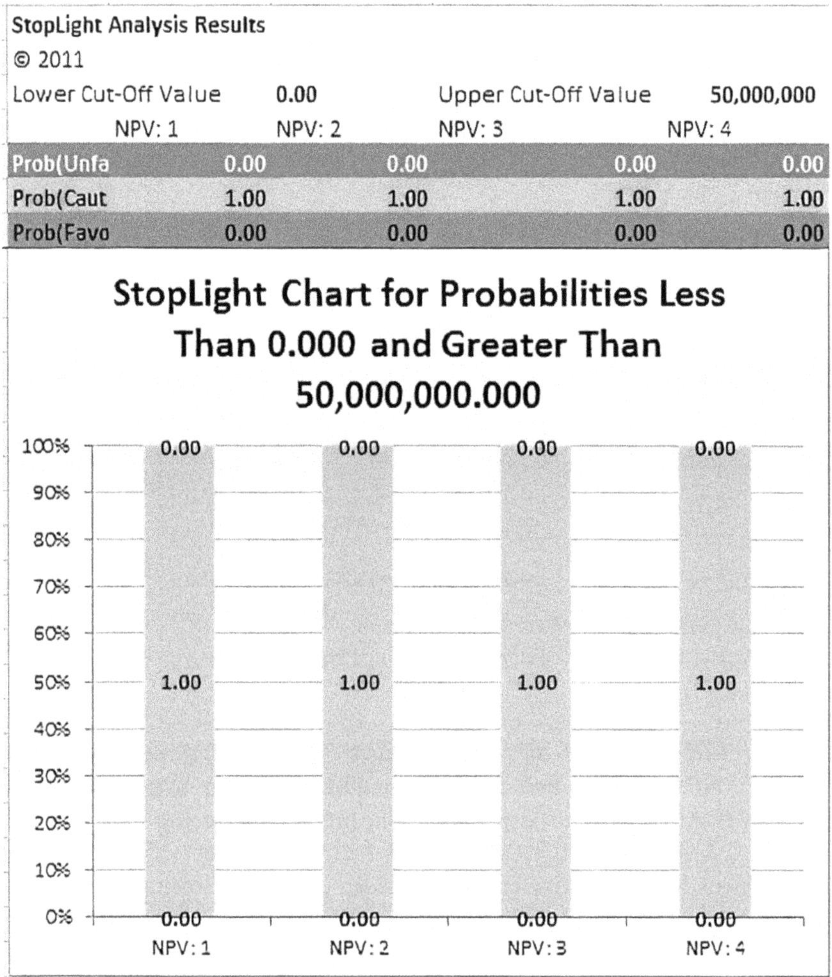

Figure 11.5 Stoplight Chart for Probabilities Less Than 0 AMD and Exceeding 100,000,000 AMD
Source: Simetar Simulations based on the interview with Yervandashat cooperative, April 2014.

Table 11.7 Probabilities of Positive NCI and Annual Cash Reserves from 2014–2018

	2014	*2015*	*2016*	*2017*	*2018*
Probability of positive annual NCI (%)	100	100	100	100	100
Probability of positive annual cash reserves (%)	100	100	100	100	100

Source: Simetar Projections based on the interview with Yervandashat cooperative, April 2014.

Table 11.8 Roy's Criteria for NCFI

	Scenarios 1	*Scenarios 2*	*Scenarios 3*	*Scenarios 4*
NCFI	0	0	0	0

Source: Simetar Simulations based on the interview with Yervandashat cooperative, April 2014.

Table 11.9 Distribution Comparison of Historical and Projected Prices of Apricot

Distribution Comparison of Dried Apricot Price per kg (AMD) & 2014 Dried Apricot Price per kg (AMD)				
Confidence Level	*95.00%*			
	Test Value	*Critical Value*	*P-Value*	
2 Sample Hotelling T^2 Test	10.42	15.87	0.153	Fail to Reject the Ho that the Mean Vectors are Equal
Box's M Test	8.00	51.00	0.127	Fail to Reject the Ho that the Covariance Matrices are Equivalent
Complete Homogeneity Test	48.00	60.48	0.130	Fail to Reject the Ho that the Mean Vectors and Covariance Matrices are Equivalent, Respectively* * Based on asymptotic distribution

Source: Simetar Analysis based on the interview with Yervandashat cooperative, April 2014.

indicating their equivalence, with 95 percent confidence level. Furthermore, the complete homogeneity test assesses whether the mean vectors and covariance matrices are equal. The two components were observed to be equal because the test fails to reject the null hypothesis that the components are equivalent. This result indicated that the mean vectors and covariance matrices are equivalent, with 95 percent confidence level. In conclusion, the tests actually validated our random numbers.

Table 11.10 presents a multivariate distribution validation test, which compares the correlation matrix of the simulated output with the input (assumed) correlation matrix. This test is useful for validating multivariate probability distributions, particularly non-normal multivariate distributions. Based on Student "t" test statistics for comparing the corresponding correlation coefficients in two matrices because the estimated "t" values are less than the critical "t" value of 1.96, the correlation coefficient test fails to reject the null hypothesis. This result indicates that the estimates of parameters associated with the prices of dried apricot, black plum, red plum, and peach with the yields of dried apricot, red plum, and peach are statistically significant, with 95 percent confidence level.

Table 11.10 Test of Correlation Coefficients of Historical and Simulated Data

Test Correlation Coefficients							
Confidence Level		*95.00%*					
Critical Value		*1.96*					
	2014 Dried Black Plum Price per kg	2014 Dried Red Plum Price per kg	2014 Dried Peach Price per kg	2014 Total Dried Apricot Yield	2014 Total Dried Red Plum Yield	2014 Total Dried Peach Yield	2014 Total Dried Black Plum Yield
2014 Dried Apricot Price per kg (AMD)	1.74	1.43	1.43	0.55	1.74	1.14	1.37
2014 Dried Black Plum Price per kg (AMD)		1.43	1.43	0.55	1.74	1.14	1.37
2014 Dried Red Plum Price per kg (AMD)			1.79	0.48	1.83	0.64	1.81
2014 Dried Peach Price per kg (AMD)				0.48	1.83	0.64	1.74
2014 Total Dried Apricot Yield					0.53	0.59	0.05
2014 Total Dried Red Plum Yield						0.88	0.92
2014 Total Dried Peach Yield							0.32

Source: Simetar Analysis based on the interview with Yervandashat cooperative, April 2014.

RECOMMENDATIONS

After discussing the characteristics and problems of introducing agricultural cooperatives in the Republic of Armenia as well as the overall situation of the cooperative industry in the nation, several relevant recommendations are proposed to promote the growth and development of cooperatives in Armenia.

First, cooperatives as entities must have legal protection in terms of concise and detailed specification of roles and responsibilities among both members and other stakeholders. Tax advantages should be specified based on the overall size of the cooperatives and the number of members.

Second, special educational programs should be specifically and separately developed for cooperatives' governing bodies and members. Furthermore, the members who are not interested in the specific subject should not attend that training. In this case, the capabilities and interest of each member are considered. Meanwhile, the governing bodies should be more specialized.

Finally, the members have to contribute to the common equity of the cooperative to stay self-sufficient and viable, even in the absence of external support by donor organizations.

CONCLUSION

This study explored whether the success of cooperatives can be explained by social capital. The hypothesis was that the members support the cooperatives because they trust their fellow members as well as their leadership. To facilitate the analysis, a survey was conducted among the cooperative members of Yervandashat, Armavir region. An ordered logit model was used to estimate the findings, which indicated social capital in the membership. On the one hand, the members, who consider cooperatives to be an efficient business form, have social ties to other members. On the other hand, the leadership enjoys extensive social capital. The cooperative is considered a social unit rather than a business enterprise. The members' support to the cooperative society is explained by the social capital within the memberships. The development of cooperatives does not only aim to maximize profit but also plays a decisive role in building trust. This trust enhances the efficiency of operations and fosters investment in ideas and human and physical capital.

Cooperatives are gradually influencing rural Armenia. They have high potential to become one of the basis of Armenia's agricultural and economic development, particularly in the rural areas where the united force of farmers can change their lives and the overall livelihood of their community. However, in Armenia, cooperatives as organizational models are not yet sustainable. Most members benefit from developing their individual farms, but the idea of cooperatives as an entity is not appropriately developed yet. This derives risks such that after donor organizations leave, cooperatives are dissolved because most members are not motivated to stay. The experience of many registered but nonfunctioning cooperatives in Armenia has shown this effect.

The first reason is the imperfection of the law on cooperatives that would define necessary and sufficient specifics of its operation and provide legal protection both within cooperatives and in interactions with other stakeholders. This would also protect ownership rights and responsibilities of the members as well as enable cooperatives to have diplomatic relationships with other legal entities, such as processors.

Second, there have been many cases where locals have confused cooperative enterprises with once-prevalent collectives from the Soviet Union period. This caused expectations for government aid. Meanwhile, the members did not contribute to the formation of a common equity of the cooperatives. Nonetheless, the members should focus on the cooperatives' self-help, self-reliance, and self-responsibility aspects rather than waiting for external support.

The government should not intervene in the creation and governance of cooperatives as they contradict the principle of independence. Instead, there should be improved partnerships between cooperatives and their stakeholders, including the government. In the case of Armenia, the government still has to undertake many activities in terms of taking actions to create a favorable legal and economic environment for the development of cooperatives.

NOTES

1. Database is available upon request.
2. Both questionnaires are available upon request.
3. The excel file with all the calculations is available upon request.

REFERENCES

Armenian Legal Informative System. *Armenian Law on Consumer Cooperatives.* Accessed on February 21, 2014, http://www.arlis.am/documentview.aspx?docid=94.

BSC Business Support Center LLC. *Assessment of the Armenian Dried Fruit and Vegetable Supply Chain*, 2012. Accessed on April 4, 2014, http://docshare02.docshare.tips/files/20815/208154420.pdf.

Business 24. *Refinancing Loan Was Set at 7.5%.* Accessed on March 10, 2014, http://www.b24.am/finance/46883.html.

Fabio, Sabatini, Francesca Modena, and Ermanno C. Tortia. "Do Cooperative Enterprises Create Social Trust?" *Small Business Economics* 42, no. 3 (2012): 621–641, http://link.springer.com/article/10.1007%2Fs11187-013-9494-8#page-1.

Geoffrey, Marczyk, David DeMatteo, and David Festinger. *Essentials of Research Design and Methodology*. Hoboken, NJ: John Wiley & Sons, 2005.

Golovina, Svetlana, Sebastian Hess, Jerker Nilsson, and Axel Wolz. "Social Capital in Russian Agricultural Production Cooperatives." *Post-Communist Economies* 26, no. 4 (2014): 522–536. https://doi:10.1080/14631377.2014.964465.

Institute for Digital Research and Education (IDRE) UCLA. *Stata Data Analysis Examples Ordered Logistic Regression*. Accessed on May 5, 2014, http://www.ats.ucla.edu/stat/stata/dae/ologit.htm.

International Co-operative Alliance (ICA). *Co-operative Identity, Values, and Principles*. Accessed on January 15, 2014, http://ica.coop/en/what-co-op/co-operative-identity-values-principles.

Invest in Armenia. *Value Added Tax*. Accessed on January 17, 2014, http://www.investinarmenia.am/en/value-added-tax.

KPMG. *Armenia-Income Tax*. Accessed on January 17, 2014. https://www.kpmg.com/global/en/issuesandinsights/articlespublications/taxation-international-executives/armenia/pages/income-tax.aspx.

Movsisyan, Suren. *The Role of Cooperatives in the Development of Agriculture in Armenia, Asian Countries & EU (Worldwide case studies)*. Berlin, Germany: Institute for Cultural Diplomacy Germany, 2013.

Movsisyan, Suren. "The Problems of Armenian Brandy Makers," *Annals of Agrarian Science* 3, no. 4 (2015): 94–98.

National Assembly of the Republic of Armenia. *1996-2012 Civil Law*. Accessed on January 20, 2014. http://www.parliament.am/legislation.php?sel=show&ID=1556&lang=eng.

National Statistical Service of the Republic of Armenia. *Time series*. Accessed on February 10, 2014. http://armstat.am/en/?nid=126&id=03001&submit=Search.

National Statistical service of the Republic of Armenia. *Prices and Price Tariffs*. Accessed on February 18, 2014, http://www.armstat.am/file/article/f_sec_3_13_5.pdf.

Parliament of the Republic of Armenia. *The Law of the Republic of Armenia on Value Added Tax*. Accessed on February 18, 2014, http://www.parliament.am/legislation.php?sel=show&ID=1607&lang=eng.

Ribera, Luis A., Brad Roberson, James W. Richardson, and Clyde Munster. "Economic Feasibility of a Mobile Fast Pyrolysis System for Sustainable Biocrude Oil Production." *International Food and Agribusiness Management Review* 14, no. 3 (2011): 1–16.

Richardson, James, Keith Schumann, and Paul Feldman. *Simulation & Econometrics to Analyze Risk*. Texas: College Station, 2008, http://www.afpc.tamu.edu/courses/622/files/technical/Simetar%20Users%20Manual%202008%20Complete.pdf.

Richardson, James, and Mapp, Harry P. "Use of Probabilistic Cash Flows in Analyzing Investments Under Conditions of Risk and Uncertainty." *Journal of Agricultural and Applied Economics* 8, no. 2 (1976): 19–24. https://EconPapers.repec.org/RePEc:cup:jagaec:v:8:y:1976:i:02:p:19-24_01.

SAS Supermarket. *Dried Fruit Prices*. Accessed on March 10, 2014, https://sas.am/products/%D4%BE%D5%AB%D6%80%D5%A1%D5%B6%D5%AB_%D5%B9%D5%AB%D6%80_%D5%AF%D5%A3__206336/.

The Government of the Republic of Armenia. *RA Sustainable Development Strategy of Agriculture and Village for 2010-2020*. Accessed on March 14, 2014, http://www.minagro.am/doc/agstrategy_arm3.pdf.
United Methodist Committee on Relief Armenia (UMCOR). Community Association Program, 1994–2007. http://umcorarmenia.am/search/node/cooperatives.
United States Overseas Cooperative Development Council (OCDC) & United States Agency for International Development (USAID). *Measuring Cooperative Success*. Accessed on February 4, 2014, http://www.ocdc.coop/pdf/metrics.pdf.
Urutyan, Vardan. *Cooperative Legislation Reform: Guidelines for Armenia*. ICARE Foundation, 2013. Accessed on February 18, 2014. https://www.icare.am/uploaded_files/Coop%20Legislation%20Study%20-%20ARM%20FINAL(1).pdf.
Urutyan, Vardan, and Narek Vardanyan. *Necessity of Legal Reforms Aimed at Sustainable Development of Cooperatives in Armenia*. ICARE Foundation, 2012. Accessed on February 18, 2014. https://www.icare.am/uploaded_files/Necessity%20of%20coop%20legal%20reforms_UrutyanVardanyan_ENG.pdf.
Urutyan, Vardan, and Samvel Avetisyan. *Agricultural Cooperative*. Yerevan: Asoghik, 2011.
Vardanyan, Narek. *Legal Reforms Needed for the Effective Development of Cooperatives in Armenia*. Yerevan, Armenia: Open Society Foundation, 2011.

Chapter 12

Benefits and Challenges of Agricultural Marketing Cooperatives in Moshi District, Tanzania: The Experience from Mweka Sungu, Mruwia, and Uru North Njari Cooperative Societies

Gratian Cronery Rwekaza and Paulo Anania Fute

The International Cooperative Alliance (ICA 1995) defines a cooperative as an autonomous association of people voluntarily united to meet their common economic, social, and cultural needs and aspirations through a jointly owned and democratically controlled enterprise. Bibby (2006) argued that cooperatives are internationally recognized as enterprises that are democratically owned and controlled by their members. Among all, agricultural cooperatives have been a successful and common aspect of rural life (Brennan and Luloff 2005).

Sub-Saharan Africa encounters many development challenges, including extreme poverty and unemployment, diseases, low productivity, and the lack of assured better future. International Labour Organization (2012) described that to survive in this increasingly complex world, poor producers and workers must become more competitive, be aware of their rights, and voice their opinions. One of the most effective methods of engaging in such activities is to join forces through their own democratic organizations. Cooperatives represent a viable form of a member-owned and member-controlled organization that can help the poor compete in the market and bring significant social benefits and changes.

Cooperatives have been important in the development of Tanzania for several years. They have experienced many successes and failures during this period, but no other institution has united so many people for a common cause. Following the Arusha Declaration, cooperatives became the main tool for building self-reliance during the Ujamaa period. However, following the introduction of free markets, cooperatives struggled to compete with the private sector, and many could not provide their members with the required services. The United Republic of Tanzania (2002) addressed this problem by introducing a new Cooperative Development Policy to help cooperatives regain their importance in the economic lives of people (Tanzania Federation of Cooperatives [TFC] 2006).

To meet their complete potential, Tanzania's cooperatives need to enroll members who can participate and actively engage in the activities of their organization. Traditionally, the dominant cooperative in mainland Tanzania is the one that focused on the marketing of farmers' agricultural crops. This type of a cooperative has been dominant in terms of the members and volume of trade since the establishment of cooperatives in the 1920s. Cooperatives developed historically, in Tanzania and elsewhere in the world, because they represent a valuable with almost no form of collective organization, at a high disadvantage when taking their products or crops to the market (Bibby 2006).

For several years, cooperatives have remained an effective strategy for people to control their economic livelihood. Cooperatives provide a unique tool for achieving one or more economic goals in an increasingly competitive economy. In the current environment where market access is poor and market information is inadequate, by not being involved in collective organizations, individual small farmers are left in a weak position. This not only affects the farmers but also the entire economy (Ainebyona and Tiruhungwa 2012).

Typically, successfully managed agricultural cooperatives are considered to have great potential in rural development, particularly in agricultural development. Bello (2005) argued that in the present era where people feel powerless to change their lives, cooperatives represent a strong, vibrant, and viable economic alternative. Cooperatives are formed to meet members' mutual needs; they are based on a strong idea that a group of people can achieve goals that none of them can achieve individually.

The history of the coffee sector is closely associated with the cooperative movement. During the 1920s, expatriate coffee growers formed a union to market their coffee. The first marketing cooperative of native cultivators was established in Kilimanjaro in 1932, primarily to promote coffee as a cash crop among peasant farmers. Subsequently, cooperatives grew in size and number, but they were confined to regions producing export crops (Baffes 2003).

The coffee cooperatives were among the most dominant agricultural cooperatives in Tanzania. Tanzania Coffee Board states that in 2015, approximately 450,000 families undertook direct coffee cultivation, accounting for 90 percent of the total coffee producers. The remaining 10 percent coffee was supplied by the estates. Indirect coffee cultivation was undertaken by 6 percent (2.4 million) of the country' population; this number is currently estimated to be 40 million. In Tanzania, arabica coffee is grown on the slopes of Mount Kilimanjaro and Mount Meru in the northern areas, under the shade of banana trees, truly an exotic location for this east African coffee. They are also grown in Southern Highlands of Mbeya and Ruvuma regions, where the coffee is both intercropped with bananas and grown as pure stand. Arabica coffee accounts for 70 percent of the total coffee production in Tanzania. Robusta coffee is grown in the western areas along Lake Victoria in the Kagera region; this crop constitutes 30 percent of the total coffee production in Tanzania. Compared with individual producers, coffee cooperatives are the most dominant organizations engaging in coffee productivity.

The most important agricultural cooperatives in the Moshi Rural district are those dealing with coffee production and marketing. In their operations to serve members' socioeconomic interests, agricultural cooperatives in this district benefit their members. However, these cooperatives experience various challenges, which retard their capacity to serve their members. Furthermore, the capacity of any cooperative to achieve its goals and benefit its members as well as be able to overcome challenges depends on the key success factors affecting the overall operation of the cooperatives. This chapter focused on identifying various benefits, challenges, and success factors in (coffee) agricultural marketing cooperatives (AMCOS) in Moshi Rural district. Specific references are made from three cooperative societies: Mweka Sungu, Mruwia, and Uru North Njari.

OBJECTIVES

The main objective of this study is to describe the challenges and benefits of coffee AMCOS in Moshi Rural district. To achieve this objective, the authors focused on the following specific objectives:

i. To identify the social benefits of coffee cooperatives to the members.
ii. To identify the economic benefits of coffee cooperatives to the members.
iii. To identify the challenges encountered by coffee cooperatives in Moshi Rural district.

SIGNIFICANCE OF THE STUDY

The study describes the concerns related to the benefits and challenges of AMCOS engaged in coffee production in Moshi Rural district. Therefore, this research clearly indicates the cooperative societies of various stakeholders and their members, policymakers, nongovernment organizations and government to comprehensively present the benefits of AMCOS as well the main challenges encountered by them.

The study also provides a basis for future studies by various scholars and researchers interested in studying the potential role and benefits of AMCOS as well as the encountered challenges.

OPERATIONALIZATION OF THE STUDY

The study is based on the experiences acquired by the authors from their field visits to three AMCOS of Uru Njari, Mruwia, and Mweka Sungu. Therefore, the study has a multiple case design. The cases were selected based on accessibility and better comparison because they have different performance levels.

The data were collected through interviews, focus group discussions, and observations and documentary reviews, where both primary and secondary data were collected. To a large extent, the study applied a qualitative approach, and in few scenarios, a quantitative approach was applied. A total of twenty respondents were enrolled, comprising chairpersons, vice chairpersons, secretaries, board members, and some cooperative members from the three cases.

DISCUSSION

Profiles of the Selected Case Studies

Uru North Njari AMCO Society

Uru North AMCOS is among the AMCOS established in Moshi Rural district. Its history can be traced to 1954, when this cooperative society was established; it is in this year that all villagers were cooperative members as mentioned by the Ujamaa and Ujamaa Village Act of 1975 (United Republic of Tanzania). The cooperative existed for some decades until being divided into three societies, namely Uru Ngoma, Msumi, and Uru North Njari AMCOS. The Uru North Njari AMCO society was formed in 1993, with a registration number KLR 422. Until 2013, the society had approximately 780 members. The current membership is different from the previous one because presently, only coffee growers are cooperative members since this cooperative deals with coffee production and marketing.

AMCOS are managed by the board (five members), two employed staff (a secretary and clerk and a security guard), and the annual general meeting comprising all members. The Uru North Njari AMCO society is also a member of the Kilimanjaro Native Cooperative Union (KNCU), which helps this society by providing marketing assistance, loans, transport services, and funds to pay initial payments to the members' product (coffee) brought to the cooperative. The cooperative also has 500 hectares of coffee land that is now operated by settlers. The farm is divided into two main farms: Machari and Usagara (Uru) estates. The settlers pay 2 million Tshs annually, from which 60 percent is devoted to social services (health and education), and 40 percent is given to the members.

Mruwia AMCO Society

The Mruwia AMCO society originated from the old cooperative called Uru East Cooperative Society. The increase in demand for new cooperatives in this area resulted in the establishment of the Mruwia AMCO society in June 1995 (registration number: KLR 482). This cooperative is a member of the KNCU. Because of the improving quality and increasing productivity of coffee, the members felt the need to be independent from the KNCU.

After being dissatisfied with the role of the union, the society joined the new union called Kilimanjaro New Cooperative Initiative–Joint Venture Enterprise (KNCI JVE), which is also called G-32. The society presently has approximately 707 active members.

Kibosho Mweka Sungu AMCO Society

The Mweka Sungu AMCO society originated from the existing cooperative called Kibosho East Rural Cooperative Society (now called the Kimasio AMCO society). The Mweka Sungu AMCO society was established in 1955 and was called Kibosho Mweka Sungu Rural Cooperative Society. This society serves the two villages of Mweka and Sungu.

This society deals with the production of coffee (through its members) and supplying farm inputs to the members. The society currently has 778 active members.

BENEFITS OF COFFEE AGRICULTURAL COOPERATIVES TO THE MEMBERS

The benefits of cooperatives are difficult to determine. Some benefits are tangible or direct, as in the case of net margins or savings. Others are intangible or indirect, such as cooperatives' effect on market price levels, quality, and service. The benefits are greater than some types of cooperatives or in specific areas. Most benefits are evaluated in economic terms, but some may be socially evaluated (Mather and Preston 1990). Based on the three analyzed cases, the authors identified the following benefits:

Social Benefits

Increased Access of the Members (and Families) to Social Services

The improved income of cooperative members has led to the trickling down of the effects to the members. The income from coffee sales enables the members (and families) of Mruwia, Mweka Sungu, and Uru North Njari AMCOS to access better social services, such as paying for health services and educational expenses for their family members and children in secondary schools, colleges, and vocational training centers. Furthermore, the members can pay for other services, such as electricity and water bills.

Birchall and Simmons (2009) reported that some cooperatives run low-cost insurance schemes for the members to cover medical treatment or funeral expenses or form welfare committees to finance medical expenses. They help the members to access education to develop their skills and knowledge of young people and encourage them to save. Birchall (2004) argued that cooperatives increase the members' incomes and promote the status of women and encourage girls to complete their education. They also assist in providing other services, such as water supply, dispensaries and hospitals, and medicine and equipment.

Improved Housing Conditions

In the interviews and discussion, the respondents revealed that the income received from the sale of coffee helps to improve their housing conditions. However, it was found that cooperative members could not build new houses by using the income from coffee sale alone but by combining other sources of income, such as selling food crops, running small businesses, and livestock keeping. The members could mostly repair their houses, such as roofing new iron sheets, painting, and other decoration as well as buying furniture and installing water and electric supply systems.

A comparison of the older and younger members revealed that the older members could previously build new houses (in the 1970s to early 1990s) compared with the new members, namely those who joined from nearly the early 2000s until the day of higher outputs of coffee from members' individual farms, which were conducive to climate as well as minimal competition and better prices. Birchall and Simmons (2009) found that in the provision of improved housing and living conditions, cooperatives provide loans for building new homes and improving the condition of members' houses. Cooperatives often offer special loans for the development of water supplies and sanitary facilities, which have been popular.

Provision of Agricultural Education

Cooperative societies are similar to schools; they are organizations for equipping members with various skills and knowledge to perform their work appropriately and be active cooperative members. Mruwia, Mweka Sungu, and Uru North Njari AMCOS provide agricultural education to the members, such as teaching more effective farming methods for both coffee and food crops and animal keeping skills and demonstrating how to treat coffee with various environment-friendly and chemical methods, spacing, planting, and processing of coffee or crops that are unfriendly or friendly to coffee, and storage of coffee and other concerns arising daily. These efforts aim to increase productivity from members' farms. Nonfarming education is also being provided to the members, such as encouraging them to attend various seminars on entrepreneurship and to establish or engage in small businesses and other farming and nonfarming activities.

Improved Food Security

Agricultural cooperatives help to ensure members' food security. The income received from the sale of coffee helps the members to access (buy) enough food. The three cooperatives also educate the members on more effective farming practices for both coffee and food crops (e.g., banana, beans, and maize), thus helping to obtain good harvest to meet their personal and family food consumption needs.

Cooperatives contribute to food security by helping small farmers, fisher folk, livestock keepers, forest holders, and other producers to overcome numerous challenges encountered in their endeavors to produce food (ICA and ILO 2014). Chambo (2009) indicated a close correlation between food security in countries having a long history and large cooperative organizations. However, this correlation was possible because of small farmers who had disposable cash income from cooperative activities to buy food from ordinary village markets.

Increase in Solidarity and Extending Social Protection

A cooperative society promotes solidarity among the members and protects from various risk and problems that are difficult to overcome on an individual basis. Cooperatives provide a new framework or re-enforce traditional mutual support habits, which are mostly event or hazard related (Develtere et al. 2008).

The members cooperate in personal lives by working together in their farms; finding foods for their domestic animals; and helping each in various personal and family problems, such as failure to pay school fees, accidents, sickness, burial and marriage ceremonies and other good and bad moments experienced by any of the members. This is possible because the members have a shared vision and common goals; hence, solidarity and the spirit of helping each other are their common ways of life as true co-operators.

Cooperatives' Concern for the Communities

The findings identified that the three analyzed cooperatives devote part of their annual budget to social responsibilities in their areas. Specifically, the Mweka Sungu AMCO society presently supports fifty-two secondary school students from poorest families and orphans Mweka and Sungu. These students include children and relatives of the members and nonmembers. The cooperative also operates a business of selling affordable farm inputs to both members and nonmembers at similar prices.

The three AMCOS receive a share of the lease fee from settlers (Chibo estates, now known as Kilimanjaro Plantations) who are farming their lands. These societies have allocated 60 percent of such lease for supporting social services in the communities (education and health) and 40 percent to the members. The Uru North Njari AMCO society receives 2 million Tshs from settlers for Machari and Usagara (Uru) estates and the Mruwia AMCO society receives approximately 3.5 million Tshs from settlers. Maghimbi (2010) reported that in some areas, such as Uru North, the cooperative provides services to the community that increases the community's quality of life, for example, building schools, water resources, and a dispensary as well as caring for orphans. Thus, both members and nonmembers benefiting from cooperative societies in their areas.

Economic Benefits

Improved Members' Income

The respondents from the three AMCOS indicated that the establishment of their cooperatives played a major role in improving their general levels of income. These cooperatives enabled the members to obtain a place to sell their crops (coffee) and earn money from such sales. This has consequently enabled the members to earn money to support their family and personal needs, access services, and buy assets and other basic needs. Hence, the members can overcome poverty to build a good living standard and live above the income poverty line.

Mather and Preston (1990) and Birchall and Simmons (2009) have reported that cooperatives conduct various business activities to help improve the income of the members and help them escape from the income poverty traps.

Birchall (2003) argued that cooperatives can reduce poverty and increase income if their values and principles are respected.

Easy Access to and Availability of Affordable Farm Inputs

Mruwia, Mweka Sungu, and Uru North Njari AMCOS have reduced the burden of members' access to farm inputs. Cooperative members previously had to travel to Moshi Municipal or Himo for affordable inputs or otherwise had to buy at them higher prices from the local retailers in their areas. These cooperatives understood the demand of their members by working with the government and other stakeholders and are helping their members to obtain affordable and high-quality and quantity farm inputs, such as fertilizers, agrochemicals (pesticides and fungicides), storage facilities, seeds, and other necessary inputs. These efforts have resulted in increased coffee productivity by the three societies.

Chambo (2009) revealed that agricultural cooperatives facilitate the supply of required agricultural inputs so that the production of commodities is timely to enhance productivity. Mather and Preston (1990) described that farm supply cooperatives provide supplies that ensure the highest value-in-use for the farmers.

Increase in Assets and Properties of Cooperatives and Their Members

This study identified the increase in assets and properties. The three analyzed cooperatives were observed to have taken a good decision in acquiring various assets by using the profits made from their activities since their establishment. The three cooperatives have almost similar assets and properties, including warehouses, vehicles (minibus, tractors, and lorries at the Mweka Sungu AMCO society), rental houses for business, and office facilities.

The profits made from coffee sales and other dividends shared have enabled the members to buy both movable (furniture, televisions, radio, and other home assets) and immovable assets (mainly land and farm plots). Nembhard (2002) reported that successful cooperative businesses create wealth and help their members accumulate wealth; a strategy to enhance an individual member's wealth and to provide easier access to the member's investment is the use of a revolving payment system or minimum vestige.

Provision of Employment

Cooperatives provide employment to both members and nonmembers (staff, secretaries, security guards or watchmen). Maghimbi (2010) argued that the quality of employment in cooperatives may be low. Though, the standard of living of the members in villages (peasants) is low but better compared with that of nonmembers. The standard of living of the members was measured by observing their housing; dressing; schooling of their children; freedom from debts; and ownership of bicycles, radios, and mobile phones. It was also measured by analyzing the socioeconomic activities in which they are engaged. Develtere et al. (2008) identified three levels of employment effects: (1) direct effects or wage employment: the personnel and staff of primary and secondary cooperatives and of supportive institutions ("induced employment" through government cooperative departments and cooperative colleges), (2) indirect effects or self-employment: the members whose membership has a substantial role in guaranteeing a decent income, and (3) multiplier or spillover effects: nonmembers whose professional activities are only viable through the transactions they have with cooperatives (e.g., tradesmen or suppliers of agricultural inputs and fertilizers). The ICA and ILO (2014) indicated that cooperatives play a significant role in employment creation and income generation. Roelants et al. (2014) reported that cooperative enterprises generate partial or full-time employment involving at least 250 million individuals worldwide, either in or within the scope of cooperatives. Cooperative organizations provide employment opportunities to the teeming population of the rural populace, which markedly facilitate the socioeconomic development of both urban and rural areas (Ibrahim 2001). Similarly, Madane (2002) and Gordon (2004) have stated the tangible benefits of using cooperatives as a community and economic development tool, including increased economic traffic, employment opportunities, support for essential community structures, and potential declines in out-migration.

Similar to other organizations, cooperative societies need some permanent and employed staff who will render their services, such as professionalism, efforts, and time, to help them realize their goals and perform well. Cooperatives must also employ people having various skills, extensive knowledge, and experience. Apart from professional people, cooperatives also employ semiskilled people capable of performing some nonprofessional activities, such as security guards (watchmen). Mweka Sungu, Mruwia, and Uru North Njari AMCOS were found to have employed some personnel to assist the board members engaged in professional activities. However, the number and type of the employed staff differ in these cooperatives based on their varying needs and financial well-being. For instance, the Uru North Njari AMCO society has employed a manager, treasurer (volunteering), and security guard, whereas the Mruwia AMCO society has four staff: an accountant, a manager, a coffee inspector, and a security guard. The Mweka Sungu AMCO society has a manager, two gardeners (for supervising the office surroundings), and a security guard (watchman).

However, this study also found that all staff employed in the three cooperatives were from within the cooperative and are not paid regular salaries but honoraria; only the security guards (watchmen) are paid wages. This is because these cooperatives do not have adequate financial capacity to employ full-time salaried staff, such as professional accountants, clerks, managers, marketing officers, and other staff members. Therefore, they use available internal skilled personnel, such as retired professional from public or private sectors and any other members willing to work as volunteers. Furthermore, in the Mweka Sungu AMCO society, their lorry and minibus have provided jobs to the youth in the area as drivers and conductors.

Marketing of Members' Produce

In Mruwia, Mweka Sungu, and Uru North Njari AMCOS, the provision of marketing services for members' crops is very helpful. The members enjoy the economies of scale by selling through their cooperatives and benefit from the low cost incurred because they perform all processes by using their cooperative as one economic unit.

Marketing cooperatives assist their members in increasing the sales volume by approaching new and bigger markets with greater bargaining power. Therefore, the members receive better prices for their goods and have increased personal profit (Zeuli and Cropp 2004). Borzaga and Calera (2012) and Nembhard (2014) reported that when cooperatives address market failure, they improve the "functioning" of the economic system and well-being of a large group of people and improve market competitiveness. Chambo (2009) described that cooperatives also provide an assured market for commodities produced by isolated small farmers in rural areas.

CHALLENGES ENCOUNTERED BY COFFEE AGRICULTURAL COOPERATIVES

In this study, the authors managed to identify various challenges encountered by AMCOS, specifically in Moshi Rural district which are as follows:

Decrease in Coffee Productivity and Quality Challenges

The accessibility to markets and better price facilitated by AMCOS highly depends on the level of productivity and quality of the produce. In Mweka Sungu and Uru North Njari AMCOS, the respondents indicated decreased productivity of coffee. This was found to be because of climate changes in the region, accompanied by intensive solar radiation, low rainfall, coffee diseases, inadequate capacity to obtain farm inputs at the correct quantity and time, and the domination of old (more aged) coffee plants that have low yield. The members also decided to grow other crops instead of coffee because of price uncertainties in local and foreign markets.

Ponte (2001) and Baffes (2003) indicated that a clear shift from high to low qualities well before the policy changes in the 1990s. The reasons for the declines appear to be the nationalization of estates, aging coffee trees, run-down central pulperies, farmers being forced to perform primary processing, the spread of coffee berry disease after 1975 to all arabica coffee-growing areas of the country, and the failure to introduce new disease-resistant high-yielding varieties.

Old System of Farming

The traditional farming system remains dominant in Moshi Rural district. The mixed farming system is dominant among the natives mostly because of land scarcity to grow different crops at different farms. In the same farms, coffee plants are mixed with beans, maize, and banana plants. This causes congestion and competition for nutrients; hence, coffee does not grow well.

The field visit revealed that farmers perform mixed farming because of the scarcity of land to separately grow coffee and food crops. Furthermore, the members are not aware of the trend of coffee prices in world markets and hence fear to experience loss if they decide to grow more coffee than food crops. This has also created a serious challenge in adapting organic coffee farming practice that demands a reduced number of banana plants and no cocultivation with other crops in the same farm.

Cost Implication of Planting New or Replacing Old Coffee Plants

One of the strategies for increasing productivity from coffee cooperatives in Moshi Rural district is introducing new coffee seedling and species that have high yield and are tolerant to drought and diseases. However, the initiative for this transformation highly depends on members' willingness to adapt and incur the costs associated with this initiative. In this study, a major challenge preventing the members from accepting organic farming is the cost related to transforming from inorganic to organic coffee farming.

All respondents from Mweka Sungu and Uru North Njari AMCOS and few from the Mruwia AMCO society reported being challenged by high costs for cutting and digging out old coffee plants, by the reduced number of banana plants to allow more space for coffee and the subsequent digging of new pits for planting new coffee plants, and time required to plant these new plants.

Late Payment of Members' Money after Selling Coffee

The members of Mruwia, Mweka Sungu, and Uru North Njari AMCOS encounter the challenge of late payment for their coffee once they sell through their cooperatives. In the Mruwia AMCO society, such complaints are mainly temporary because the cooperative uses bank loans (obtained from KCBL) to buy coffee from farmers instead of depending on KNCI JVE. In Uru North Njari and Mweka Sungu AMCOS, such a problem is very serious; these cooperatives depend on KNCU for funds to buy coffee from the members. Considering financial problems (because huge debts) of the union, it typically fails to pay adequate amounts of money for coffee collected from members. This discourages the members to sell their coffee through their cooperatives, and they decide to sell to private buyers, thus minimizing revenues of their cooperatives.

Price Fluctuations in Local and Foreign Markets

Price fluctuations in local and foreign markets are another challenge encountered by cooperatives and have discouraged production. Therefore, some members diversify into growing more food crops, keeping livestock, and engaging in small businesses. Low prices result in little profit (and sometime losses) to the members because they cannot effectively cover the costs of production, such as that of preparing the farms; labor work; harvesting; transport; and access to farm inputs such as fertilizers, agrochemicals, and storage facilities. For instance, from 2010 to 2014, the prices fluctuated from 1500 Tshs to 5000 Tshs per kg of coffee. Unstable markets also influence the unions. For example, similar to other cooperatives under the KNCU, the union sometime pays more money to the members. However, in comparison with the world market, the prices are low. When the KNCU obtains loans from banks (mostly the CRDB bank), it fails to repay its loans, hence increasing its debts. Furthermore, the members' incomes are largely affected by such price instabilities because they find themselves only covering production cost with little surplus remaining. The prices also decrease because of a low quality of their produce.

Milford (2004) provided that constantly changing prices indicate that coffee farmers worldwide live in a situation of uncertainty, which complicates planning the future. Therefore, in most cases, low prices are because of overproduction and low quality. Similarly, Kodama (2007) indicated that coffee farmers are particularly exposed to the international economy compared with domestic staple food farmers. They experience from export price fluctuations determined by foreign markets, which are out of their control.

Debt Burden to Societies after Required to Share the Union's Debts

The respondents from Mruwia, Uru North Njari, and Mweka Sungu AMCOS reported that their cooperatives have to pay a share of the union debts for funds obtained from banks, particularly the CRDB bank. Currently, the union has a debt of approximately 3 billion Tshs. Each primary cooperative is required to contribute to paying this debt. For example, the Uru North Njari AMCO society was allocated to pay 16,774,660 Tshs, where 16,624,210 Tshs is the debt from members' advanced payment. This has happened because the union bought coffee at higher prices from the members. On sending this stock to the world market, the prices suddenly dropped, hence creating loss and failure to repay the loan. Furthermore, 150,450 Tshs is the debt for sugar that the union had given on credit to be sold to the primary societies, including the Uru North Njari AMCO society. Because the Mruwia AMCO society has separated from the KNCU and joined KNCI JVE, it refused to contribute to the debt payment.

Heavy debt reduces the cooperatives' net surplus and increases the burden of the cooperatives' members. The members also indicated that the union leaders do not serve interests of members of the primary societies. The union is even borrowing from banks without involving the members before making decisions and is even involved in an intensive misuse of funds and believed to plan selling the farm belonging to the primary societies.

Inadequate Provision of Education and Training

The scarcity of adequate budget for training the members, board, and staff is creating a challenge for the development of Mweka Sungu, Mruwia, and Uru North Njari AMCOS. With uncertain profitability (because of low productivity), the cooperatives are not receiving sufficient revenues to conduct all activities, including the training and provision of education to the members, board, and committee and staff members. The members were observed to not be well-versed with cooperative education, such as the understanding of member rights and responsibilities and their power and presence of overdependence on leaders for all affairs of the cooperative instead of direct participation.

As mentioned by the TFC (2006), cooperative education is necessary for developing enlightened and responsible cooperative leaders who can maintain cooperative values and operate efficient business enterprises; improve the management, business, and entrepreneurial skills of the employees and committee members; and ensure that the members are informed and aware of the nature of cooperative's economic activities, their duties, and responsibilities and benefits of the cooperative membership. Ainebyona and Tiruhungwa (2012) indicated that educating, training, and re-training the members, particularly the officers, are always a challenge to cooperatives, mostly in developing countries. Nyoro and Komo (2005) indicated that, as the main decision-makers of cooperatives, farmers should be trained and be well sensitized on important concerns to ensure that they make informed decisions. Financial constraints hinder the organizations from training their members.

Excessive Deductions on Members' Coffee Sold

Excessive deductions discourage members and minimize their net profit and income from coffee sales in coffee auctions. These include deductions by Coffee Research Institute, expense of transport and escorting coffee to the curing machine, insurance charges, empty bag fees, processing fees at coffee curing machine, union and primary societies' levies, Moshi Rural district levies, health insurance, overpayment charges, price stabilization funds, bank charges, and loan interest. These deductions are a burden to farmers; hence, some farmers even decide to sell to private buyers.

"Free Rider" Effect

The respondents, particularly from Mweka Sungu and Uru North Njari AMCOS, indicated experiencing the challenge of free riders. Free riders are basically dormant cooperative members who have not yet paid the minimum required number of shares and other contributions but still sell their coffee through the cooperative and enjoy other benefits, such as access to subsidized farm inputs (fertilizers, storage facilities, and agrochemicals [pesticides and fungicides]) for coffee production and even receiving various education and training services when opportunities arise. Free riders lead to dormant members, loss of revenues because of unpaid fees and other contributions, and selling coffee to private buyers in case of low prices in cooperatives. They affect the close relations among the members and freely use resources.

The Food and Agriculture Organization (1998) established that in most cases when the cooperative becomes a large group, there are increased chances of the free-rider effect. Briefly, some members try to obtain the maximum possible resources from the cooperative without contributing a fair share. Cooperative, particularly a growing one, should try to develop group management systems that discourage the free-rider effect, such as limiting large numbers of minimally contributing members.

Poor Record Keeping and Accounting Systems

The success of cooperatives relies on appropriate record keeping of the cooperatives and the members. Failure to appropriately maintain records, such as financial and sales records, contracts, and other vital documents result in a poor record of the daily transactions, sales, income and expenditures, and agreements made with other organizations or individuals.

Poor record-keeping was identified in all three cases. Mweka Sungu and Uru North Njari AMCOS were observed to not appropriately maintain their financial records, including writing financial reports following better financial (reporting) standards. This is mainly attributed to few skilled staff members, such as accountants, managers, loan officers, and other leaders, who would perform these professional activities. Furthermore, the low financial capacity of cooperatives to pay for external auditors and lack of professional accountants and managers lead to failure in preparing audited financial reports and maintaining updated financial reports. The Mruwia AMCO society indicated good progress in financial records because of a professional accountant.

Bruynis et al. (2001) indicated that accurate financial statements must be prepared and distributed on a timely basis to the management team. Financial problems occur because of poor accounting systems and lack of appropriate records on transaction made by cooperatives. Therefore, funds are lost or misused without notice by the members. The TFC (2006) indicated that appropriate records and performance reports were not maintained and audited accounts were not presented regularly at the Annual General Meetings.

Less Participation and Membership of Women and Youth

Apart from other factors, the achievements of cooperatives depend on the level of participation and membership of the youth and women. Mweka Sungu, Mruwia, and Uru North Njari AMCOS have many adult men members because the customary land laws have prevented women and the youth from accessing land and using them for coffee production. Therefore, men enjoy complete access to land and use the youth and women to prepare the farms, dig pits, and plant coffee as well as treat and prevent coffee diseases and assisting in harvesting. Men only actively participate during the selling (marketing) activities and collection of the sales revenues.

This relates to the study by Ainebyona and Tiruhungwa (2012) who found that the participation of women is limited in both membership and leadership of primary cooperatives' activities in Kilimanjaro.

Technological Constraints

The studied cooperatives lacked the use of computers in their operations. They still use manual systems for performing their activities, such as maintaining financial records and other reports. This may lead to a risk of loss of information and possibility of fund misappropriation, such as staff leaders taking authorized loans and stealing cooperative funds. Similarly, in the comparative study of 450 cooperatives in Tanzania and Sri Lanka, Simmons and Birchall (2008) identified that the main constraints of cooperatives in Tanzania include the lack of technical knowledge and access to new technology.

Limited Capacity to Supply Adequate and Timely Farm Inputs to Members

A main target of cooperatives in Moshi Rural district is maximizing coffee productivity (and certainly, food crops) from members' farms. Cooperatives supply farmers with affordable and subsidized farm inputs, such as fertilizers, agrochemicals (pesticides and fungicides, etc.), storage facilities, seeds, and other farm equipment. The main challenge in Mruwia, Mweka Sungu, and Uru North Njari AMCOS is that the type of some inputs supplied, particularly agrochemicals and fertilizers, do not meet the demand of the members and mostly do not reach the members on time. Most farmers lack information on the correct type of farm inputs to use and their appropriate time of application. Key inputs, such as seed, pesticides, fertilizers, and equipment, are still not affordable by most rural farmers. Low affordability reduces the application of these farm inputs and eventually reduces the yield that farmers get from their coffee farms.

Management Challenges

Appropriate management practices and capacity are essential for the success of cooperative societies. Poor management leads to the failure of various goals and plans, losing direction because of the lack of clear vision and even problems in the management of funds and other resources, and poor planning because of the lack of strategic planning. Management problems were identified in the cases, particularly in Mweka Sungu and Uru North Njari AMCOS. The problems exist because of poor planning, failure to diversify into other income-generating activities, poor record-keeping, failure to influence changes among members (convincing them to adapt organic coffee farming), and inadequate training on managerial skills.

These factors delay the delivery of expected benefits to the members. Baka (2013) identified that because of weak management, cooperatives require assistance in hiring qualified and experienced employees who can overcome the new challenge of competition with other businesses.

Free Market Challenge (Competition)

Market liberalization, similar to other local enterprises, has affected cooperative societies mostly in terms of price instability and competition. Mweka

Sungu, Mruwia, and Uru North Njari AMCOS reported encountering the challenge of competition from other coffee producers, such as Kilimanjaro Plantations (Chibo estates), and other cooperative societies in the region and nationwide. This creates difficulty for cooperatives to ensure maintaining quality and producing large quantities of coffee. Furthermore, private buyers are affecting the sales volume of coffee through cooperatives because the members sometimes decide to sell all or part of their coffee to these private buyers and organization. Private buyers, such as Doman, sometimes offer higher prices (slightly) exceeding the indicative buying prices offered by cooperative societies. This causes loss of revenues (primary society levies) of the cooperative societies.

Not all cooperatives have the leadership and financial abilities to effectively deal with other firms in the marketplace. Many agricultural cooperatives have little or no influence on the basic price level for the farm products or supply of items (Mather and Preston 1990).

Financial Deficit

The study also revealed that the three cooperative societies, particularly Mweka Sungu and Uru North Njari AMCOS, encounter the challenge of inadequate financial resources. The budget deficit obstructs these cooperatives to diversify their income-generating activity to provide more income benefits to the members. The shortage of funds has mostly been because of overdependence on revenue (tariffs) from coffee sales, the presence of many members who have not yet met the minimum number (amount) of shares, and the presence of non-trustworthy members selling coffee to private buyers and hence reducing the revenue amount of their cooperatives.

Zeuli and Radel (2005) indicated that cooperative members must own a portion of their organization. Equity constraints are a challenge for all cooperatives, but they might be particularly severe for cooperatives in limited resource communities, where the members do not have the surplus financial resources to invest in business ventures, cooperatives, or other organizations. The United Republic of Tanzania (2005) identified that the lack of adequate capital and sustainable finances are challenges encountered by cooperative societies.

Other Challenges

This study identified the following other challenges: the presence of union leaders who are not serving the interests of the members, lack of entrepreneurial skills among the members, resistance to change, decline in the size of arable land because of the need of space (land) for building houses and burial activities for the families of the members, inadequate understanding of cooperative laws and policies, inadequate knowledge among the members regarding their rights and responsibilities, low educational levels of leaders (e.g., committee and board members) and staff, and the limited capacity of cooperatives to employ professional staff.

CONCLUSION AND RECOMMENDATIONS

Conclusion

Cooperatives mostly experience various challenges because of their limited capacity and mechanisms to overcome threats to sustain their operations and activities and offer expected socioeconomic benefits to the members. The development of cooperative societies in this era of globalization highly depends on the internal capacity of cooperatives. The capacity of cooperatives must be developed to be in a safe position to operate, well strategize their operations, compete, and bring more benefits to their members and the wider community and nation.

Recommendations

Based on the identified challenges, the studied cooperatives may implement the following strategies to overcome the encountered challenges:

Cooperative Joint Venturing

Liberalization makes cooperatives vulnerable to various economic shocks and lack of influence in the market. Apart from strengthening the capacity of unions, "Cooperative Joint Ventures" must be emphasized, namely two or more cooperatives must join and perform some business or activities together and share resources, surplus, and profits acquired. The joint ventures will facilitate increasing the bargaining power of the cooperatives, acquire more power to influence the market (e.g., influence prices and increase supply and quantities of coffee sold), and minimize costs of operations (e.g., share transport, warehousing, insurance, processing costs. and other expenses). Thus, typically, cooperatives will benefit from the economies of scale.

Warehouse Receipt Systems

The Mruwia AMCO society was found to practice the warehouse receipt system. The cooperative uses its coffee preserved in the warehouse as collateral to take loans from banks, particularly KCBL, hence finding its own funds to finance its activities, such as buying members' coffee when the harvest season is due. Therefore, if the same practice can be initiated and effectively applied to other cooperatives, it may help in securing adequate funds for cooperatives and the members, prevent cooperatives from experiencing losses and little surplus because of lower prices, and even increase safety for members' coffee until they get better prices.

Cooperative Entrepreneurship

Cooperative entrepreneurship is a form of joint entrepreneurship. Because cooperatives aim to fulfill the needs of the members, a better strategy for sustainability and benefiting more members is by establishing new cooperative ventures. This may attract the commitment of the members and lead to a sense of collective ownership, rather than pure self-gaining. However, starting businesses requires the members to be ready to face and share risks and benefits. Following bylaws, cooperative values and principles, and appropriate management are essential for the businesses to be successful. Cooperatives in Moshi Rural district and those at regional and national levels should design businesses to produce goods and services that are or are not being provided by other companies and provide them at affordable prices.

Roles and Limits of the Union

The KNCU was observed to cause some problems to coffee cooperatives in Moshi Rural district. Among the three analyzed cooperatives, Mweka Sungu and Uru North Njari AMCOS are members of the KNCU. These two societies indicated some of the union-based challenges, such as the misuse of the union's funds and a poor involvement of primary cooperatives in making major union decisions, such as decision to borrow and using primary societies to pay union's debts. Furthermore, it acts as a middleman instead of being a representative of cooperatives in marketing the coffee of the members, whereas cooperatives only act as buyers. The union has become more powerful than primary societies it formed. To reduce or remove complaints from the members, it is better for cooperatives to be granted and to let them decide to obtain complete autonomy to perform most functions performed by the union, including coffee supervision, processing, and marketing, and be able to borrow directly without involving the union. The KNCU should only be the overseer or supervisor and adviser of primary cooperatives and not a final decision-maker.

Extended Training and Education Programs

Cooperatives must invest in the provision of training and education. The training and education programs must address the specific capacity-building needs of the board, staff, and members. Various seminars must be held, and the members or staff must be sent for short- and long-term training programs in various institutions, such as colleges and universities and other institutions, to equip the members, board, and staff with the necessary skills and knowledge required for the smooth operations of cooperatives. For example, training on strategic and business planning, financial management and accounting skills, and risk management and marketing skills must be provided. Furthermore, training must be ensured on the awareness of rights and responsibilities of the members, board, and staff as well as on legal concerns such as cooperative policies and laws.

Diversification of Coffee Products

To overcome the risks of price fluctuations and unreliable coffee markets, agricultural (coffee) cooperatives must diversify coffee products and businesses. For example, cooperatives, individually or jointly, may establish coffee bars in various areas, where people may sit and drink the locally processed coffee. They may also establish units for coffee roasting to provide materials to coffee vendors.

Extend Credit Services and Supply of Subsidized Farm Inputs to Members

Improving the productivity of the coffee farms of the members, among other factors, highly depends on the availability of funds to finance the members' agricultural activities (coffee production). Therefore, cooperatives, by working with cooperative banks and the government, must determine the best strategies to assist farmers with agricultural credits. A supply of various subsidized farm inputs, such as fertilizers, pesticides, fungicides, storage facilities, chemical pumps or sprayers, and tools, would enable farmers to adequately buy and apply these inputs, thus increasing coffee productivity in Moshi Rural district.

Government Interventions

There should be more supportive business environment including cooperative legal (policies and laws) and economic (price stabilization) environments to enable cooperatives to flourish. Market-focused cooperative policy should be in place such as supporting cooperatives to access foreign markets, engaging in value addition, ensuring better prices for their products, providing funds at competitive interest rates, and so on.

Inclusion of Women and Youth in Cooperative Development

It will be vital for cooperatives to involve women and youth in their activities and management by enrolling most of the population and enhancing the realization of a larger multiplier effect. Efforts need to be directed in eliminating cultural issues hindering their participation, and developing attractive business activities and extending value chain where youth can participate.

Terminating Free Riders in Cooperatives

Cooperative development and sustainability highly depend on the activeness of the members. It is vital for agricultural cooperatives to eliminate free riders. This can be ensured by regularly inspecting the membership registry, omitting the names of inactive members, preventing inactive members from voting and making decisions.

Involving in Fair Trade Agreements

The concept of fair trade aims to build "a system of trade, in which the partners deliberately seek to establish a more direct relationship between groups of producers and consumers in the two worlds and a greater understanding among consumers of the need of the producers for support for their independent development" (Brown 1993). Fair trade is often called "alternative trade" because it aims to establish a trade network alternative to the commercial market. Once cooperatives receive their fair-trade certification for their coffee, they can obtain better prices for their coffee exports in various markets among fair trade members.

REFERENCES

Ainebyona, R. R., and R. M. Tiruhungwa. *Relevance and Key Performance Indicators of Cooperative Unions in Serving Primary Cooperatives in Tanzania: A Case of Kilimanjaro Native Cooperative Union (KNCU).* Research Report Series 1, no. 9 (2012): 90–118.

Baffes, John. *Tanzania's Coffee Sector: Constraints and Challenges in a Global Environment.* Africa Region Findings & Good Practice Infobriefs 56, 2003.

Baka, O. Leonard. "The Challenges Facing Co-operative Societies in Kenya A Case Study: Kenya Planter Co-operative Union (KPCU)." *Public Policy and Administration Research* 3, no. 11 (2013): 34–43.

Bello Dogarawa, Ahmad. *The Role of Cooperative Societies in Economic Development.* Germany: University Library of Munich, 2005.

Bibby, Andrew. *Tanzania's Cooperatives Look to the Future*, 2006. Accessed on March 30, 2015, www.andrewbibby.com.

Birchall, Johnston, and Richard Simmons. *Co-operatives and Poverty Reduction: Evidence from Sri Lanka and Tanzani*a. Co-operative College 13, 2009.

Birchall, Johnston. *Cooperatives and the Millennium Development Goals.* Geneva: International Labour Office (ILO), 2004.

Birchall, Johnston. *Rediscovering the Cooperative Advantage: Poverty Reduction Through Self-Help*. Geneva: International Labour Organization (ILO), 2003.

Borzaga, Carlo, and Giulia Galera. "The Concept and Practice of Social Enterprise. Lessons from the Italian Experience." *International Review of Social Research* 2, no. 2 (June 2012): 85–102. https://doi:10.1515/irsr-2012-0019.

Brennan, Mark A., and Luloff A.E. "A Cooperative Approach to Rural Development in Ireland: Cultural Artifacts and the Irish Diaspora as an Example." *Journal of International Agricultural and Extension Education* 12, no. 1 (Spring 2005): 15–25.

Brown, Michael Barratt. *Fair Trade: Reform and Realities in the International Trading System*. London and New Jersey: Zed Books, 1993.

Bruynis, Christopher, Peter D. Goldsmith, David E. Hahn, and Willaim J. Taylor. "Critical Success Factors for Emerging Agricultural Marketing Cooperatives." *Journal of Cooperation* 16 (2001): 14–24.

Chambo, Suleman A. *Agricultural Co-operatives: Role in Food Security and Rural Development*. (Paper presented at the Expert Group Meeting on Co-operatives, Moshi, Tanzania), 2009.

Develtere, Patrick, Ignace Pollet, and Fredrick Wanyama. *Cooperating out of Poverty: The Renaissance of the African Cooperative Movement*. Geneva: ILO, 2008.

Food and Agriculture Organization (FAO). *Agricultural Co-operative Development: A Manual for Trainers*. Rome: FAO, 1998.

Gordon, Jessica. "Non-traditional Analysis of Co-operative Economic Impacts: Preliminary Indicators and A Case Study." *Review of International Co-operation* 97, no. 1 (2004): 6–47.

Ibrahim, Yahaya. *Basic Aspects of Cooperative Studies*. Kano: Munawwar Books International, 2001.

International Cooperative Alliance (ICA). *Statement on the Cooperative Identity*, 1995. https://www.ica.coop/en/cooperatives/cooperative-identity.

International Cooperative Alliance and International Labour Organization. *Cooperatives and the Sustainable Development Goals: A Contribution to the Post-2015 Development Debate – A Policy Brief*. Brussels and Geneva: ICA and ILOCOOP.

International Labour Organization (ILO). *Co-operative Enterprises Build a Better World*. Dar es Salaam: International Labour Office, 2012.

Kodama, Yuka. *New Role of Cooperatives in Ethiopia: The Case of Ethiopian Coffee Farmers Cooperatives*. African Study Monographs 35 (2007): 87–108.

Madane, V. Madhav. "Co-operative Rejuvenation Through Self-help Groups and Other Alternatives." *Review of International Co-operation* 95, no. 1 (2002): 104–113.

Maghimbi, Sam. *Cooperatives in Tanzania Mainland: Revival and growth*. Coop AFRICA. Working Paper No. 14. Dar es Salaam: ILO, 2010.

Mather, James Warren, and Homer J. Preston. *Cooperative Benefits and Limitations: Farmer Cooperatives in the United States*. United States Department of Agriculture/ Rural Business- Cooperative Service. Cooperative Information Report 1, Section 3, 1990.

Milford, Anna. *Coffee, Co-operatives, and Competition: The Impact of Fair Trade*. Bergen: Chr. Michelsen Institute Development Studies and Human Rights, 2004.

Nembhard. Jessica G. "Cooperatives and Wealth Accumulation: Preliminary Analysis." *American Economic Review* 92, no. 2 (2002): 325–329.

Nembhard, Jessica G. *White paper on Benefits and Impacts of Co-operatives*. New York: John Jay College, 2014.

Nyoro, K. James, and Isaac Komo. *An Analysis of Success, Failure and Demand Factors of Agricultural Co-operatives in Kenya*. Strategies and Analysis for Growth and Access (SAGA), Policy Brief, February, 2005.

Ponte, Stefano. *Coffee Markets in East Africa: Local Responses to Global Challenges or Global Responses to Local Challenges?* Working Paper 01.5. Copenhagen: Center for Development Research, 2001.

Roelants, Bruno, Eum Hyungsik, and Elisa Terrasi. *Cooperatives and Employment: A Global Report*. CICOPA, 2014. https://cicopa.coop/wp-content/uploads/2018/03/cooperatives_and_employment_a_global_report_en__web_21-10_1pag.pdf.

Simmons, Richard, and Johnston Birchall. "The Role of Co-operatives in Poverty Reduction: Network Perspectives." *Journal of Socio-Economics* 37, no. 6 (December 2008): 2131–2140.

Tanzanian Federation of Cooperatives. *Co-operatives and Development in Tanzania: A Simplified Guide to the Co-operative Development Policy and the Co-operative Societies Act of Tanzania Mainland*. Tanzanian Federation of Cooperatives in Collaboration with the Cooperative Development Department, 2006.

United Republic of Tanzania, *The Cooperative Reform and Modernization Program*. CRMP: 2005–2015, April 2005.

United Republic of Tanzania. *Tanzania Co-operative Development Policy*. Dar es salaam: Government Publishers, 2002.

United Republic of Tanzania. *Villages and Ujamaa Villages Act 1975*. Dar es Salaam: Government Publishers, 1975.

United States Department of Agriculture. *Cooperative Benefits and Limitations: Farmer Cooperatives in the United States*. Cooperative Information Report 1 Section 3, 1990.

Zeuli, Kimberley, and Robert Cropp. *Co-operatives: Principles and Practices in the 21st Century*. University of Wisconsin Extension, Madison: Publication A1457, 2004.

Zeuli, A. Kimberley, and Jamie Radel. "Cooperatives as a Community Development Strategy: Linking Theory and Practice." *Journal of Regional Analysis and Policy* 35, no. 1 (2005): 1–12. https://doi:10.22004/ag.econ.132302.

Chapter 13

Emerging Issues in the Management of Cooperatives in India

Tapas R. Dash

Cooperatives have been flourishing for more than two centuries in the world by attracting democratic-minded people to their fold. Serious research has firmly established cooperation as a more productive and efficient approach to almost any task than competition (Williams 2007). Cooperation came into existence as an off-shoot of the industrial revolution of the eighteenth century in Europe, led by Great Britain. The enormous use of machines and a series of changes in the production systems during the industrial revolution (1750–1850) replaced human labor to a great extent. To protect the working class from exploitation, Robert Owen (1771–1858), William King (1786–1865), and Charles Fourier (1772–1837) explored an alternative as a result of which the cooperative movement began in the modern world in the later part of the eighteenth century (Sharada 1986). However, the modern cooperative movement in the world dates back to August 15, 1844, when a small group of twenty-eight weavers in England with a share capital of 28 pounds started a store of their own called "The Rochdale Equitable Pioneers Society" (Bailey 1960). The Rochdale Pioneers established a great tradition and marked the beginning of the world of the cooperative movement. The Rochdale store was not the first society of its kind as the dock-yard workers of Woolwick and Chathom had set up the first cooperative flour mill as early as in 1760. Yet, the Rochdales are called "Pioneers" because they founded the first permanent successful store and gave a final shape to the cooperative principles, propagated them, and imparted them dignity and glory (Bedi 2001). While the cooperative movement in the developed world sprang up in reaction to the industrial revolution in the eighteenth and nineteenth centuries, the movement in the developing countries was based on the need for creativity in response to the rapid decolonialization during the second half of the twentieth century. Cooperation facilitates mass voluntary participation in an organized way to enlist the support of millions of small farmers, artisans, craftsmen, and cottage and small-scale enterprises (Jha 1969). Today, cooperatives in many countries are significant social and economic actors in their national economies by contributing to the well-being of various sections of the society.

The success of cooperative model which brings communities out of poverty, allows individuals to pool their resources and skills together to work toward a common economic goal. This model depends upon adhering to the seven core principles of cooperation adopted by the International Cooperative Alliance (ICA) in 1995, which includes: (1) voluntary and open membership, (2) democratic member control, (3) members' economic participation, (4) autonomy and independence, (5) education, training and information, (6) cooperation among cooperatives, and (7) concern for community.

Cooperation in India has been recognized as part of the pattern of Indian socialism, especially interpreted in terms of rural society (Margaret 1981). Cooperatives are pivotal institutions for bringing socioeconomic development for an inclusive growth in rural areas (Mukherjee 2012). Cooperation in a vast country like India is of great significance because (1) it is an organization for the poor who wish to solve their problems collectively, (2) it is an institution of mutual help and sharing, (3) it softens the class conflicts and reduces the social cleavages, (4) it reduces the bureaucratic evils and follies of political factions, (5) it overcomes the constraints of agricultural development, and (6) it creates a conducive environment for small and cottage industries (Prakash 2011).

By operating in various areas of the economy such as credit, production, processing, marketing, housing, dairy, urban banking, sugar, and handlooms and textiles, and so on, the cooperative sector has been playing a significant role toward the progress of the country's socioeconomic development. In spite of their high level of commitment to uplift the standard of living of their members, cooperatives in India face several problems and challenges. Based on the above backdrop, this chapter is mainly designed with an intention to further continue the discussion on the problems and challenges of cooperatives in India along with strategies for the development and management of cooperatives in the country. First, we begin the chapter by briefly describing the progress of cooperatives in India. Second, we carry out a discussion on the problems and challenges for cooperatives in the country, followed by strategies dealing with the emerging issues for the development and management of cooperatives. Finally, we conclude with managerial insights.

PROGRESS OF COOPERATIVES IN INDIA

The cooperative movement in India was mainly organized against the exploitation of unscrupulous money-lenders to exonerate the farming community. The enactment of Cooperative Societies Act 1904 enabled the formation of agricultural credit cooperatives in rural India under the active support of the government. Since then, the cooperative movement has made significant progress in cooperative credit. Further, the growth of the cooperative movement in its manifold ways gained impetus since the commencement of the socioeconomic planning process in the country. Over a period of time, the movement is seen as one of the largest movements in the world. With the presence of 854,355 cooperatives (177,605 credit cooperatives; 676,750 noncredit cooperatives) having a total membership of more than 290 million covering 98 percent of the rural areas in 2016–2017 (NCUI 2018), cooperatives significantly contribute to almost all areas of economic activities in the country. In addition to the agricultural credit, cooperatives have made their presence in other sectors such as real estate, power, insurance, health care, tourism, and so on. The movement which had initially started with a limited spectrum of activities in the field of rural financing, made an all-pervasive effect in penetrating into every sphere of economic activity of the nation generating 13.3 percent of direct employment and 10.9 percent of self-employment in 2016–2017 (NCUI 2018). In agriculture, during the same period, the total credit disbursed by cooperatives was 13.4 percent, and the short-term agricultural credit disbursed by cooperatives to small and marginal farmers was 19.1 percent. Thus, Indian cooperative movement which is considered as the world's largest movement has been widely acknowledged as an instrument toward achieving the socioeconomic transformation of the Indian society with special attention on the people living in rural areas. It is a movement of mass involvement, an approach toward equity and justice (Dash 1998).

In India, the cooperative sector has been considered as a balancing force between public and private sectors as it combines the virtues of both the private sector, that is, freedom and flexibility, and the public sector, that is, social commitment for the welfare of the community (Barua and Choudhury 1998). Further, the involvement of people in the planning process through cooperatives has strengthened the democratic fiber of the nation. Though the century-old Indian cooperative movement has been considered as a significant instrument of socioeconomic development, the period of globalization and liberalization has forced it to face multiple problems and challenges of a market-oriented economy. It has also been observed that even though the quantitative growth of Indian cooperatives appears sound, the qualitative aspect of the movement is still a missing link.

EMERGING PROBLEMS AND CHALLENGES OF COOPERATIVES

In spite of the significant contribution in boosting the socioeconomic conditions of their million members, the century-old cooperatives in India are not free from multifarious problems and challenges. Despite the tremendous growth of the cooperatives, the overall progress of the movement is not very impressive. Confronted with lack of active participation of members in the management of cooperatives, lack of mobilization of internal resources, limited capital, overdependence on government assistance, mounting over-dues in cooperative credit institution, lack of professional management, bureaucratic control, and interference in the management, and so on, have proved to be harmful to their growth and do not meet the rising expectations of their members. Therefore, the real challenge for the cooperatives today is to retain their competitive positions in the liberalized economy and establish their relevance in the society.

Inadequate/Lack of Active Participation of Members

It has been largely felt that sustainability of cooperatives mostly depends on the active participation of their members in social activities. This can be seen in terms of the members' involvement in the affairs of the cooperatives, their attitude toward the cooperatives, the role clarity and division of powers of decision and control within the members.

Emphasizing the importance of both management and governance, Groeneveld (2015) states that "there is no substitute for competent management and good governance. Indeed, how cooperative banks tackle all challenges is largely determined by the set up and functioning of the representative democracy, that is, how and to what extent members participate in strategy, control, supervision, policy and decision-making."

The failure of the voice option (members' participation) has been the outcome of what Brett (1993) has called "bounded rationality" among the cooperative members stemming from extreme asymmetries in information. In the context of India, government officials, political leaders, and managers of development agencies frequently impose their wills on cooperatives and as a result, the value of voice has been entirely lost.

Politicization of the Cooperative Movement

Theoretically, the cooperative movement has nothing to do with politics. But the Indian cooperative movement has become politicized with politicians replacing genuine people's interests in the cooperative movement. Wresting control of the cooperative societies has become a political prestige for leaders. This, in turn, has led to alleged inclusion of bogus members in a majority of cooperative societies at the time of cooperative elections. Cooperatives have been much politicized as the political party in power has found these organizations effective enough to meet their political ends. In 1965, the Mirdha Committee while assessing the growth of cooperative movement had observed that government policy of deliberate expansion of cooperatives had led to politicization of cooperatives and entrenchment of vested interests in their management.

In many occasions, the selection of beneficiaries, particularly getting loans from cooperative societies is mostly done on political considerations, and when the payment of loans arises, there is always an intervention from the local leaders. Sometimes, before election, to gain the support of the people, political leaders declare to waive the loans of the members if they will come to power. Also, when a cooperative body loses, it is kept continued by the political leaders to serve their own interests. Thus, political interference acts as a formidable obstacle to the growth of cooperative movement in India.

Overdependence on Government Assistance

The cooperative movement in India was initiated by the enactment of Cooperative Societies Act 1904, and right from the beginning, the government has patronized the movement. During the first five-year plan (1951–1954), the All India Rural Credit Survey Committee (AIRCS) was appointed and the recommendations of the committee led to the emergence of state partnership at all levels of cooperatives in the form of share capital contribution, and provision of technical, managerial and financial assistance to different kinds of cooperatives. Thus, there was a paradigm shift in the state's approach to cooperatives with the implementation of the recommendations of the AIRCS in the year 1954. With government involvement, cooperatives came to be perceived as agencies of the State rather than an autonomous member-based economic enterprises.

The state-controlled cooperatives, which depend on government subsidies lack vitality and flexibility required to adjust to market-driven environment. Based on the observations of the Mirdha Committee 1965, the Conference of State Ministers of Cooperation in 1969 recommended stringent provisions in cooperative legislation which destroyed autonomous and democratic character of cooperatives. As cooperatives have started being increasingly dependent on the government for both financial as well other, state interventions in their management eventually increased. Due to the government's interference in cooperative activities, "self-help," a basic thrust of the cooperative society has gone out. Further, senior positions in cooperatives are agreed to be manned by officers on deputation from government departments. Thus, government control has not only weakened cooperative leadership but also stalled the growth and development of cooperatives. The decade up to the 1990s marked active government intervention, which led to the degeneration of cooperatives from autonomous member-driven bodies to appendages of the state (Misra 2006).

Limited Operational Coverage

Primary cooperative societies are mostly small in their size and meant for single purpose only. Their development has suffered as they only have a few members and solely operate in one or two villages. Due to limited coverage of the geographical area, their resources remain limited, for which it becomes impossible for them to expand their means and business base. Further, as most of the societies are single purpose, they are unable to take a total view of the need of the people and are not in a position to make optimal use of their resources.

Poor Linkage among Different Cooperatives

Cooperatives in India have mostly failed to show a strong horizontal and vertical linkage among themselves to develop an integrated structure. Apart from structural linkages, there are no sustained business relationships among various tiers in the movement. The units in various tiers have started working at cross purposes for the existence of themselves. As a result, cooperatives have failed to compete effectively with the private sector and meet the desired expectations of their members. To strengthen cooperative credit system, Capoor Committee in 2000 had suggested for the voluntary amalgamation of cooperatives based on the economies of scale and revitalization package for cooperatives to be based on financial, operational, organizational, and systematic considerations. Further, the Advisory Committee on Flow of Credit to Agriculture and other related Activities from the Banking System, known as Vyas Committee, in 2004 had suggested to strengthen the linkages between production and marketing by increasing pledge finance, credit for marketing, and introduction of advances against warehouse receipts.

Poor Level of Planning and Ineffective Monitoring

Lack of proper planning has crippled a number of primary cooperative societies in the country. Many cooperatives at the grass-root level function without a plan and do not have a clear goal for their achievement. In addition, in the rural areas, they do not give much attention in monitoring their performances against the standard set in terms of the goals. Thus, the poor level of planning and ineffective monitoring have crippled the cooperatives for which they are not able to act as change agents for the rural people. Therefore, to make cooperatives viable, at first, the need is to initiate and develop planning at micro level.

Poor Recovery of Loans

The main challenges for financial cooperatives according to Groeneveld (2015) include the adherence to an expression of cooperative values and principles and member participation, as well as future commercial performance, capitalization, achievement of operational excellence, and stricter regulatory and supervisory requirements.

In the Indian scenario, the history of the cooperative credit system has been the history of alternating periods of growth, stagnation, reorganization, yet quantitatively, the achievement of the cooperative system is significant. Unfortunately, one of the major constraints has been the poor recovery of loans. For Primary Agricultural Credit Societies (PACS), in 2007–2008, while the total overdue was INR 15,415 crores, it had reached INR 53,293 crores in 2016–2017 against the total demand of INR 200,464 crores in the country. The collection rates vary largely both at intra-state and inter-state levels and the amount of over-dues has been on a rising scale due to the poor recovery of loans. Majority of the cooperative societies have been incurring losses year after year and are financially vulnerable.

Weak Human Resource Management

The approach of cooperative enterprises to human resource management does not significantly change in spite of their enhanced size in terms of their business as well as diversified activities. In most cases, the elected nonofficial managements have never seriously thought about the need to strengthen the management by professionals or by imparting intensive training for improving the skills or filling the gaps in knowledge and skills of their existing personnel. Besides, qualified and experienced personnel do not feel attracted to work in the cooperative organizations due to their poor working conditions. As a result, the weak human resource management system in cooperatives has finally affected their performance in an adverse way.

Lack of Professionalization

The success of cooperatives largely depends on the efficiency of their operations. Although the importance of professionalization is accepted by cooperatives in principle, it continues to be ignored in practice. Due to the lack of professional management, a large number of cooperatives in the country have fallen into the hands of competition with the private sector.

A major inhibiting factor in this regard is the practice of filling up the senior positions in cooperatives by bringing officers on deputation from government departments. This results in thwarting the growth of professional managers from within. So long as members do not demand high-level performance from their cooperatives and pressures are not built on cooperatives to excel in the market place, professionalization is very unlikely to materialize.

Indian cooperatives are also unable to evolve strong communication and public relation strategies that can promote the concept of cooperation among the masses (Prakash 2011). Apart from these problems, cooperatives in their respective sectors have been facing a number of challenges as follows:

i. Competition: Multinational companies have started taking full advantage of the borderless world without hindrance of the national boundaries to undertake large-scale economic activities, which will further dominate the world market in the coming days. This scenario has posed tremendous threats to the cooperative movement's ability for survival.
ii. Resource constraints: In the liberalized economic system, since the government has gradually withdrawn support, many cooperatives have faced difficulties in generating their own resources and have to completely reorganize themselves to survive and succeed in the competitive environment.
iii. Lack of concrete direction: With such a huge and diversified cooperative structure in the country, the most significant challenge is to provide proper direction toward which cooperative movement should move with firm determination.
iv. Lack of policy support: Structural weaknesses of cooperative institutions coupled with the lack of proper policy support have neutralized their positive impacts and resulted partly in mismanagement and inefficiency.

STRATEGIES FOR DEVELOPMENT AND MANAGEMENT OF COOPERATIVES

In the light of the multifarious problems covering their organizational, managerial, and operational weaknesses and challenges, if the Indian cooperative movement has to sustain and strengthen, a viable strategy for cooperative development under present market conditions needs to be introduced. Thus, cooperatives have to reorient their strategies in the context of the present competitive environment and as such the following strategies are suggested:

i. The foremost question of sustainability in cooperatives is the active participation of its members in business and other activities. The first task is to restore the confidence of the members on cooperatives, which has been lost due to gross negligence and extension of poor services by the cooperatives to the members. A genuine attempt is required to ensure accountability and demonstrate honesty and transparency in the system. Increased participation can gradually be built up through the adoption of better business strategy and an improvement in the management of cooperatives. More importance to the participation in cooperatives, both in the governance processes and cooperative legislation has to be considered on a priority basis.
ii. In the present environment, cooperatives should become more "market friendly" and "members' friendly" to meet their organizational goals. Cooperatives at all levels should make efforts to reorient their functions according to the market demands. The government needs to recognize that cooperatives are formed and managed by members and not subjected to government intervention in their internal management. The powers vested in the government to direct and supervise cooperatives should be reviewed periodically. The aim should be to give more autonomy to the cooperatives. Hence, cooperative legislation should suitably be altered for creating level field conditions for cooperatives in relation to their competitors (Upadhyaya 2008).
iii. Development of proper horizontal and vertical linkages among the cooperatives is necessary to strengthen their positions against competitors as well as to effectively serve members. To be effective and successful, cooperative federation must continuously achieve two interrelated goals: strengthen the autonomy of its affiliates, enhance viability, and improve the ability to serve its members; and remain an economically viable, innovative, and competitive enterprise. In this context, the supportive interlinkages, management processes, decision-making organs, and governance structures should be evolved (Upadhyaya 2008).
iv. It is strategically important to initiate and develop planning at a micro level to make cooperatives as viable units. To make cooperatives function effectively, the development of solid need-based plans with clear goals is necessary. Besides, it is equally important to monitor the performances of the cooperatives against the standard set in terms of the goals in a periodic manner.
v. For ensuring that the cooperatives meet the expectations of their members as well as the beneficiaries, it is necessary to devise strategies to

upgrade the quality of the human resources. This aims not only to ensure efficient management but also higher productivity in cooperatives. Thus, human resource development appears to be one of the most effective answers to the search of the solution that improves the quality of existing manpower in the cooperative system.

vi. Cooperatives need to develop appropriate strategies in mobilizing resources to meet their requirements, particularly for the expansion and diversification of their business. In the light of the present competitive environment, the whole spectrum of cooperative values and principles needs to be reviewed to give space and avenues for resource mobilization. One of the mechanisms could be a kind of preferential shares from resourceful members and deposits from nonmembers.

vii. The success of cooperatives depends upon the capacity of their members to a large extent. Therefore, it is necessary to evolve strategies of intensive training and education of the members to enable them to participate in the development process. The composition of boards at different levels often needs to be changed, whereby persons with business experience should become the board members (Upadhyaya 2008).

viii. Professionalization in the management of cooperatives needs to be strengthened to ensure efficiency in their operations. The practice of appointing officials in cooperatives on deputation from government departments should be stopped due to the lack of their accountability. Functionaries of cooperatives need to be well-trained to consolidate their positions. While the managers in cooperative enterprises without a business acumen should be replaced, new managers should be offered performance-related rewards. Boards must empower managers to serve the community on a faster and timely basis.

According to Taimni (1998), cooperatives in the South Asian region have to strive to:

i. make optimum use of all resources and continuously enhance the productivity of the resources;

ii. ensure highest efficiency while providing services to members;

iii. improve management capabilities and competencies through effective organizational designs and structures;

iv. mobilize capital and lay greater stress on internal capital formation and accumulation;

v. develop and retain human resources—members, leaders, staff, and managers;

vi. forge strategic alliance with key institutional actors in new environments;

vii. evolve and sustain integrated, vertical structures;
viii. increasingly focus on directly enhancing socioeconomic conditions of their members by undertaking value-added operations;
ix. encourage members' participation through improved and diversified services;
x. strictly adhere to the values of honesty, openness, care, and concern for the community and environments; and
xi. develop and retain symbiotic relations with the government.

According to Mukherjee (2012), "Cooperatives in our country face many challenges and problems. Their performance across sectors, activities, and regions is variable. They need to reorient by improving their efficiency and develop professionally to meet requirements of their core clientele."

CONCLUSION

In the present liberalized environment, while the public sector has been synchronizing in their activities, the private sector has failed to make an impressive impact in the development of the rural areas and particularly, the socioeconomic conditions of the disadvantaged and marginalized sections of the society. Therefore, there is great hope on the cooperative sector to provide benefits to the members by enlarging its base. Upon realizing the importance of the cooperative sector, the government of India has time to time changed policy directives to support cooperatives in their operations. In 2012, the government has taken a big initiative for cooperatives by bringing in the 97th amendment to the Constitution, which enables democratic and autonomous functioning. By this amendment, the right to form cooperatives has been made a fundamental right. Indian cooperatives need to bring in professionalism for which State laws need to be amended in line with the Central legislation to ensure that the country's six lakh cooperatives work as autonomous, self-reliant, and democratic bodies (Mukherjee 2012).

As cooperatives are the only alternatives for the large sections of society for the betterment of living of their members, removing all sorts of constraints in the operations of cooperative enterprises assumes greater significance. Strategies should be devised to revitalize the weaker cooperatives and strengthen the operational cooperatives to effectively deliver goods and services as per the needs of the communities. It is important to protect the autonomy of the cooperatives and carry out activities without diluting democratic characteristics of the institutions. Managers of the cooperatives must not consider cooperatives at par with private entities, rather they should exercise more caution while delivering their services to the members of the cooperatives. We need to keep in mind that cooperatives are owned and controlled by members for their benefits. To ensure competitiveness, cooperatives must be managed professionally. In the light of mismanagement, ensuring good governance among cooperatives has assumed greater importance.

REFERENCES

Bailey, Jack. *The British Co-operative Movement.* London: Hutchinson University Library, 1960.

Barua, Nayan, and A. J. Choudhury. "Emerging Economic Scenario: Challenges before the Cooperatives." In *Co-operatives and Economic Development*, edited by Tapas R. Dash and K.K. Sen, 101–13. Jaipur: Rawat Publications, 1998.

Bedi, Raghubans. D. *Theory, History and Practice of Co-operation.* Meerut: R. Lall Book Depot, 2001.

Brett, Edwin A. "Voluntary Agencies as Development Organizations: Theorizing the Problem of Efficiency and Accountability." *Development and Change* 24, no. 2 (1993): 269–304.

Dash, Tapas R. "Regional Variations in Co-operative Development – A Taxonomic Approach." In *Co-operatives and Economic Development*, edited by Tapas R. Dash and K.K. Sen, 59–67. Jaipur: Rawat Publications, 1998.

Groeneveld, Hans. "Member-based Enterprises: The Spotlight on Financial Services Co-operatives." Inaugural address at TIAS School for Business and Society at Tilburg University on 13 February 2015. Tilburg, Netherlands: Tilburg University, 2015.

Jha, D. *Development of Co-operation for Economic Development: An Interdisciplinary Approach.* Pune: Vaikunth Mehta National Institute of Co-operative Management, 1969.

Margaret, Digby. *An Assessment of Indian Co-operative. New Delhi*: RBSA Publications, 1981.

Misra, Biswa Swarup. "Performance of Primary Cooperatives in India: An Empirical Analysis." *Indian Economic Journal* 53, no. 4 (2006): 95–113.

Mukherjee, Pranab. "States must amend Cooperative Laws to make them Autonomous: President." http://www.thehindubusinessline.com/economy/states-must-amend-cooperative-laws-to-make-them-autonomous-president/article4178351.ece.

National Co-operative Union of India. *Indian Co-operative Movement – A Statistical Profile- 2018.* New Delhi: NCUI, 2018.

Prakash, Daman. "Roadblocks before Cooperatives." http://www.indiancooperative.com/blog/roadblocks-before-cooperatives/.

Sharada, V. *The Theory of Co-operation.* Bombay: Himalaya Publishing House, 1986.

Taimni, K. K. "Challenges before Co-operatives in South Asia: Building a Comparative Advantage." Sustainable Development Department, Food and Agriculture Organization (1998): 1–6.

Upadhyaya, P. K. *Economic and Financial Performance of Fishery Cooperatives – A Study of Fishery Cooperatives around Chilika Lake, Orissa.* Unpublished Ph.D. Thesis. Bhubaneswar: Department of Analytical and Applied Economics, Utkal University, 2008.

Williams, Richard C. *The Co-operative Movement: Globalization from Below.* Aldersgate, England: Ashgate Publishing Ltd., 2007.

Index

About the Editor and Contributors

EDITOR

Tapas R. Dash is a professor and research advisor at CamEd Business School, Phnom Penh, Cambodia. Earlier he served as a professor and senior vice president of academic and university affairs at Build Bright University, Cambodia, and a faculty member of the Institute of Cooperative Management, National Council for Cooperative Training, New Delhi, India. He has had the privilege of commissioning a number of research and consultancy projects funded by the international and national organizations including the Royal Government of Cambodia. Currently, some of his important consultancies are funded by the Swiss Agency for Development and Cooperation (SDC), International Labor Organization (ILO), USAID Cambodia Green Future Activity, East-West Management Institute (EWMI), Plan International Cambodia, People in Need (PIN), Advocacy and Policy Institute (API), and Cambodia Development Resource Institute (CDRI) among such other institutions. As an international expert, presently he is involved in designing the National Program Phase II (2021–2030) of the Sub-National Democratic Development (SNDD), Royal Government of Cambodia. Tapas is the co-editor of Cooperatives and Economic Development (Rawat Publications, India) and Educational Access and Excellence (Allied Publishers, India). He is the founder editor-in-chief of the International Journal of Business and Development Research, and currently, the editor-in-chief of the Journal of Accounting, Finance, Economics, and Social Sciences. He can be contacted at tapas_dash@yahoo.co.in/dranjan@cam-ed.com.

CONTRIBUTORS

Jan Danica S. Asma is an assistant professor at the Institute of Cooperatives and Bio-Enterprise Development, College of Economics and Management (CEM), University of the Philippines Los Baños (UPLB). She teaches cooperative management and enterprise development. Her research interests are in the fields of cooperative management, rural development, and technological innovations. She can be contacted at jsasma@up.edu.ph.

Franci Avsec has worked for more than thirty-seven years for the Cooperative Union of Slovenia as a legal adviser, starting as a probationer under the mentorship of professor Emil Čeferin. In 1997, he began to lecture on cooperatives, and agricultural and business law at universities in Maribor and Ljubljana. Currently, he is partly employed as an associate professor in the Faculty of Economics and Informatics at the University of Novo Mesto and also works as a freelance adviser and researcher. His publications mainly focus on agricultural and cooperative law, cooperative history, and the current development of cooperatives in Slovenia and abroad. He can be contacted at franci.avsec@siol.net.

Stefan Bäckman is a lecturer of Agricultural Economics in thc Department of Economics and Management, Faculty of Agriculture and Forestry, University of Helsinki, Finland. He teaches microeconomics, macroeconomics, and linear programming. He is specialized in the efficiency and productivity of agricultural production with a special interest in precision agriculture and artificial intelligence. He can be contacted at stefan.backman@helsinki.fi.

Faustine K. Bee is a professor and vice chancellor of the University of Dodoma, Tanzania. Prior to his current position, he was vice chancellor of Moshi Co-operative University, Tanzania. His research relates to cooperatives and livelihoods in Tanzania. He can be contacted at faustine.bee@udom.ac.tz.

Tafuteni Nicholaus Chusi is a lecturer, researcher, and consultant in the Department of Development Finance and Management Studies at the Institute of Rural Development Planning, Dodoma, Tanzania. Her research interests are on women entrepreneurship and SME development, and capital markets and development. She has taken a number of researches and consultancies on cooperatives, strengthening producers, processors, and market associations. She can be contacted at tnc0917@gmail.com.

Tapas R. Dash is a professor and research advisor at CamEd Business School, Phnom Penh, Cambodia. Earlier he served as a professor and senior vice president of academic and university affairs at Build Bright University, Cambodia, and a faculty member of the Institute of Cooperative Management, National Council for Cooperative Training, New Delhi, India. He has had the privilege of commissioning a number of research and consultancy projects funded by the international and national organizations including the Royal Government of Cambodia. Currently, some of his important consultancies are funded by the SDC, International Labor Organization (ILO), USAID Cambodia Green Future Activity, EWMI, Plan International Cambodia, PIN, Advocacy and Policy Institute (API), and CDRI among such other institutions. As an international expert, presently he is involved in designing the National Program Phase II (2021–2030) of the SNDD, Royal Government of Cambodia. Tapas is the co-editor of Cooperatives and Economic Development (Rawat Publications, India) and Educational Access and Excellence (Allied Publishers, India). He is the founder editor-in-chief of the International Journal of Business and Development Research, and currently, the editor-in-chief of the Journal of Accounting, Finance, Economics, and Social Sciences. He can be contacted at tapas_dash@yahoo.co.in/dranjan @cam-ed.com.

Paulo Anania Fute is an assistant lecturer in the Department of Cooperative Development and Management and head, Department of Extension and Outreach Programmes, Institute of Continuing Co-operative Education (ICCE), Moshi Cooperative University, Tanzania. His areas of interest are cooperative management and development studies. He has been involved in developing cooperative management programs at certificate and diploma levels, and has intensively carried out field works and training in various primary cooperatives in Tanzania. He can be contacted at ananiapf@yahoo.com.

Greg MacLeod was a well-known Cape Breton priest, community activist, and educator. He became a professor of Philosophy at the College of Cape Breton in 1974, which eventually turned into Cape Breton University. MacLeod later became one of the founders of a community economic development organization—New Dawn Enterprises and BCA Group (Banking Community Assets) in 1989. MacLeod passed away in 2017 after a lengthy illness.

Suren Movsisyan is an economics doctorate from the Armenian National Agrarian University. He studied at the Institute for Culture Diplomacy in Berlin, and worked as a researcher in Copenhagen Business School-funded project. Suren is cited in the world's top universities, and research institutions in fifteen languages across thirty-five countries. Currently, he is a startup advisor, and founder and CEO of Algorithm. He can be contacted at suren@ movsisyan.dk.

Emmanuel Maro Nyankweli is an experienced rural development specialist, currently working as an associate professor at the Mwalimu Nyerere Memorial Academy, Dar es Salaam, Tanzania. Earlier he served at the Ministry of Education, Science and Technology as a deputy director of Higher Education, and at the Institute of Rural Development Planning, Dodoma, where he instructed both undergraduate and postgraduate students. His research experiences are on cooperatives and agricultural value chain in Tanzania, African policy analysis, China–Africa trade relations, climate change and environment, African mineral resource, and the governance of non-state socio-protection services. He can be contacted at emmanuel.nyankweli@gmail.com.

Karen P. Quilloy is an assistant professor at the Institute of Cooperatives and Bio-Enterprise Development, CEM, UPLB. She teaches courses on cooperatives and conducts several research and extension activities in the field of cooperative and enterprise development. Her other research interests include food security, agricultural marketing, and rural development. She can be contacted at kpquilloy@up.edu.ph.

Niranjan Roy is a professor and the head of the Department of Economics at the Assam University, India. He was the former dean of the Mahatma Gandhi School of Economics and Commerce, Assam University. His area of specialization includes agricultural economics, environmental economics, and social sector issues. He has published widely and participated in a number of international conferences. He can be contacted at royniranjan3@gmail.com.

Ravinder Rena is a professor of Economics and an internationalization project leader at the NWU Business School, North-West University, South Africa. He also serves as an adjunct professor of Economics for Masters and Doctorate Programs at the Monarch Business School, Monarch University, Hagendorn, Zug, Switzerland. He has written ten books and published more than 120 articles in reputed peer-reviewed journals. He can be contacted at drravinderrena@gmail.com.

Andrés Eduardo Ruggeri is a social anthropologist from the Universidad de Buenos Aires (UBA), Argentina. Since 2002, he has been the director of the Programa Facultad Abierta (Open Faculty Program), a group-based program, in the Division of Philosophy and Letters of the UBA that is dedicated to researching, supporting, and advising worker-recuperated enterprises. With this program, he has coordinated four national studies of recuperated enterprises and several volunteer projects organized through the University. In 2004, he had helped create the Documentation Center for recuperated enterprises that operates in the Chilavert Printers Cooperative. He is the author and/or the coauthor of various books on the subject of recuperated enterprises, some of them are translated to English, Italian, Greek, French, and other languages. Currently, he teaches at the Universidad Nacional Arturo Jauretche (UNAJ) in Florencio Varela, Buenos Aires province. He can be contacted at andres.ruggeri@gmail.com.

Gratian Cronery Rwekaza is a lecturer in the Department of Management, Moshi Co-operative University, Tanzania. His areas of research interest are cooperative management, community development, microfinance, organizational development, and micro, small, and medium enterprises among others. He can be contacted at gratiancronery@gmail.com.

Satyendra Singh is a professor of Marketing and International Business in the Faculty of Business and Economics at the University of Winnipeg, Canada, a conference chair of the Academy of Business and Emerging Markets (ABEM), and an editor-in-chief of the Journal of Academy of Business and Emerging Markets (JABEM). He has published widely in reputed international journals and presented papers at international conferences such as the American Marketing Association, Academy of Marketing Science, British Academy of Management, European Marketing Academy, World Marketing Congress, Administrative Sciences Association of Canada, among many others. Satyendra is the author of Market Orientation, Corporate Culture and Business Performance (Ashgate, UK) and Business Practices in Emerging and Re-emerging Markets (Palgrave, USA). He has also edited the Handbook of Business Practices and Growth in Emerging Markets (World Scientific, Singapore). His latest book is on Luxury and Fashion Marketing: A Global Perspective (Routledge, UK, 2021). He can be contacted at s.singh @uwinnipeg.ca.

John Sumelius is a professor of Production Economics and Farm Management in the Department of Economics and Management, Faculty of Agriculture and Forestry, University of Helsinki, Finland. His expertise covers quite a broad range of issues relating to farm management, food supply chain, agri-environmental issues, food security, and agricultural development in the developing world, economic analysis of farms and rural industries, productivity, efficiency, and rural livelihoods. He can be contacted at john.sumelius@ helsinki.fi.

Vera Zamagni is a professor of Economic History at the University of Bologna, Italy and an adjunct professor at SAIS Europe of the Johns Hopkins University. She was a member of the Italian National Research Council

(1994–1999) and the Italian Agency for University evaluation (2011–2013), and the vice-president of the Emilia-Romagna Region (2000–2002) and the NGO Cefa since 2003. Her publications include more than 140 essays and 20 volumes in Italian, English, Spanish, and German, covering the economic history of Italy since the unification, with special references to the reconstruction of national income estimates, regional disequilibria, state intervention, business history, cooperative movement, European integration, role of family in the society, and so on. She can be contacted at vera.negri@unibo.it.

Lightning Source UK Ltd.
Milton Keynes UK
UKHW021459110521
383532UK00002B/31

9 781498 555227